THE TORAH / LAW IS A JOURNEY

USING COGNITIVE
AND CULTURALLY
ORIENTED LINGUISTICS
TO INTERPRET AND
TRANSLATE METAPHORS
IN THE HEBREW BIBLE

IVANA **PROCHÁZKOVÁ**

CHARLES UNIVERSITY
KAROLINUM PRESS, 2021

KAROLINUM PRESS
Karolinum Press is a publishing department of the Charles University
www.karolinum.cz

© 2021 by Ivana Procházková

First edition

Designed by Jan Šerých
Set and printed in the Czech Republic by Karolinum Press

Cataloging-in-Publication Data is available from the National Library of the Czech Republic

This publication is part of the research held at the Protestant Theological Faculty of Charles
University in 2017–2019 within the grant project project Metaphorical conceptualization
of the conceptual area of the law, justice, judgement and righteousness in the poetic texts
of the Old Testament canon, no. 17-17435S supported by the Czech Science Foundation.
It is published with the financial support of the Progres Q01—Theology as a way of interpreting
history, traditions and contemporary society.

The book was peer reviewed by Iva Nebeská (Faculty of Arts, Charles University) and Martin Prudký
(Protestant Theological Faculty, Charles University).

ISBN 978-80-246-2
ISBN 978-80-246-4 (pdf)
ISBN 978-80-246-1 (epub)
ISBN 978-80-246-8 (mobi)

CONTENTS

INTRODUCTION

> *Metaphor is the application of an alien name*
> *by transference either from genus to species,*
> *or from species to genus, or from species to species,*
> *or by analogy, that is, proportion.*
> (Aristotle, *Poetics*)

Since Aristotle offered this definition of metaphor, possibly the oldest on record, metaphor theory has undergone a long evolution. Metaphors are no longer understood primarily as instruments of poetic language, as linguistic adornment. Today, we are more likely to read that we "think" and "get to know things" through metaphors; that we "evaluate" and "experience" the world around us and even perhaps "live" through the linguistic tool of the metaphor.

Scholars of linguistics, literary theorists, philosophers and others have offered a range of theories to suggest how metaphors work and how to identify, classify and interpret them. This present contribution to the scholarly debate is anchored in the methodology of cognitive and culturally oriented linguistics, a field that has been developing since the 1980s. Although cognitive linguistics has developed largely in the direction of language exploration, it is now far from being a single discipline and includes a wide range of approaches and theories.

Chapter one is theoretical and offers a basic overview of the theories on which our analysis of metaphorical expressions concerning the law, righteousness and justice in the Old Testament will be based. The theory of the conceptual metaphor, the theory of incarnation, the theory of mental images, and the theory of conceptual blending are all briefly introduced.

The principal focus, however, is on Hebrew metaphorical expressions concerning one of the key Old Testament concepts, namely, תורה *the Torah / Law* and related Hebrew concepts from the semantic area of *Law, Righteousness, and Justice*. The aim is to identify the Hebrew conceptual metaphors used in the chosen semantic area and to explain the meaning of the respective metaphorical expressions. Metaphorical vehicles (expressions whose use in the text signals the presence of a metaphor) and generic narrative structures (bundles of metaphorical vehicles connected by function) as sub-positions of conceptual metaphors of a narrative nature will provide the primary methodological tool for the exploration of conceptual metaphors in the Hebrew text and in language in general.

The language of laws in the general sense, and especially the language of "the Law" in the Hebrew biblical canon, is highly formalised. Legal texts are subject to stringent requirements of factual and formal clarity and accuracy. Metaphorical meaning, however, is intentionally ambiguous, dynamic and multi-layered, and envisages a wide range of connotations regarding the concepts and phrases used in metaphorical expressions. Our focus will be on the types of legal text used in the Old Testament Hebrew canon and how they function.

Chapter two presents an overview of the metaphors involved in the conceptualisation of the Hebrew expression תורה *the Torah / Law* and related terms in the Hebrew Old Testament. Each conceptualisation is described through metaphorical vehicles, and in some cases through generic narrative structures as partial positions of a single conceptual metaphor. The metaphorical expressions selected from the Old Testament canon include not only those which represent conventional uses of the conceptual metaphor but also innovations that are unique to the respective author.

Regarding the metaphorical conceptualisation of the key term תורה *the Torah / Law*, the book will explore whether there is any hierarchy or factual connection between the metaphors with respect to how often they are used and whether there are any mutual internal relations: we believe there may be a "centre" and a "peripheries." Metaphors for the Torah such as honey, gold, sun and light are well known, especially in the Psalms, and are further developed by Jewish and Christian oral and written traditions. We will explore whether a potential centre of metaphorical conceptualisation is formed by these or other conceptual metaphors and will investigate whether this centre somehow corresponds to the etymology of the Hebrew expression תורה *the Torah / Law*. The first step towards describing and interpreting the meaning of each metaphorical expression is to identify the conceptual metaphor.

Where a metaphor occurs in an exegetically controversial place, the analysis could contribute to the interpretation of these passages of text, and chapter three is devoted to this aspect of the application of cognitive-linguistic analysis. Selected metaphorical statements related to תורה *the Torah / Law* in Jeremiah, Zephaniah and Proverbs will be subjected to more detailed analysis, which will then be used to interpret these passages.

The use of cognitive-linguistic analysis and the interpretation of metaphorical expressions has proved highly effective in the field of translation. Chapter three will also, therefore, look at translations of selected metaphorical expressions in Jeremiah and Zephaniah into modern Czech and English.

Just as Europe witnessed the cultivation of Christian, Renaissance and Baroque cultures, we now live in a "culture" of human rights. The liberal secular-humanist notion of human rights often claims to be a central shared value, a moral value, the highest good for Europe or even the whole world. The French Catholic theologian René

Cassin compared human dignity, freedom, equality and brotherhood to the pillars of a temple: the "temple" of the *Universal Declaration of Human Rights*, in whose formulation he had a significant hand.[1] The case study in the final chapter is devoted to an analysis of the conceptual metaphors that contribute to the concept of human rights in the contemporary English-language teaching manual *Compass: Manual for Human Rights Education with Young People*. Here we will use the same methods as those used in the analysis and interpretation of metaphorical expressions in the Hebrew Old Testament. The analysis of the metaphors in *Compass* will contribute to the debate on the possible biblical (Jewish and Christian) origins of the whole idea, nature and culture of human rights. As we shall see, metaphors and other concepts and patterns of thought used in *Compass* bear undeniable signs of having been inspired by passages from the Bible and various aspects of Christian teaching.

---

1   Micheline Ishay, *The History of Human Rights. From Ancient Times to the Globalization Era* (Berkeley: University of California Press, 2008), 5.

CHAPTER 1

THE IDENTIFICATION, ANALYSIS AND INTERPRETATION OF METAPHORICAL EXPRESSIONS IN THE HEBREW TEXT OF THE OLD TESTAMENT: STARTING POINTS AND METHODS

Scholars have used a broad range of methods and approaches to analyse and interpret metaphorical expressions in the Hebrew text of the Bible. One rapidly developing field of study in this regard, especially in the Anglo-Saxon world, is cognitive linguistics. This book will build on the development of cognitive and culturally oriented linguistics over the past four decades. Polish anthropological and culturally based linguistics, or ethnolinguistics (Jerzy Bartmiński, Ryszard Tokarski, Alicja Pajdzińska, etc.),[2] works with the notion of *the linguistic image of the world* (in Polish *językowy obraz świata*) and has been developing since the 1980s, initially independently of Anglo-American cognitive linguistics. Our preferred term of cognitive and culturally oriented linguistics covers a variety of approaches often associated with particular researchers or themes.

In 1980 Lakoff and Johnson caused a considerable stir, not only in the academic world, with their book *Metaphors We Live By*.[3] The work was published at a time when scholars in the field of metaphor theory were re-evaluating existing research in light of Max Black's *interaction theory*,[4] which revised the long-accepted *substitution theory* of metaphor. Around since the time of Aristotle, substitution theory states that a metaphor is a substitute that represents the transfer of the meaning of a word or phrase to one that is non-original; it is applied primarily in artistic or poetic language. Black's interaction theory states that *focus* and *frame* interact within metaphorical statements: metaphor is a process during which a word (*focus*) that is being used metaphorically is incorporated into a new *frame*, thereby providing insight into the metaphor; the metaphor organises our understanding of the subject of the metaphor (*focus*). Lakoff and Johnson and others speak of the *source domain* organising the information within the *target domain*. According to Black, we view the framework of metaphorical testimony through a focal point. In cognitive linguistics, a metaphor's ability to organise our view of the framework and to structure the *frame* (the target domain) through a *focus* (the source domain) is later called *mapping* or conceptualis-

2   See, for example: Janusz Anusiewicz, *Lingwistyka kulturowa. Zarys problematyki* (Wrocław: Wydawnictvo Uniwersytetu Wrosławskiego, 1995); Jerzy Bartmiński, *Językowe podstawy obrazu świata* (Lublin: Uniwersytet Marii Curie-Skłodowskiej, 2007); Jerzy Bartmiński, *Jazyk v kontextu kultury* (Prague: Karolinum, 2016).
3   George Lakoff and Mark Johnson, *Metaphors We Live By* (Chicago: University of Chicago Press, 1980).
4   Max Black, *Models and Metaphors. Studies in Language and Philosophy* (Ithaca: Cornell University Press, 1962).

ation. This in turn led to the *conceptual metaphor theory*, the key concept of Lakoff-oriented cognitive linguistics.[5]

Lakoff and Johnson insisted that the metaphor reaches far beyond the field of poetic and literary language, and provided a convincing array of examples to demonstrate that metaphors are used widely in everyday communication. There is no sharp line between poetic metaphors, conventional metaphors used in everyday language, and lexicalised metaphors: in whatever sphere, the principle remains the same. Above all, a conceptual metaphor is the way in which we view and structure (conceptualise) one mental area on the basis of another. For Lakoff and Johnson, however, the conceptual metaphor is much more than a single metaphorical expression: it is the way in which we conceptualise individual concepts or even whole conceptual areas. The conceptual metaphor is realised through individual metaphorical expressions, conventional or innovative, in everyday language or in literature, and was later shown even to be active in areas such as non-verbal communication and iconography. Lakoff and Johnson showed that abstract terms for phenomena not commonly available to us through physical—sensory—contact are understood, experienced and spoken about through metaphors.

Cognitive and culturally oriented linguistics emphasises, therefore, that a metaphor is not a single concept but the realisation of the process of thinking and evoking similarity and the acceptance of analogy. A metaphor structures or organises the *target domain* on the basis of the *source domain*. According to Lakoff this takes place through the *image schema* of the source domain. *Image schemas* are models or mental patterns that enable conceptualisation of the target domain. Some such *image schemas* were described in *Metaphors We Live By*, such as schemas based on our corporeality (our bodily experience in relation to objects, our orientation in space, etc.), schemas that are *experiential gestalts*.[6]

In *The Body in the Mind* (1987), Johnson described image schemas such as CONTAINER, PART–WHOLE, CENTRE–PERIPHERY, CONNECTION, JOURNEY, START–FINISH.[7] In *Women, Fire, and Dangerous Things* (1987), Lakoff described four types of cognitive model through which conceptualisation takes place; metaphor is one of these models.[8] In the world of literary texts, where several conceptual metaphors can be involved in the construction of metaphorical meaning, Fauconnier and Turner developed the *conceptual blending theory* (elsewhere the *conceptual integration theory*), which describes

---

5   George Lakoff, *Women, Fire, and Dangerous Things. What Categories Reveal about the Mind* (Chicago: University of Chicago Press, 1987).

6   "Experiential gestalts are multidimensional structured wholes. Their dimensions, in turn, are defined in terms of directly emergent concepts. That is, the various dimensions (participants, parts, stages, etc.) are categories that emerge naturally from our experience." Lakoff and Johnson, *Metaphors We Live By*, 60.

7   Mark Johnson, *The Body in the Mind. The Bodily Basis of Meaning, Imagination, and Reason* (Chicago: University of Chicago Press, 1987).

8   "In the conceptual system, there are four types of cognitive models: propositional, image-schematic, metaphoric, and metonymic. Propositional and image-schematic models characterize structure; metaphoric and metonymic models characterize mappings that make use of structural models." Lakoff, *Women, Fire, and Dangerous Things*, 153–154.

the blending of the elements and inter-relationships of two or more mental spaces.[9] The authors went on to develop the mental spaces theory, originally set out by Turner in *The Literary Mind* (1996).[10] Turner uses the term *parable* rather than metaphor and unlike Lakoff and Johnson emphasises the narrative character of a metaphor.

In the wake of Lakoff and Johnson's seminal work, numerous researchers explored conceptual metaphors in both literary and everyday language. Metaphors generally fell into one of two broad categories: those which have a universal physical and spatial-experiential basis and can be found in various historical, linguistic and cultural contexts; and those linked to a specific socio-cultural, religious and, occasionally, geographical context (*socio-cultural metaphor*).

Zoltán Kövecses is one of the leading linguists dedicated to the study of the conceptual metaphor.[11] Other scholars explore metaphorical conceptualisations and their motivation and function in a particular area of social or cultural life, especially in the fields of politics and law.[12] Another interesting area of research is the comparison of metaphorical conceptualisations in different languages. The relevance of new concepts of the metaphor has also been demonstrated by the exploration of metaphors in visual communication and sign language for the deaf. The very same metaphors that occur in language have been documented in children's drawings, the fine arts, films, cartoons and comics, and in non-verbal communication (gestures, facial expressions, etc.).[13] Cognitive and culturally oriented concepts of the metaphor are also considered in psycholinguistics, where metaphor is seen as an important tool of human perception and a means of organising experience (physical, mental, social, spiritual), memorising, and understanding and experiencing reality.[14]

---

9   Gilles Fauconnier and Mark Turner, *The Way We Think: Conceptual Blending and the Mind's Hidden Complexities* (New York: Basic Books, 2003).
10 Mark Turner, *The Literary Mind. The Origins of Thought and Language* (New York: Oxford University Press, 1996).
11 Zoltán Kövecses, *Metaphors of Anger, Pride, and Love: A Lexical Approach to the Structure of Concepts* (Amsterdam: John Benjamins, 1986); Zoltán Kövecses, *Emotion Concepts* (New York: Springer, 1990); Zoltán Kövecses, *Metaphor and Emotion* (Cambridge: Cambridge University Press, 2000); Zoltán Kövecses, *Metaphor: A Practical Introduction* (Oxford: Oxford University Press, 2002); Zoltán Kövecses, *Metaphor in Culture. Universality and Variations* (Cambridge: Cambridge University Press, 2005); Zoltán Kövecses, *Where Metaphors Come From. Reconsidering Context in Metaphor* (Oxford: Oxford University Press, 2015); Zoltán Kövecses and Peter Szabo, "Idioms: A View from Cognitive Semantics," *Applied Linguistics* 17, no. 3 (1996): 326–355.
12 One of the more recent monographs is Michael Hanne and Robert Weisberg, eds., *Narrative and Metaphor in the Law* (Cambridge: Cambridge University Press, 2018).
13 Alan Cienki, "Metaphoric Gestures and Some of Their Relations to Verbal Metaphorical Expressions," in *Discourse and Cognition: Bridging the Gap*, ed. Jean-Pierre Koenig (Stanford: CSLI, 1998), 198–204; Charles J. Forceville, "The Identification of Target and Source in Pictorial Metaphors," *Journal of Pragmatics* 34, no. 1 (2002): 1–14; Alice Deignan, *Metaphor and Corpus Linguistics* (Amsterdam: John Benjamins, 2005); Karen Sullivan, "Frame-Based Constraints on Lexical Choice in Metaphor," *Proceedings of the Annual Meeting of the Berkeley Linguistics Society* 32, no. 1 (2006): 387–399; Karen Sullivan, "Grammar in Metaphor. A Construction Grammar Account of Metaphoric Language," doctoral dissertation, University of California, 2006; Karen Sullivan, *Mixed Metaphors: Their Use and Abuse* (London: Bloomsbury Academic, 2016); Alan Cienki and Cornelia Müller, *Metaphor and Gesture* (Amsterdam: John Benjamins, 2008).
14 See, for example: René Dirven and Wolf Paprotté, eds., *The Ubiquity of Metaphor. Metaphor in Language and Thought* (Amsterdam: John Benjamins, 1985); Sam Glucksberg, "The Psycholinguistics of Metaphor," *Trends in Cognitive Sciences* 7, no. 2 (2003): 92–96; Markus Tendhall, *A Hybrid Theory of Metaphor: Relevance Theory and Cognitive Linguistics* (Basingstoke: Palgrave Macmillan, 2009).

The role of the *conceptual metaphor* is a subject of much scholarly discussion. Cognitive and culturally oriented linguistics foregrounds its cognitive function, whereby the metaphor captures and passes on the results of human cognitive activity, that is, results which remain within natural cognitive processes but which are not caught within the existing form of the language system. The metaphor represents a new semantic quality that cannot be achieved by other linguistic means. Another important function of the metaphor is the expression of meaning in a compressed form.[15]

The literature on cognitive and cultural linguistics is extensive. The first significant review was *An Introduction to Cognitive Linguistics* by Ungerer and Schmidt (1996). This was followed by *Cognitive Linguistics* by Croft and Cruse (2004), *Cognitive Linguistics: An Introduction* by Evans and Green (2005), and *The Oxford Handbook of Cognitive Linguistics* edited by Geeraerts and Cuyckens (2007).[16] In its forty-nine chapters, the *Oxford Handbook* outlines basic concepts such as embodiment, experimentalism, the prototype theory, the radial categories theory, mental spaces, conceptual metaphors, and the conceptual integration theory. It also includes several sections on cognitive grammar and identifies places where the subject matter overlaps with psychology, philosophy, political science and sociology. It provides a comprehensive bibliography.

The most recent large-scale project is *The Cambridge Handbook of Cognitive Linguistics* (2017),[17] which includes contributions from significant scholars in the field such as Laura Janda, Nick Enfield, Kurt Feyaertes, Karen Sullivan, Mark Turner, and Ronald Langacker. The compendium covers matters such as cognitive-linguistic methodology, written language and gestures, and the relationship between language, cognition and culture, and has chapters devoted to the embodiment theory, inter-subjectivism, various aspects of linguistic analysis (phonological, semantic, grammatical, pragmatic, structural grammar), overlaps between cognitive linguistics and cognitive psychology, sociology and neuroscience, and of course metaphors. Part IV on Conceptual Mappings includes contributions from Eve Sweetser (conceptual mappings), Karen Sullivan (conceptual metaphors), Jeannette Littlemore (metonymy), Todd Oakley and Esther Pascual (the conceptual blending theory), Raymond Gibbs Jr. (embodiment), Elena Semino (corpus linguistics and metaphor), and Teenie Matlock (metaphor, simulation and fictive motion). Like its Oxford counterpart, the publication offers a rich bibliography.

---

15   See, for example: Jens Allwood and Peter Gärdenfors, eds., *Cognitive Semantics: Meaning and Cognition* (Amsterdam: John Benjamins, 1999); Alan Cienki, "An Image Schema and Its Metaphorical Extensions—Straight," *Cognitive Linguistics* 9 (1998): 107–149; Annalisa Baicchi, "The Relevance of Conceptual Metaphor in Semantic Interpretation," *Rivisteweb. The Italian Platform for the Humanities and Social Sciences* 1 (2017): 155–170.
16   Friedrich Ungerer and Hans-Jörg Schmid, *An Introduction to Cognitive Linguistics* (New York: Longman, 2006); William Croft and Alan Cruse, *Cognitive Linguistics* (Cambridge: Cambridge University Press, 2004); Vyvyan Evans and Melanie Green, *Cognitive Linguistics. An Introduction* (Edinburgh: Edinburgh University Press, 2006); Dirk Geeraerts and Hubert Cuyckens, eds., *The Oxford Handbook of Cognitive Linguistics* (Oxford: Oxford University Press, 2007), 188–213.
17   Barbara Dancygier, ed., *The Cambridge Handbook of Cognitive Linguistics* (Cambridge: Cambridge University Press, 2017).

Prominent cognitivist-oriented linguists in the sphere of Czech language include Irena Vaňková,[18] Lucie Saicová Římalová,[19] Iva Nebeská, Jasňa Šlédrová, and Lucie Šťastná;[20] Zbyněk Fišer applies cognitivist approaches in translation studies.[21]

Theologians employ cognitive-linguistic approaches in biblical studies, dogmatics, pastoral theology and religious studies. Research in biblical theology has been carried out along the lines of the conceptual metaphor theory since the 1980s, first by Sallie McFague,[22] and more recently by Bonnie Howe,[23] Claudia Bergmann,[24] Regine Hunziger-Rodewald,[25] Brent Strawn,[26] Pierre van Hecke,[27] and others. In the context of the New Testament parables of the kingdom of God, Crossan pointed out that metaphors can introduce new and previously unknown meanings, concepts and insights, and are capable of conveying new realities and new religious, social and cultural experiences.[28]

Comparative studies have revealed similar metaphorical approaches to key concepts in various archaic cultures and religious systems. This also applies to the Hebrew terms that will be the subject of our examination of the Old Testament, and of the expression תורה *the Torah / Law* and other terms related to it. These are consensuses that can be explained only through linguistics.[29]

The universal dimension of some conceptual metaphors, such as the metaphor of the *journey*, which we will address here in relation to the Torah, probably stems from the anchoring of such concepts in the universal physical human experience of the existence of the human body in time and space, and in the physical nature of the structure of our pre-conceptual and conceptual experience. This aspect is noted by

---

18 Irena Vaňková, *Nádoba plná řeči. Člověk, řeč a přirozený svět* (Prague: Karolinum, 2007).

19 Lucie Saicová Římalová, "Představová schémata a popis jazyka. Schéma cesty v češtině," *Bohemistyka* 9 (2009): 161–176; Saicová Římalová, Lucie, *Vybraná slovesa pohybu v češtině. Studie z kognitivní lingvistiky* (Prague: Karolinum, 2010); Irena Vaňková et al., *Co na srdci, to na jazyku. Kapitoly z kognitivní lingvistiky* (Prague: Karolinum, 2005).

20 Irena Vaňková, Jasňa Pacovská, and Jan Wiendel, eds., *Obraz člověka v jazyce a v literatuře* (Prague: Filozofická fakulta Univerzity Karlovy, 2010); Irena Vaňková and Lucie Šťastná, eds., *Horizonty kognitivně-kulturní lingvistiky*, vol. 2, *Metafory, stereotypy a kulturní rozrůzněnost jazyků jako obrazů světa* (Prague: Filozofická fakulta Univerzity Karlovy, 2018); Irena Vaňková, Veronika Vodrážková, and Radka Zbořilová, eds., *Horizonty kognitivně-kulturní lingvistiky*, vol. 1, *Schémata, stereotypy v mluvených a znakových jazycích* (Prague: Filozofická fakulta Univerzity Karlovy, 2017); Irena Vaňková and Jan Wiedl, eds., *Tělo, smysly, emoce v jazyce a v literatuře* (Prague: Filozofická fakulta Univerzity Karlovy, 2012); Jan Wiedl, ed., *Lidský život a každodennost v literatuře* (Prague: Filozofická fakulta Univerzity Karlovy, 2016).

21 Zbyněk Fišer, *Překlad jako kreativní proces. Teorie a praxe funkcionalistického překládání* (Brno: Host, 2009).

22 Sallie McFague, *Metaphorical Theology: Models of God in Religious Language* (Philadelphia: Fortress Press, 1982).

23 Peter Bonnie Howe, *Because You Bear This Name. Conceptual Metaphor and the Moral Meaning of 1 Peter* (Leiden: Brill, 2006).

24 Claudia D. Bergmann, *Childbirth as a Metaphor for Crisis. Evidence from the Ancient Near East, the Hebrew Bible, and 1QH XI, 1–18* (Berlin: Walter de Gruyter, 2008).

25 Regine Hunziger-Rodewald, *Hirt und Herde. Ein Beitrag zum alttestamentlichen Gottesverständnis* (Stuttgart: W. Kohlhammer, 2001).

26 Brent Strawn, *What Is Stronger than a Lion? Leonine Image and Metaphor in the Hebrew Bible and the Ancient Near East* (Fribourg: Academic Press, 2005).

27 Pierre van Hecke, ed., *Metaphor in the Hebrew Bible* (Leuven: Leuven University Press, 2005).

28 John Dominic Crossan, *In Parables. The Challenge of the Historical Jesus* (San Francisco: Harper & Row, 1985).

29 See Jiří Starý and Tomáš Vítek, "Zákon, právo a spravedlnost v archaickém myšlení," in *Zákon a právo v archaických kulturách*, ed. Dalibor Antalík, Jiří Starý, and Tomáš Vítek (Prague: Filozofická fakulta Univerzity Karlovy, 2010), 13–54.

cognitive and cultural linguistics. The *embodiment theory* states that our conceptual structures arise from and depend upon our pre-conceptual experience.[30] Lakoff further states that, "The core of our conceptual systems is directly grounded in perception, body movement and experience of a physical and social character."[31]

Modern cognitive linguistics offers methodological tools for the exegesis of metaphorical expressions in biblical studies. It enables scholars to study the processes involved in the construction of the meaning of metaphorical expressions and whole conceptual metaphors, to discern their function in the text, and to observe the semantic development of various terms, as well as semantic changes and their motivation. Cognitive-linguistic exploration in theology works with both universal metaphors and those that are closely tied to particular socio-cultural, religious or geographical contexts, and also with metaphors that are specific to a particular literary form of the Bible, a genre, an author, or a literary collection.

1.1 METHODS USED IN THE ANALYSIS AND INTERPRETATION OF HEBREW METAPHORICAL EXPRESSIONS RELATING TO THE TERM תורה THE TORAH / LAW, AND IN THE EXPLANATION OF MEANING

Our focus will be conceptual metaphors and their realisation in metaphorical expressions in the Hebrew text of the Old Testament which relate to one of the key biblical concepts, namely the term תורה (*the Torah / Law*). We will describe approaches to explaining the meaning of metaphorical expressions in the Hebrew text of the Old Testament using the methods of cognitive and culturally oriented linguistics. We will identify metaphorical expressions in the text and the conceptual metaphors that lie behind them. One possible application of this analysis is the detection of those elements in a passage of text which have significance for translation into modern languages, that is, the identification of the core meaning that must be preserved as precisely as possible in the target language.

The various theories and specifics of meaning are the concern of semiotics, semantics and pragmatics, but they are also relevant in the areas of anthropology, psychology and philosophy; meaning is also dealt with in art, literature and other cultural disciplines. Linguistic semantics uses the terms *meaning* and *meaning levels*.[32] The study of

---

30 "Experience is thus not taken in the narrow sense of the things that have 'happened to happen' to a single individual. Experience is instead construed in the broad sense: the totality of human experience and everything that plays a role in it—the nature of our bodies, our genetically inherited capacities, our modes of physical functioning in the world, our social organization, etc." Lakoff, *Women, Fire, and Dangerous Things*, 266.

31 Ibid., 14.

32 Meaning can be lexical, grammatical, or pragmatic. The meaning of a word can be broken down into several components, such as conceptual (denotational; cognitive), collocative, connotational, social, emotive (affec-

meaning is also at the heart of cognitive and culturally oriented linguistics, which to-gether with cognitive and culturally oriented semantics, pragmatics and poetics, offers a number of ways to describe the meaning of a word or utterance or even a complete literary work. What is key is the perceived connection with the human mind and the anthropological, ethnological and cultural constants. Cognitive and culturally oriented linguistics, and the semantic theories that go with it, have strongly criticised linguistic objectivism and structural theories of language.[33] In place of linguistic objectivism, Lakoff, Johnson and others talk about the *theory of the intersubjective system of mean-ing-making* or the *experiential realism theory*.[34] "Experiential realism" assumes that all our thinking, all our conceptual systems, are anthropocentric and conditioned by our physicality (human physical and sensory capabilities) and our social and cultural ex-periences.[35]

The Czech cognitive linguist Irena Vaňková suggests that cognitive linguistics emphasises the close interconnection of language processes with cognitive and emo-tional processes, as well as with the sensory and physical experience of the world, with all human experience: "with 'the whole person in us.' Furthermore, meaning—not only lexical, but also grammatical and pragmatic—has a physical, experiential and subjective, or rather inter-subjective basis in the cognitive conception."[36] Criticism of linguistic objectivism and objectivist semantic theories rests mostly on the study of colour categorisation, human biological categories, and the study of the categorisation of emotions and prototype phenomena in language.

As we have already noted, Polish anthropological and culturally based linguistics (Bartmiński, Tokarski, Pajdzińska, and others) is rooted in ethnology and ethnolin-guistics and uses the umbrella term *the linguistic image of the world*. According to the Lublin linguist Bartmiński, the cognitive definition of meaning is a *story of an object*,[37] which indicates the characteristics of a subject that the linguistic and cultural commu-nity considers essential. By contrast, cognitive linguistics of predominantly American origin (for example, Croft, Fauconnier, Janda, Johnson, Kővecses, Lakoff, Langacker, Turner) has its roots in the theory of artificial intelligence, psychology, neurology and psycholinguistics, and explores cognitive structures and the organisation of con-sciousness assisted by the kind of analysis of cognitive strategies that people use in language manifestations and to preserve information and think, learn and understand.

---

tive; emotional), reflected, and thematic-rhematic. For more detail, see Svatova Machová and Milena Švehlová, *Sémantika & pragmatická lingvistika* (Prague: Pedagogická fakulta Univerzity Karlovy, 2001), 17.

33   See, for example, Lakoff, *Women, Fire, and Dangerous Things*, part II.

34   See Vaňková et al., *Co na srdci*, 59–66; Lakoff, *Women, Fire, and Dangerous Things*, 261–268; Vaňková, *Nádoba plná řeči*, 56–57.

35   For more on this, see Lakoff, *Women, Fire, and Dangerous Things*, 14–16; Vaňková et al., *Co na srdci*, 24–26, 37–66, 195; Vaňková, *Nádoba plná řeči*, 56–57.

36   Vaňková et al., *Co na srdci*, 79–80.

37   Jerzy Bartmiński, "Definicja kognitywna jako narzędzie opisu konotacji," in *Konotacja*, ed. Jerzy Bartmiński (Lu-blin: Uniwersytet Marii Curie-Skłodowskiej, 1988), 169–183.

Language is perceived primarily in its relation to the human ability to acquire knowledge and to think. The explanation of meaning is therefore de facto a description of the process of conceptualising. Meaning is therefore identical to the mental representation of a concept in the human mind.[38]

Anna Wierzbicka, a Polish linguist living in Australia, developed a distinctive approach to describing meaning, which she defines as what people think of when they encounter a word, how they understand it, and what they mean when they use the word. Wierzbicka maintains that all languages contain a relatively small number (approximately 60–100) of universal semantic primes. These primary semantic units are then used to explain the meaning of other passages of text.[39] Vaňková talks about the cognitive definition of meaning, which concerns, "how an average subject (characteristic, activity, etc.) is perceived by an average native speaker of a given language, what it means, which aspects of its appearance and function, characteristics, activities and states associated with it are characteristic and significant."[40] All the available information provided by language (transferred meanings, phraseology, typical collocations) and the texts of this language are taken into account. Describing the meaning of a word is a complex business. It involves, among other things: (i) taking into account its etymology, its motivation, the inner form of the word, the secondary and transferred meanings, the meanings of word derivatives, used phrases, and connotations (including connotations in texts of a given linguistic and cultural sphere); (ii) naming the meaning stereotype; and (iii) formulating prototypical scenarios. The explanation of meaning is then a complete picture of knowledge of the subject and its characteristics and activities in a given linguistic and cultural sphere.[41]

Offering even the most basic overview of the literature on meaning, even one limited to linguistic and cognitively oriented disciplines, is well beyond the scope of this book. However, the connection with the human mind and with anthropological, ethnological and cultural constants will all be taken as essential components of any explanation of the meaning of metaphorical expressions related to the term תורה *the Torah / Law*. We present here only those theories and methods from cognitive and culturally oriented linguistics that have been used to identify metaphorical expressions related to תורה *the Torah / Law* in Old Testament texts, that is, theories and methods that have been used to describe the meaning of these metaphorical expressions and to describe the conceptual metaphors which lie behind them. These include:

38 Lakoff, *Women, Fire, and Dangerous Things*, 12.
39 A definition of the phrase *to feel afraid* can be described as follows: • I felt afraid. = • I felt something because I thought something » sometimes a person thinks: » "something bad can happen to me now » I do not want this to happen » because of this I want something » I do not know what I can do" » because this person thinks this, this person feels something bad • I felt (something) like this because I thought something like this. See Anna Wierzbicka, *Emotions across Languages and Cultures. Diversity and Universals* (Cambridge: Cambridge University Press, 1999), 14.
40 Vaňková et al., *Co na srdci*, 82.
41 In the Czech context, several authors, including Vaňková, Nebeská, Saicová-Římalová, and Šlédrová, have developed this concept of language and meaning, largely along the lines of Bartmiński and other Lublin linguists.

- the conceptual metaphor theory (Lakoff, Johnson, Kövecses)[42]
- embodiment theory[43]
- the mental spaces theory (Fauconnier) and the conceptual blending theory (Fauconnier, Turner)[44]

These theories are being developed and modified by numerous scholars but have their fair share of critics and opponents. Space does not permit a full discussion; the relevant discourse has been reflected on in the Oxford and Cambridge *Handbooks*, and elsewhere.

EMBODIMENT THEORY

We will assume that not only the general meaning but also the metaphorical meaning is anchored physically, socially and culturally. We will see in concrete conceptual metaphors used in Hebrew Old Testament texts that physical, social and cultural experience is an important basis of metaphorical conceptualisations. Hebrew terms such as תורה (*the Torah / Law*), צדק / צדקה (*justice*), and משפט (*judgment*), and even some highly abstract concepts, are often structured by the metaphorical mapping of terms and domains that reflect people's immediate physical, social and cultural experience. In order to explore the meaning of many conceptual metaphors in the Hebrew Old Testament, it is essential to know the cultural, religious and social environment not only of ancient Israel but of the entire Middle East. Metaphorical concepts that are the same as or similar to those used in the biblical text also appear in cults, social structures, and materialist and spiritual cultures.

THE MENTAL SPACES THEORY

This theory was suggested by Fauconnier in the mid-1980s to explain the construction of meaning in natural languages. Fauconnier understood mental spaces as partial complexes constructed during the process of thinking and speaking for the purpose of understanding and action.[45] Unlike the semantic area, the mental space is a matter of mind and language and its primary function is understanding.[46]

---

42   See Geeraerts and Cuyckens, *Oxford Handbook*, 188–213; Kövecses, *Metaphor: A Practical Introduction*.

43   See Geeraerts and Cuyckens, *Oxford Handbook*, 25–47; Dancygier, *Cambridge Handbook*, 449–462.

44   See Geeraerts and Cuyckens, *Oxford Handbook*, 170–187, 351–393; Dancygier, *Cambridge Handbook*, 379–384, 423–448.

45   "Mental spaces are very partial assemblies constructed as we think and talk for purposes of local understanding and action. They contain elements and are structured by frames and cognitive models." Geeraerts and Cuyckens, *Oxford Handbook*, 351.

46   According to Fauconnier, mental spaces contain elements that are structured by both frameworks and cognitive models. Fauconnier's mental spaces theory follows Fillmore's semantic conception of scenes and frames (see Geeraerts and Cuyckens, *Oxford Handbook*, 171–177). Cognitive models are structures that organise the content

In his conceptual metaphor theory, Lakoff uses *domain* rather than *mental space*, but the two terms mean essentially the same thing. For Lakoff, the basis of the metaphor is the structuring of the *target domain* through the *source domain*. When analysing metaphorical expressions, we will use Lakoff's *domain*. As noted above, Lakoff describes four basic cognitive models (propositional, image-schematic, metaphoric, and metonymic) based on the principle of the content on which the thinking is structured.[47] Turner, on the other hand, as well as replacing the term *conceptual metaphor* with the word *parable*, which he describes as having a narrative character and defines as a projection of one story onto another, uses the mental spaces theory and introduces the terms *input spaces, generic spaces* and *blended spaces*.[48]

THE CONCEPTUAL BLENDING THEORY

Also known as *conceptual integration*, this is the theory of the blending of two or more mental spaces, their elements and their inter-relationships to create a new, third space. In *The Way We Think*, Fauconnier and Turner used the mental spaces theory to interpret the construction of metaphorical meaning. They understand the metaphor as a specific case of the conceptual integration of at least two, but usually more, mental spaces. The network of source mental spaces is projected onto the target space and the whole network consists of *input spaces, generic spaces* and *blended spaces*. The mental spaces theory and the conceptual blending theory make it possible to explain the meaning of metaphorical expressions, behind which stand multiple conceptual metaphors. Another advantage of this multi-space model over the theory of metaphor described by Lakoff and Johnson in *Metaphors We Live By* is that the structure of mental spaces can be described dynamically, narratively.

The multi-space model assumes that the meaning of metaphorical expressions and of whole texts is shaped by numerous processes of the blending of metaphors and of metaphorical metonymy. To set out the mental spaces theory, Fauconnier used the well-known tale of Achilles and the tortoise,[49] one of a series of paradoxes attributed to the fifth-century BC Greek philosopher Zeno of Elea.[50]

---

of our thinking. The cognitive model as a whole, or any part of it, can be linked to a conceptual category. The product of these cognitive models is therefore the whole category structure as well as individual categories, but also prototypes. By framework, Fauconnier understands a set of verbal expressions, grammatical rules or linguistic categories that can give rise to a particular mental idea in a particular situation.

47   See Lakoff, *Women, Fire, and Dangerous Things*, 154.
48   See Turner, *The Literary Mind*.
49   Achilles is to race a tortoise in a hundred-metre race. Because Achilles is ten times faster than the tortoise, the tortoise is given a ten-metre head start. When the race starts, Achilles begins to catch up. When he has run ten metres, he reaches the place where the tortoise started. At this point, the tortoise has moved one metre, so is one metre ahead of Achilles. When Achilles covers that one metre, the tortoise is still ahead, but now only by ten centimetres. When Achilles reaches that point, the tortoise is one centimetre ahead of him. And so on to infinity. Although the tortoise's lead is shrinking, it is still in the lead. So, Achilles can never win the race.
50   Zeno shared Parmenides's belief that there is only one being. There is therefore no movement and no change: both are an illusion. This statement was supported by Zeno's paradoxes of the racetrack, the arrow, and Achilles

Achilles sees a tortoise. He chases it.
He thinks that the tortoise is slow and that he will catch it.
But it is fast. If the tortoise had been slow, Achilles would have caught it.
Perhaps the tortoise is really a hare.[51]

Likewise, to interpret the construction of metaphorical meaning, Turner uses the proverb,
While the cat's away, the mice will play.
The proverb can be understood as a *generic space*, an abstract structure which is shared by *input spaces* and has its own conceptual existence. It can be manipulated in favour of the construction of the *target space*, but the *source space* is not affected by such manipulation. The *generic space* can be applied to a variety of *target spaces*. The narrative concerning people who cease to follow the orders of their superior once his or her back is turned has its own conceptual potency and using it does not interfere with the source mental space—a story about mice and a cat.[52]

To explain how the mental spaces theory can be applied to the construction of meaning, Turner also uses the example of personified death,[53] often portrayed as a skeleton (or an old woman or man). In legends, fairy tales, fictional works, poetry, and indeed in everyday language in the English-speaking world, *Death* is the Grim Reaper, who appears to the dying wielding a scythe. Turner, Lakoff, and Fauconnier and Turner in *The Way We Think*, have all analysed this scythe-wielding skeleton.

To use a biblical example, the meaning of the metaphorical statement we find in Psalm 44:6 is formed by the blending of the conceptual metaphors GOD IS A WARRIOR (A WARRIOR FIGHTS THE ENEMY) and GOD IS A BULL (A BULL GORES).[54]

Ps 44:6 בך צרינו ננגח בשמך נבוס קמינו:
Through your name we tread down [literally **trample**] our assailants.[55]

The Hebrew word that indicates the use of the conceptual metaphor GOD IS A BULL is the verb root נגח (in PI *to pick up with its horns*). The words that indicate the conceptual metaphor GOD IS A WARRIOR are the nouns צרים *enemies* and the participle of the verb קום *assailant*. The verb בוס (in Q *to tread, trample*) appears in both the semantic area פר *Bull*

---

and the tortoise, which assume that an infinite series of numbers cannot have a finite sum (hence Achilles will never catch up with the tortoise).

51 This text was probably created by Fauconnier and then interpreted using mental spaces. See Geeraerts and Cuyckens, *Oxford Handbook*, 356–362.

52 Turner, *The Literary Mind*, 87.

53 Ibid., 79–86.

54 We will write conceptual metaphors according to established usage with small capital letters (e.g. GOD IS A KING; THE TORAH / LAW IS A JOURNEY). In describing the construction of the meaning of metaphorical expressions, we will use Lakoff's terms *conceptual domain*, *source domain* and *target domain*. In describing the meaning of metaphorical expressions in which two or more conceptual metaphors are applied, we will use the conceptual blending theory.

55 Unless otherwise stated, all English translations of the Hebrew text are from the *New Revised Standard Version*. Alternatives have sometimes been added in brackets in order to maintain the integrity of the metaphorical conceptualisation.

and the semantic area מלחמה *war*.[56] The verb root בוס in Q therefore signals the ongoing conceptual integration of the two conceptual domains.

A HOLISTIC UNDERSTANDING OF MEANING: UNDERSTANDING CONNOTATIONS

Connotation is an important component of the meaning of metaphorical expressions, especially connotations associated with both *source domain* and *target domain* expressions, and those associated with lexical expressions involved in metaphorical projection. Vaňková points out that in cognitive and culturally oriented linguistics, meaning is understood holistically and requires the formation of an integrated picture of all knowledge concerning the relevant subject in a given linguistic and cultural sphere;[57] it therefore requires a consideration of connotation. The structural concept of meaning is usually limited to its denotational component and any description tends to be as economical, unambiguous and "closed" as possible. In seeking to meet the requirements of linguistic objectivism, the structural concept of meaning reduces that meaning both deliberately and considerably. The typical dictionary definition of meaning describes only the "satisfactory" or objective properties of an object or activity, or the nature of its relationships. Cognitivists consider such explanations insufficient. Language objectivism and structural expressions of language can have a devastating effect on metaphorical meaning, which is reduced to those characteristics shared by all positions and variants of the conceptual metaphor, whereas in fact, in its breadth of meanings, the metaphor can bring new understanding and new insights.

Cognitive and culturally oriented linguistics, semantics, pragmatics and poetics offer a variety of ways to describe the meaning of words, utterances (including metaphorical words and utterances), and entire literary works. The aim is not to define meaning denotationally, on the basis of structural signs, but to expect connotations and to assume that meaning is anchored physically, experientially, socially and culturally.

We can use Psalm 102:11 to show the importance of connotations to an understanding and exploration of the meaning of metaphorical expressions:

Ps 102:11 מפני־זעמך וקצפך כי נשאתני ותשליכני׃

... because of your indignation and anger;
for you have **lifted me up and thrown me aside**.

The meaning of this Hebrew metaphorical expression is closely linked to the socio-cultural and geographical context in which it originated and depends on an understanding of connotations. The pair of Hebrew verbs נשא (in Q *to lift up, to take up,*

---

56   It also occurs in other contexts within the Hebrew Old Testament canon. For example, *treading wine in a vat* (Isa 63:6).

57   According to the cognitive definition of the term (Vaňková et al., *Co na srdci*, 82).

to raise, to erect) and שׁלך (in HI to throw, to cast into, to cast away) indicates the use of metaphorical metonymy of the metaphor GOD'S WRATH IS AN EAGLE. In the Bible, as in other literature, the eagle plays a significant role in religious and royal symbolism. The metaphor of the eagle (or GOD IS AN EAGLE) has an important theological use in the Hebrew biblical canon. The Hebrew term נשׁר is usually translated *eagle* or *vulture*, but here in Psalm 102:11 it may be the name of the great Eurasian mountain vulture *Gypaetos barbatus*. Identifying the metaphor used here requires knowledge of this predator's behaviour, especially the way it hunts its prey, which is to circle at high altitudes looking for carcasses (its main source of food) or other possible prey. Unlike other vultures, *Gypaetos barbatus* is able to fly away with its catch, taking even large bones high up into the high mountains, where it smashes them on rocks before eating them. The bird can carry whole tortoises, breaking the shell by dropping it from a height so that it can more easily attack the meat. It also flies directly at animals on the rocks in an attempt to throw them off. It seems that experience with this bird's hunting pattern formed the basis of the metaphorical mapping of the concept of *God's wrath* in Psalm 102:11. In the metaphorical projection of the *eagle* (Hebrew נשׁר) into *God*, the Hebrew text is using the imagery of the hunting vulture. Evocation of this mental imagery is essential for conceptualisation of יהוה אף *God's anger* through the metaphors mentioned above. The affliction and suffering brought by the wrath of God (Ps 102:3; Hebrew צר) is the same as that inflicted by a mountain vulture on its prey.

We have already seen that conceptual domains: (i) are dynamic structures that cannot be identified with the semantic area: (ii) are always present during the mapping process; and (iii) can be formed by whole category structures but also by prototypes and stereotypes.[58] Nevertheless, we should offer here at least a brief definition of the semantic area תורה *the Torah / Law* in Hebrew texts of the Old Testament.

It can be assumed that passages of text with semantic areas other than תורה *the Torah / Law* may also include metaphorical expressions. Lexical expressions of the source domain that appear repeatedly in metaphorical conceptualisations will be referred to as *metaphorical vehicles*. These are always Hebrew source domain expressions that are involved repeatedly in metaphorical conceptualisation of the target domain or domains in various passages of text (even completely independent passages). Met-

---

58 The idea that categories are based primarily on shared qualities and that terms are placed in the same category when they have certain common characteristics was first criticised by Eleanor Rosch, who notes that in fact categories include examples that are "better" or "worse," and that defining categories by shared properties alone removes any such notion. In this context, cognitive semantics refers to the *centre* and *periphery* of the category. See Eleanor Rosch and Barbara Bloom Lloyd, eds., *Cognition and Categorization* (Oxford: Lawrence Erlbaum, 1978); Francisco Varela, Evan Thompson, and Eleanor Rosch, *The Embodied Mind: Cognitive Science and Human Experience* (Cambridge: MIT Press, 1991); Eleanor Rosch, "Prototype Classification and Logical Classification: The Two Systems," in *New Trends in Cognitive Representation: Challenges to Piaget's Theory*, ed. E. Scholnick (Hillsdale: Lawrence Erlbaum Associates, 1983), 73–86. The prototype phenomenon in cognitive and culturally oriented linguistics is the "best example" within the category. The prototype is then made up of the most characteristic elements or the most suitable features that represent the given category to the maximum extent. Cognitively oriented sociology, sociolinguistics, ethnology and culturology work in a similar way with the notion of *stereotype*. We speak about stereotypes when special consideration is given to the socio-cultural anchorage of a prototype. The stereotype can have different positions and variants that exist in a given linguistic and cultural circle in parallel.

aphorical vehicles signal the presence of a metaphor in a text because they are lexical expressions of a different semantic area from that which the reader perceives as the target domain. We can see this in the following verses from the Psalm 38:

יהוה אל־בקצפך תוכיחני ובחמתך תיסרני: Ps 38:2

3 כי־חציך נחתו בי ותנחת עלי ידך:

O Lord, do not rebuke me in your anger, or discipline me in your wrath.
For your **arrows** have sunk into me, and your hand has **come down** on me.

Here in Psalm 38:2–3, the metaphorical vehicle that signals the conceptualisation of *God* through the metaphor GOD IS A WARRIOR is the Hebrew noun חץ (*arrow*) in connection with the verb נחת (in Q *to go down*).

The metaphorical meaning within a particular passage of text in the Hebrew Old Testament canon will be explored through a network of correspondence that is created during metaphorical conceptualisation. In *Metaphors We Live By*, Johnson and Lakoff introduced the term *correspondence* to describe the relationship between the source and target domains of a metaphor, in other words, the relationship of entities that correspond to each other. Lakoff later described such correspondence as either *ontological* or *epistemic*.

Ontological correspondence is the correspondence between entities in the source domain and corresponding entities in the target domain. For example:

–   I blew my **top**

Here, in the conceptual metaphors THE BODY IS A CONTAINER FOR THE EMOTIONS and ANGER IS HEAT, Lakoff notes the ontological correspondence between the *vessel* in the source domain and the *head* (top of the head) in the target domain, and between the *fluid in the vessel* (source) and *emotions* (target).

Epistemic correspondence arises when knowledge of the source domain is applied to knowledge of the target domain. In the example above, when the intensity of the emotion (here anger) increases, the temperature of the liquid rises, as does the pressure in the vessel until an explosion occurs and parts of the vessel fly into the air.[59]

Similarly, in Psalm 38:2–3, we can identify the ontological correspondence between the entities חץ (*arrow*) in the source domain and קֶצֶף (*wrath*) and חמה (*rage*) in the target domain. Epistemic correspondence is carried by the verb נחת (in Q *to go down*). Just as arrows hurt and kill, the manifestations of God's wrath are felt by the psalmist to be equally devastating.

Metaphorical conceptualisations and conceptual metaphors can also be described through *generic narrative structures*, a term I introduced in 2002 to describe variants of

---

59   See Lakoff, *Women, Fire, and Dangerous Things*, 380–389.

the Old Testament metaphor GOD IS A KING.[60] The generic narrative structure, a subset of the conceptual metaphor, generates metaphorical meaning and participates in the conceptualisation of target domains.

Correct identification of the generic narrative structure specifies the principal metaphorical concept. The generic narrative structure can also be described as a bundle of metaphoric vehicles, in this case Hebrew expressions specific to one functionally linked semantic domain. Metaphorical vehicles involved in the generic narrative structure as source domain elements establish structural correlations and correspondence with target domain entities.

The core of a generic narrative structure is usually, therefore, a verb expression which provides it with its narrative character and central meaning. As a rule, nominal, adverbial and other expressions are attached to the verbal metaphorical vehicle, but only rarely to other verb expressions. In particular, conceptual metaphors that are key within a linguistic, cultural or religious environment appear in multiple positions, within which we can describe several generic narrative structures. For example, the conceptual metaphor GOD IS A SHEPHERD is a key (cardinal[61]) metaphor in the corpus of the entire biblical canon (not only the Old Testament). The *shepherd* metaphor conceptualises the entire conceptual area of *God* and is in a sense a theological concept. The meaning of the Hebrew noun רעה (*shepherd*) can be defined by several prototypes within the Old Testament Hebrew canon:[62]

- a man who owns sheep and breeds them for meat, leather, milk and wool;
- a man who sells sheep;
- a hired shepherd (who does not own the flock but works for wages);
- a man who leads a flock to grazing land;
- a man who takes care of the flock (who provides enough grazing and water; who treats sick sheep, etc.);
- a man who leads sheep into the pen for the night (e.g. by playing a whistle or a sitar);
- a man who is responsible for selecting appropriate animals for breeding;
- a man who sells individual animals or the whole flock to the slaughterhouse;
- a man who supervises the flock (who is responsible for ensuring that the sheep do not escape, looks for and brings back those who stray from the flock, and guards the flock from wild animals, thieves or other danger).

---

60   Ivana Procházková, *Hospodin je král. Starozákonní metafora ve světle kognitivní lingvistiky* (Prague: Česká biblická společnost, 2011).

61   Viktor Krupa, a Slovak linguist who specialises in metaphor and metonymy and in imagery in the languages and cultures of Oceania, works with the concept of mythological and cardinal metaphors: a mythological metaphor is cardinal if it conceptualises the whole area of religion, allows the construction of an additional cognitive apparatus, and builds a particular hypothesis about the target area. See Viktor Krupa, *Metafora na rozhraní vedeckých disciplín* (Bratislava: Tatran, 1990).

62   Ivana Procházková, "The Torah within the Heart, in the Feet, and on the Tongue: Law and Freedom in Psalm 119 from the Perspective of Cognitive Linguistics," *Communio Viatorum* 54, no. 1 (2012): 16–37. See also Procházková, *Hospodin je král*, 40–64.

Not all prototype positions are necessarily used metaphorically in language and culture, nor are they necessarily the basis of a generic narrative structure. However, as we will see later, the generic narrative structures that are central to the metaphor are always likely to correspond to one of the big prototypes that can be described within the appropriate language category.

Elsewhere I have described nine sub-positions (variants) of the conceptual metaphor GOD IS A SHEPHERD, nine generic narrative structures in the Old Testament Hebrew canon, as identified by the methods of cognitive and cultural linguistics: THE SHEPHERD LEADS THE FLOCK TO THE GRAZING LAND (e.g. Ps 23:2,6; 31:4; 43:3; 61:3; 78:52–54; 107:7,40), THE SHEPHERD WATERS AND FEEDS THE FLOCK (e.g. Ps 17:15; 36:9; 78:15–16,20,24,29; 80:6; 81:11,17; 90:14; 104:11–13; 105:40–41), THE SHEPHERD GUARDS THE FLOCK FROM THE ENEMY (e.g. Ps 12:8; 34:21; 41:3; 91:11; 121:4; 124:6; 146:9), THE SHEPHERD HEALS THE FLOCK (e.g. Ps 28:9; 91:12; 107:20; 147:3), THE SHEPHERD SEEKS AND BRINGS BACK THE LOST SHEEP (e.g. Ps 40:3; 68:23; 80:4,8,20; 107:20; 119:59,176), THE SHEPHERD CRADLES THE SHEEP (e.g. Ps 107:41; Jer 3:16; 23:3; Ezek 36:11), THE SHEPHERD LIVES IN A TENT (e.g. Ps 74:1–2; 78:60), THE SHEPHERD GATHERS THE SCATTERED FLOCK (e.g. Ps 102:23; 106:47; 107:3), and THE SHEPHERD LEADS THE SHEEP TO THE SLAUGHTER (e.g. Ps 44:12–13; Isa 53:7; Jer 12:3; 25:34; 51:40; Ezek 21:15).

These generic narrative structures relate to some of the prototypes mentioned in the list above but not to all of them. There are no references to the shepherd who owns the sheep and breeds them for meat, leather, milk and wool; or to the shepherd who leads the sheep into a pen for the night (by playing a whistle or a sitar); or to the shepherd who breeds sheep and chooses appropriate animals for breeding.

We have already noted that in *The Literary Mind*, Turner worked with the term *parable* rather than *conceptual metaphor* and emphasised its narrative character. The parable is a projection of a story, not primarily of objects, their properties, structures, or knowledge about them; the key feature is the narrative. We will also note regarding the metaphorical conceptualisations of תורה *the Torah / Law* that although nouns are the usual subjects of metaphorical conceptualisation, verbs will also play a key role in metaphorical expressions from source domains.

Narration has been at the forefront of the study of philosophy, literary science, linguistics, cognitive sciences and neurosciences since the middle of the last century, while some disciplines, for example narrative psychotherapy and narrative theology, have developed in their own directions. The story is considered one of the major anthropological and cultural categories. This is certainly true for Polish anthropologically and culturally oriented linguists (Łebowska, for example[63]), who consider it a basic mental and cognitive structure or mechanism. Narration as an act of the mind serves in all cultures to control, work with and organise experiences ("big stories" such as myths and fairy tales, but also "small stories" such as the stories of individuals and stories about everyday life and

---

63   Anna Łebowska, "Pojęcie focus w narratologii—problem i inspiracje," in *Punkt widzenia w tekście i w dyskursie*, ed. Jerzy Bartmiński, Stanisława Niebrzegowska-Bartmińska, and Ryszard Nycz (Lublin: Wydawnictwo Uniwersytetu Marii Curie-Skłodowskiej, 2014), 228.

life experiences). Stories are an essential tool for mental manipulation and are an instrument for organising experiences in the mind.[64] As mentioned above, Bartmiński refers to the cognitive definition of meaning as the *story of an object*.[65] Objects and persons are defined functionally and narratively by being incorporated into a sequence of events.

The reason for introducing the term *generic narrative structure* is similar.[66] In the generic narrative structure, the individual metaphorical vehicles (the Hebrew expressions of the source domain) are functionally linked as part of the sequence of events; they are part of the narrative. As we will see later, for generic narrative structures, verb expressions are usually determinative, that is, they organise the basic structure and related substantives, adjectives, adverbs and other terms. For example, the conceptual metaphor THE TORAH / LAW IS A JOURNEY will include the generic narrative structure TO STRAY OFF THE PATH. Within a generic narrative structure, a metaphorical vehicle can participate in the metaphorical conceptualisation of the Hebrew verb expression: סור (in Q *to turn aside, to go off, to retreat, to fall down, to abandon, to desist, to stand aloof, to leave off, to stop*; in HI *to remove*); נטה (in HI *to stretch out, to spread out, to steer sideways, to guide away*); הפך (in Q *to turn, to overthrow, to turn back to front*; in NI *to fall upon, to be overthrown*); מוש (in HI *to remove*); לוז (in Q *to escape from someone's sight*; in NI *to go wrong*; in HI *to escape from someone's sight*); or also עזב (in Q *to leave, to leave behind, to leave over*) and עבר (in Q *to pull along, to go to one's side, to move through, to pass over*). These are adopted by other expressions that may also occur in other generic narrative structures: דרך (*way, road, journey*); נתיב / נתיבה (*pathway, path*); ארח (*path, ground, dam*); מסלה (*[main] road, highway, paved way, track*); רגל (*foot, leg*); משׂכה חדק (*[path] overgrown with thorns*); הפכפך (*crooked [path, journey]*); קרב (*in the middle [of the journey]*); תחלה (*the beginning [of the journey]*), and so on.[67]

The generic narrative structure as a partial position of the conceptual metaphor or a bundle of functionally linked metaphorical vehicles is then a tool of conceptualisation which generates metaphorical meaning. The generic narrative structure TO STRAY OFF THE PATH is involved, for example, in the metaphorical conceptualisation of the Hebrew expression תורה *the Torah / Law* and related terms in Isaiah 59:7–8:

Isa 59:7 רגליהם לרע ירצו וימהרו לשפך דם נקי מחשבותיהם מחשבות און שד ושבר במסלותם:

8 דרך שלום לא ידעו ואין משפט במעגלותם נתיבותיהם עקשו להם כל דרך בה לא ידע שלום:

Their **feet run** to evil, and they **rush** to shed innocent blood;
their thoughts are thoughts of iniquity,
desolation and destruction are in their **highways**.
The **way** of peace they do not know, and there is no justice in their **paths**.
Their **roads** they have made **crooked**; no one who **walks** in them knows peace.

---

64 Dorota Fillar, "Narracyjność w badaniach interdyscyplinarnych a kategorie narracyjne w semantyce," in *Narracyjnosc jezyka i kultury*, ed. Piekarczyk Fillar (Lublin: Wydawnictwo Uniwersytetu Marii Curie-Skłodowskiej, 2014), 16–17.

65 Jerzy Bartmiński, "Narracyjny aspekt definicji kognitywnej," in *Narracyjnosc jezyka i kultury*, ed. Piekarczyk Fillar (Lublin: Wydawnictwo Uniwersytetu Marii Curie-Skłodowskiej, 2014), 100.

66 Procházková, *Hospodin je král*, 40–64.

67 For other metaphorical vehicles, see the next chapter.

The metaphorical vehicles רגל (*foot, leg*), מסלה (*main road*), דרך (*way, road, journey*), and נתיבה (*pathway, path*) are joined to the generic narrative structure TO STRAY OFF THE PATH in both verses. To identify the appropriate generic narrative structure, the verbs רוץ (in Q *to run*), עקשׁ (in PI *to twist, to make crooked*), דרך (in Q *to tread*), and also possibly מהר (in PI *to hasten, to come quickly, to go quickly*) are determinative.

As will be seen below, some generic narrative structures are used in different variants and contexts and generate metaphorical meaning repeatedly; others (like some conceptual metaphors) are used only once within the Old Testament canon and are the unique and original work of the author.

As with the conceptual metaphor, we will assume that the primary function of the metaphorical projection of a generic narrative structure into a target domain is cognitive; that a generic narrative structure is an instrument of knowledge and understanding which brings fresh knowledge and fresh understanding, reveals new relationships, and sets objects in the context of events.

The construction of the meaning of metaphorical expressions in biblical texts often involves intertextuality. Vehicles include not only individual verb expressions, phrases, or whole passages of text, but also, as we will see below, generic narrative structures. The identification of conceptual metaphors and generic narrative structures in the text is therefore a vital part of the understanding process and of the exploration of the meaning of the passage of text in exegesis.

For example, in Lamentations 3:1–3, the Hebrew verb expressions נהג (in Q a perfect verb) and הלך (in HI an imperfect verb) and the noun שׁבט act as metaphorical vehicles and signal the applied conceptual metaphor GOD IS A SHEPHERD and within it the generic narrative structure THE SHEPHERD LEADS THE FLOCK TO THE GRAZING LAND:

אני הגבר ראה עני בשבט עברתו: Lam 3:1
2 אותי נהג וילך חשך ולא־אור:
3 אך בי ישב יהפך ידו כל־היום:
I am one who has seen affliction under the **rod** of God's wrath;
he has driven and brought me into darkness without any light;
against me alone he turns his hand, again and again, all day long.

Here, the generic narrative structure THE SHEPHERD LEADS THE FLOCK TO THE GRAZING LAND is the bearer of intertextuality, which in this case plays a key role in the construction of metaphorical meaning. The best-known passage from the Psalms governed by such a generic narrative structure is undoubtedly Psalm 23. Following Hillers,[68] Villanueva[69] has described Lamentations 3:2 as an "anti-Psalm 23."

---

68   Delbert R. Hillers, *Lamentations* (New York: Doubleday, 1984), 125.
69   Federico Villanueva, *The "Uncertainty of a Hearing". A Study of the Sudden Change of Mood in the Psalms of Lament* (Leiden: Brill, 2008), 224.

The expression חשך ולא־אור (*darkness without light*)[70] within the conceptual metaphor GOD IS A SHEPHERD (more precisely within the generic narrative structure THE SHEPHERD LEADS THE FLOCK TO THE GRAZING LAND) is understood as the goal of the shepherd's leading. In the source domain, this goal is usually the source of life: נוה (*pastures*), מים מנחות (*calm places by the waters*), מנחה (*a place of rest*), and so on. In metaphorical projections, the entity נוה (*pasture*) can correspond, for example, to entities that refer to the Lord's temple, such as in Psalm 43:3–4, and here in Psalm 78:52–54:

Ps 78:52 ויסע כצאן עמו וינהגם כעדר במדבר:

53 וינחם לבטח ולא פחדו ואת־אויביהם כסה הים:

54 ויביאם אל־גבול קדשו הר־זה קנתה ימינו:

Then he led out his people like sheep and guided them in the wilderness like a flock.
He led them in safety, so that they were not afraid;
but the sea overwhelmed their enemies.
And he brought them to his holy hill, to the mountain that his right hand had won.

Against the background of these verses, in Lamentations 3:2 the phrase חשך ולא־או (*darkness without light*) is used to construct a contrasting and drastic image, like the instrument with which the shepherd leads the herd: שבט עברה (*staff of anger*; Lam 3:1). Here, the generic narrative structure is undoubtedly being used as an innovative intertextual tool and the reader (or listener) is supposed to recall texts where this generic narrative structure is used in the usual positive way.

1.2 THE METAPHORICAL CONCEPTUALISATION OF תורה THE TORAH / LAW AND RELATED HEBREW TERMS: BASIC CHARACTERISTICS OF THE SEMANTIC AREA AND THE TERMINOLOGY AND ETYMOLOGY OF THE CENTRAL HEBREW EXPRESSION

We have already noted that the essence of a conceptual metaphor is the structuring of the *target domain* through the *source domain*. Conceptual domains, both source and

---

70 The Hebrew phrase חשך ולא־אור (*darkness without light*) in verse 2 also appears, for example, in Job 12:25. Like its variants, such as ארץ חשך (*earth of darkness*; Job 10:21), it can refer in these contexts to the underworld, the grave, שאול (*Sheol*; Job 17:13). In his study of spatial metaphors in Lam 3:1–9, Eidevall used cognitive and culturally oriented linguistics to interpret this phrase in Lam 3:2 in the same way. See Göran Eidevall, "Spatial Metaphors in Lamentations 3:1–9," in *Metaphor in the Hebrew Bible*, ed. Pierre van Hecke (Leuven: Leuven University Press, 2005), 133–137. Berges mentions a possible connection between verse 2 and Isa 50:10, Isa 59:9 and Mic 7:8. See Ulrich Berges, *Klagelieder* (Freiburg im Breisgau: Herder, 2002), 187; חשך ולא־אור (*darkness without light*) is also identified with the day of the Lord and the judgment of Jerusalem (Jer 7:29; Joel 2:1–2; Judges 1:14–16; Amos 5:18). See Duane A. Garrett and Paul R. House, *Song of Songs, Lamentations* (Nashville: Thomas Nelson, 2004), 409, 411. Garrett and House connect מחשך (*darkness*) in verse 6 with the darkness of the grave but assume the metaphor of the judge lies in the background of the metaphorical expression and interpret the destruction of Jerusalem and its inhabitants (which they see as embodied in the spoken section of Lam 3:1–24) as God's judgment.

target, are dynamic structures that are always present during the mapping process. The conceptual domain תורה *the Torah / Law* cannot therefore be defined outside a particular metaphorical expression and cannot be easily identified with a semantic area. Nonetheless, as its metaphorical conceptualisations will be observed throughout the Old Testament Hebrew canon, it will be appropriate here to introduce some basic terminology to provide an overview of the Hebrew expressions for the semantic area תורה *the Torah / Law*. These are primarily substantive Hebrew terms and only secondarily verbal, adverbial and other expressions. On the other hand, metaphorical conceptualisations are seen mainly through verbs of the domain which is the source domain for the metaphor. Mapping often takes place through structures that are narrative in nature. The core Hebrew terms of the semantic area תורה *the Torah / Law* which appear repeatedly in metaphorical expressions throughout the Old Testament are listed in the following table. Their affiliation to the semantic area תורה *the Torah / Law* was tested in standard dictionaries and lexicons.[71]

Tab. 1.1

SUBSTANTIVES	
תורה	direction, instruction, law
חק	due, prescribed task, law, regulation
מצוה	order, commandment
פקודים	instructions, procedures
עלדות	witness, testimony, law, legal provision
משפט	judgment, judicial decision, verdict
צדק צדקה	accuracy, the right thing, justice, justness
צדיק	innocent, just, upright
תוכחת תוכחה	rebuke, punishment, reprimand, reproof
טוב טובה	good things, goodness, kindness

71   For example: Wilhelm Gesenius, *Hebräisches und Aramäisches Handwörterbuch über das Alte Testament*, 18th ed. (Berlin: Springer, 2013), hereafter, Gesenius 2013; Ludwig Koehler, Walter Baumgartner, and M. E. J. Richardson, *The Hebrew and Aramaic Lexicon of the Old Testament. The New Koehler Baumgartner in English*, 4 vols., trans. M. E. J. Richardson (Leiden: Brill, 1994–1999); Gerhard Botterweck, Heinz-Josef Fabry, and Helmer Ringgren, eds., *Theological Dictionary of the Old Testament*, 15 vols., trans. Douglas W. Stott (Grand Rapids: Eerdmans, 1991–2005); Jenni Westermann, *Theologisches Handwörterbuch zum Alten Testament* (Munich: Chr. Kaiser, 1984); Willem VanGemeren, *Dictionary of Old Testament Theology, and Exegesis*, 5 vols. (Grand Rapids: Zondervan, 1997); David Clines, ed., *The Dictionary of Classical Hebrew*, 8 vols. (Sheffield: Sheffield Academic Press, 1998–2011).

חטא חטאה חטאת	offence, guilt (sin, sinner)
רע	evil
עון	misdeed, sin, guilt caused by sin, punishment
עול עולה עלוה	perversity, injustice, criminal, sinner, badness, malice
שקר	lying, lie (with a legal or judicial connotation)
גנב	thief
רשע רשעה	guilty, wicked person, wrong, offence
חמס	violence, wrong
חלקלקות חלקלק	intrigues
מכשול	offence

Table 1.2

ADJECTIVES	
טוב	good, pleasant, desirable, in order, usable, qualitatively good, efficient
צדק	righteous
רע	injurious, evil
חטו	fallible, sinful
נקי	blameless
חר	guilty, criminal (uncertain: to be loaded with guilt, to be wrong; dishonest)
עקש	to be perverted

Table 1.3

VERBS	
שמר	Q to keep, to respect, to obey
נצר	Q to keep, to respect, to obey
עבר	Q to infringe, to break rules, to make a mistake
שגג	Q to infringe, to break rules, to make a mistake
עקש	PI to pervert

ישׁר	Q *to be straight, to be smooth, to be right*
שׁפט	Q *to pass judgment, to administer justice*
דין	Q *to plead one's cause, to execute judgment*
יכח	NI *to argue (in a lawsuit), to be found to be right* HI *to rebuke, to chasten, to punish*
טוב	Q *to be good, to be joyful*
עול	PI *to act unjustly*
חטו	Q *to miss, to wrong (morally), to sin, to offend*
רשׁע	Q *to (become) guilty* HI *to declare guilty*
נקה	Q *to be without blame, to remain blameless* PI *to leave unpunished, to declare to be free from punishment*
שׁקר	Q *to act against contractual terms* PI *to break faith*
ריב	Q *to carry on, to contest a lawsuit*
נגע	Q *to touch violently, to strike with*
חמס	Q *to treat violently*
רצח	Q *to kill, to murder*
גנב	Q *to steal, to purloin*

The core Hebrew expression (noun) תורה (translated into English as *the Torah / Law*, but also *code, instructions, commandments, teaching* or *direction*) is one of the key concepts in the Old Testament biblical canon and indeed in biblical theology in general. The broader theme of law, righteousness and justice can be found in almost everything written about Old Testament theology. The topic is dealt with separately[72] or in the context of covenant,[73] God's attributes and names,[74] and Old Testament morals and ethics, but also in interpretations of creation and Old Testament eschatology. All the theological testimonies of the Jewish and Christian traditions, and hence those concerning law, righteousness and justice, were formulated on the basis of the texts of the Old Testament biblical canon, which was in turn based on many centuries of the life and faith of ancient Israel and the anthropological, social, geographical, historical,

---

72 Gerhard von Rad, *Theologie des Alten Testament*, (Munich: Chr. Kaiser, 1957–1967), 1:382–393; Claus Westermann, *Theologie des Alten Testament in Gründzugen* (Göttingen: Vandenhoeck & Ruprecht, 1985), 102–132; Brevard Childs, *Old Testament Theology in a Canonical Context* (Philadelphia: Fortress Press, 1985), 51–62.
73 Walther Eichrodt, *Theology of the Old Testament* (Philadelphia: Westminster Press, 1964), 70–83.
74 Ibid., 232–239; Horst Dietrich Preuss, *Theologie des Alten Testaments* (Stuttgart: W. Kohlhammer, 1991), 196–203; Rolf Rendtorff, *Canonical Hebrew Bible. A Theology of the Old Testament*, trans. D. E. Orton (Blandford Forum: Deo Publishing 2005), 613–616, 630–636.

cultural and religious experiences of ancient Israelites. This experience is captured very particularly in metaphors.

As we shall see below, the theological testimonies of the Old Testament texts and the metaphors involved in the conceptualisation of the key Hebrew expression תורה *the Torah / Law* will to some extent correspond to etymology. The motivation of etymology is often the same as the motivation of metaphorical conceptualisation. This is because in both cases motivation is based on the same (or similar) image schemas that are anchored throughout the language culture. These schemas are often based on physical experience –experience with objects, with their origin in motion or orientation in space.

The etymology of תורה *the Torah / Law* is the subject of much academic discussion. The initial verb root, for example, is not easily identifiable (Gesenius suggests ירה[75]), although most modern standard dictionaries and lexicons do at least agree on its meaning.[76] Wellhausen sees a connection between תורה and הורה (see Joshua 18:6), that is, with the ancient practice of discerning God's will by casting lots using the Urim and Thummim.[77] Delitzsch believes תורה to be derived from the Akkadian *têrtu*, the nominal derivative of the verb translated into English as *send, transmit, convey*, as in *convey knowledge or instruction*.[78] Wellhausen and others suggest a connection to the practice of bringing an oracle. Cazelles notes the following:

> That in West Semitic *tôrah* referred originally not to instruction but to an oracle or divine decision has now been demonstrated by the discoveries at Mari, which clarify certain scattered observations of Assyriologists. The verb *wâru* corresponds to the Hebrew *yrh / wrh*, just as its derivative *têret* corresponds to *tôrâh*. Now we can finally distinguish this root from *yrh*, "throw," which becomes *w'r* as analysed by Bottéro and Finet. *Wâru* does not mean "teach" but "give orders, instructions" or "send a message / messenger." As regards *têrtu(m)* (const. *têret*), ... it may be rendered ... "omen" or "oracle."[79]

Jensen on the other hand rejects the notion of inferring the meaning of תורה from etymology and suggests understanding the Torah as a set of commandments, ordinances and teachings in the sense of the entire set of canonical Old Testament texts.[80]

---

75 Gesenius 2013. Gesenius also refers to the relative root הרי and its relation to akk. (*w*)*arû* – *führen, schicken*, ug. *Schiessen*, äth. *Warawa–werfen*: (I) Q *werfen, schiessen*; HI *werfen, schiessen*; (II) HI *tränken, benetzen*; (III) HI *lehren, unterweissen, zeigen, Zeichen geben*.

76 VanGemeren, *Dictionary of Old Testament Theology*: (I) Q *to shoot (arrow), throw, cast, set*; HI *shoot, throw*; (II) HI *made drenched, made saturated*; (III) HI *teach, instruct*. Clines, *Dictionary of Classical Hebrew*: (I) Q *throw*; HI *shoot, throw*, (II) HI *water, rain upon, cause to rain down*; (III) Q *teach*; HI *teach, instruct*; (IV) *be led*. Koehler, Baumgartner, and Richardson, *Hebrew and Aramaic Lexicon*: (I) Q *throw, shoot*; HIF *throw, cast, shoot*; (II) HIF *to water*; (III) HI *instruct, teach*.

77 Julius Wellhausen, *Skizen und Vorarbeiten* (Berlin: Georg Reimer, 1887), 394–395.

78 Friedrich Delitzsch, *Prolegomena eines neuen hebräisch-aramäisches Wörterbuch zum Alten Tesatment* (Leipzig: J. C. Hinrichs'sche Buchhandlung, 1886), 41, 47; Friedrich Delitzsch, *Assyrische Grammatik* (Berlin: Verlag von Reuther and Reichard, 1906).

79 Henri Cazelles, "Le Pentateuque comme Torah," in *Autour de l'Exode* (Paris: Cerf, 1987), 136–137.

80 Joseph Jensen, *The Use of Tôrâ by Isaiah: His Debate with the Wisdom Tradition* (Washington DC: Catholic Biblical Association, 1973).

Pavel Čech, a Czech expert on ancient Semitic languages, interprets תורה as a causative abstract derived from the verb root ירה with the meaning *to point to* and points out that the noun מורה (*teacher*) is derived from the same word and means one who directs students by their explanation: *to direct (on the way)*. A more accurate translation of תורה would then be *law* rather than *direction*. Čech also points out that according to similar rules of derivation, the noun *Talmud* comes from the verb root למד (*to teach*).[81]

The conceptual metaphor THE TORAH / LAW IS A JOURNEY, which we will identify as lying behind a series of Old Testament metaphorical expressions, especially, in its framework, within the generic narrative structure TO SHOW THE PATH (but also TO TURN FROM THE PATH, TO RETURN), corresponds to some of the hypotheses mentioned regarding the etymology of the noun תורה. Some verb expressions of the semantic area תורה *the Torah / Law*, and only in exceptional cases nominal expressions, can even be described as lexicalised metaphors. For example, the meaning of the verb root עבר is listed by standard dictionaries and lexicons in Q as *to pull along, to go one's way, to move through, to pass over, to pass by, to go over*, but also in Q *to infringe, to break the rules of the Torah, to make a mistake*. Similarly, the meaning of the verb root שגג is listed in Q as *to go astray*, but also *to infringe, to break the rules of the Torah, to make a mistake*, and the adjective עקש is rendered *twisted / crooked (journey)*, but also *to be perverted*. Some metaphorical vehicles of the conceptual metaphor THE TORAH / LAW IS A JOURNEY, that is, those vehicles of the metaphor that are central to the conceptualisation of the concept תורה as part of the Old Testament Hebrew canon, have become lexicalised or "domesticated" in the semantic area תורה *the Torah / Law*; ordinary speakers rarely realise the metaphorical use of this expression and standard dictionaries and lexicons of biblical Hebrew often mention the metaphorical meaning as its own Hebrew equivalent (usually as the third or second meaning, but sometimes the first).

In the Pentateuch, in the sense of laws, ordinances and regulations, תורה *the Torah / Law* is concentrated in three great collections: *the Book of the Covenant* (Ex 20:22–23:33), *the Deuteronomic Code* (Deut 12–26, and 28) and the *Holiness Code* (Lev 17–26 or 27), but of course countless other laws, ordinances and regulations—which Rabbinic Judaism has proceeded to systematise—are scattered throughout the Old Testament, including in the Wisdom Literature and the Prophets. Sections of text, or books or sets of books, or literary circles and the like, can have their own literary, linguistic, terminological and theological characteristics.

The whole of the Old Testament can be considered as having the status of a legal document. Equally, tradition understands the whole set of sacred Judaic texts as a vassal covenant between God and his people. Rabbinic Judaism, which prevailed after the fall of the Temple in AD70, is largely a legal system: being a Jew means signing a contract and observing the law. The term *oral Torah*, the authoritative interpretation by Jewish scholars of the *written Torah*, was introduced later. In the broadest sense, therefore, the Torah represents the entire literary production of all Jewish culture over

---

81   Pavel Čech, "Zákon ve Starém zákonu," in *Zákon a právo v archaických kulturách*, ed. Dalibor Antalík, Jiří Starý, and Tomáš Vítek (Prague: Filozofická fakulta Univerzity Karlovy, 2010), 161–176.

several centuries, which arose from the need to interpret the *written Torah*, to clarify and formulate its meaning, and to give precise instructions on its application.

However, יהוה תורה *the Torah / Law of the Lord* is not just a *law* in the legal sense: as a set of commandments and teachings it narrates the biblical account of God's will and God's deeds. It is therefore, in the broadest sense, both the totality and the promulgation of God's revelation.

The laws, ordinances and regulations of the Old Testament cover numerous spheres: national and international treaties; regulations concerning property and inheritance; the legal status and rights of different groups within the population (priests, foreigners, slaves, prisoners, women, and citizens with limited rights—such as eunuchs); laws and regulations ensuring the proper functioning of the administrative apparatus; commercial, labour and criminal laws; religious and ritual regulations (regarding what is ritually clean and unclean, rules regarding the offering of sacrifices, rules regarding the ordination of priests, regulations regarding holy days and what to do on them, etc.); and examples of judicial practice.

These are laws and regulations that originate in the earliest oral tradition, in customary law and in tribal communities; others come from the separate kingdoms of Israel and Judah, and the newest from the Assyrian, Babylonian, and ultimately the Roman rule over Palestine. The legal texts were therefore collected, edited, commented on and supplemented in very different cultural, social and political contexts. Of course, these contexts also form the source domains, that is, the experiential basis of the conceptual metaphors.

As we have already noted, in general, and also in the texts of the Old Testament canon, the language of laws and regulations is specific and highly formalised. It consists of established implicative and irrefutable formulas and set phrases for oaths, curses, witness statements, legal actions and court judgments. The focus here will be on passages of text which we can classify as metaphorical expressions. The first signal that a metaphor may be involved in constructing the meaning of a passage of text is when different non-legal expressions, from a semantic area other than תורה *the Torah / Law*, are used within a single statement.

Metaphorical expressions therefore appear not only in poetic texts but also in legal texts, particularly in the preambles to collections of laws and in the final summaries. In more general considerations of compliance with and violation of the law, and in texts concerning the meaning of the law, these expressions concern topics which today are dealt with in the areas of legal theory and the philosophy of law. Metaphorical expressions often reveal how the authors of the relevant texts in *the Torah / Law* understood their function in society and in culture and testify to the status enjoyed by *the Torah / Law* in the system of values and what society saw and appreciated in it.

CHAPTER 2

METAPHORICAL CONCEPTUALISATION OF תורה *THE TORAH / LAW* AND RELATED TERMS

To identify and explain the meaning of metaphorical expressions, each with its own particular form and content, we will use the methods of cognitive and culturally oriented linguistics as described in the previous chapter. These methods help to provide a more precise analysis of metaphorical expressions and are a useful tool for analysing and interpreting the text of which the metaphorical expression is a part—sometimes, as we will see, even contributing to the interpretation of exegetically contested points.

The language of the laws in the Hebrew biblical canon is distinctive and often quite formalised. Parts of it appear as set formulas (implicative, apodictic, etc.) or set phrases used in oaths, curses, witness statements, legal actions and court judgments, but we also find numerous metaphorical expressions in the Psalms and throughout the Wisdom Literature and the Prophets. Here, they appear in texts that reflect more general "legal" questions, such as the source or significance of a particular law and the reason for violating or observing it, questions regarding its universality or particularity, or a more general awareness of the law. In other words, questions which today are studied within the fields of legal theory and the sociology, psychology or philosophy of law. Because metaphors help us to understand abstract or complex social, religious and cultural phenomena and ideas, these metaphorical expressions have much to say about the place occupied by the Torah / Law in the society's value system, about what it was that society valued in the law, and about how the authors of certain biblical passages understood its function within the society and culture.

Metaphors "speak" about these complex and abstract phenomena and ideas by suggesting a similarity to the objects, processes and events of everyday life, to entities that we experience through movement or through our senses as human beings; by evoking similarities to the physical perception of darkness and light, hunger and thirst, to the activities of daily life in the home (weaving, washing, dressing, undressing), work in the fields and the different ways of earning a living, and the natural cycles of life.

One example of how the methods of cognitive and culturally oriented linguistics can contribute to an interpretation of exegetically disputed passages can be shown by a cognitive-linguistic analysis of the metaphorical expression in Ps 76:11.[82]

82   For a more detailed cognitive-linguistic analysis of this metaphorical expression, see Procházková, *Hospodin je král*, 166–189.

Ps 76:11 כי־חמת אדם תודך שארית חמת תחגר׃

Human wrath serves only **to praise you**,
when you bind the last bit of your wrath around you.

The Hebrew expression תודך is usually understood in HI as the imperfect 3. fem. singular of the verb root ידה *to praise, to give thanks*,[83] where the subject of the verb is usually assumed to be שארית חמת *the last bit of wrath; remains of wrath of God* or *human wrath*.[84] Emerton,[85] on the other hand, suggests that the subject of the verb is "the Lord" and that the Hebrew verb is a derivative of the root דוך / דכך *to smash, to shatter*,[86] and proposes the following translation:

Surely, thou **dost crush** the wrath of man.
Thou dost restrain the remnant of wrath.

The New English Bible, The Revised English Bible, Goulder, Jacquet and Eaton (in Goulder), Anderson (in Tesh and Zorn), Kraus,[87] and others lean towards a further variant in which אדם is read and translated as "Edom" rather than "man" and חמת as "Hamath" instead of "wrath."[88] *The New American Bible* also has.

Even wrathful Edom praises you;
the remnant of Hamath keeps your feast.

Verse 11 seems to offer the greatest single challenge to interpretation in Psalm 76 (commentators at least have much to say about it), but there is also a great deal of mixing of conceptual metaphors in the construction of metaphorical expressions in the rest of the psalm. In verses 4–7, we can identify the conceptual metaphors GOD IS A WARRIOR,[89] GOD IS A LION / LIONESS,[90] GOD IS THE KING and GOD IS THE SUN.[91] Some of the Hebrew expressions could be considered tools of conceptual blending as they represent more than one conceptual domain: the conceptual domains אש מלחמה WAR-

---

83   Wilhelm Gesenius, *Hebräisches und Aramäisches Handwörterbuch über das Alte Testament*, 17th ed. (Berlin: Springer, 1962), hereafter, Gesenius 1962: *loben, preisen*.

84   Frank-Lothar Hossfeld and Erich Zenger, *Psalms* (Minneapolis: Fortress, 2005), 2:385.

85   John Emerton, "A Neglected Solution of a Problem in Psalm LXXVI 11," *Vetus Testamentum* 24 (1974): 136–146.

86   Koehler, Baumgartner, and Richardson, *Hebrew and Aramaic Lexicon: smash, shatter*; Gesenius 1962: *zerschmettern (Bäume, Hörner, Bogen, Knochen, Masseben . . .), smash into fragments*.

87   See Michael D. Goulder, *The Psalms of Asaph and the Pentateuch: Studies in the Psalter III* (Sheffield: Sheffield Academic Press, 1996), 91–94, 136–146; S. Edward Tesh and Walter D. Zorn, eds., *The College Press NIV Commentary. Psalms*, vol. 1 (Joplin: College Press Publishing, 1999); Hans-Joachim Kraus, *Psalmen I. Psalmen 1–59*, 5th ed. (Neukirchen-Vluyn: Neukirchener, 1978), 481–482.

88   These translators and biblical scholars understand the terms either as symbols of the northern and southern borders of Israel (symbols of the enemies of Israel who will be subjected to the rule of Israel / the Lord), or as a response to the historical events of the 8th century, as representatives of the Assyrian coalition.

89   The following Hebrew expressions can be classified as metaphorical vehicles: קשת *bow*; מגן *shield*; חרב *sword*; מלחמה *war, battle*; אבירי לב *stout-hearted*; אנשי־חיל *warriors*.

90   This Hebrew term can be classified as an example of the metaphorical vehicle טרף *prey (of a lion or lioness)*.

91   These two Hebrew terms can be classified as examples of the metaphorical vehicle פתח נאור (NI *to be lit up, to shine*, etc.).

RIOR and אֲרִי / לָבִיא LION / LIONESS both include the Hebrew expressions שׁבר (in PI to shatter, to smash), גערה rebuke, threaten, growl and שׁלל (in HITPO to be despoiled, to become prey). The meaning of these Hebrew expressions thematically links the metaphorical concepts used and also refers to the central motif of the psalm, namely the fear and awe commanded by God, God-king, God-lion, God-warrior and God-judge.

The verbal expression תחגר, a derivative of the verb root חגר (in Q to gird oneself [with armour; sword, dagger]) can then create a correspondence between נשׁק weapons, or חרב a sword (and variants) from the source domain and the entity שׁארית חמת remains of wrath in the target domain. We can now interpret the metaphorical expression in Ps 76:11 as a threat which is followed in verse 12 by the warning that "God-warrior" is ready to go into battle at any time or to slay his enemies, that is, those who refuse to submit to his sovereignty. In the construction of the metaphorical meaning in the second part of verse 11, the use of the generic narrative structure THE WARRIOR ARMS (HIMSELF) FOR THE FIGHT is quite obvious; the same generic narrative structure also creates a suitable framework for interpretation of the first part of the verse.

The same generic narrative structure, and similar terminology, was used by the author or authors in the construction of the metaphorical expression in Ps 109:19. Through the entity נשׁק weapons, or חרב sword, the entity קללה curse is conceptualised in the target domain.

וַיִּלְבַּשׁ קְלָלָה כְּמַדּוֹ וַתָּבֹא כַמַּיִם בְּקִרְבּוֹ וְכַשֶּׁמֶן בְּעַצְמוֹתָיו: Ps 109:18
¹⁹ תְּהִי־לוֹ כְּבֶגֶד יַעְטֶה וּלְמֵזַח תָּמִיד יַחְגְּרֶהָ:

He clothed himself with cursing as his coat,
may it soak into his body like water, like oil into his bones.
May it be like a garment that he wraps around himself,
like a belt that he wears every day.

Most analysis and interpretation of the problematic metaphorical expression in Ps 76:11 reinforces Emerton's suggestion[92] that the Hebrew verb תורך is a derivative of the verb root דוך / דכך to pound, to crush, to crumble.[93] We can see, therefore, that the methods of cognitive and culturally oriented linguistics make a valuable contribution to the complex linguistic and theological debate surrounding this exegetically controversial verse.

We can state quite unequivocally that the conceptual metaphor THE TORAH / LAW IS A JOURNEY is central to the whole Old Testament corpus. We will describe this metaphor primarily through generic narrative structures (functionally linked bundles of metaphoric vehicles; Hebrew expressions specific to the semantic area Journey) and annotated tables using the structural correlations and correspondences that arise

---

92 Emerton, "A Neglected Solution."
93 Blahoslav Pípal, *Hebrejsko-český slovník ke Starému zákonu*, 2nd ed. (Prague: Ústřední církevní nakladatelství, 1974): *break, shatter, break up, crush*; Czech Ecumenical Translation: *to fragment*; Kralice translation: *break into pieces*; Koehler, Baumgartner, and Richardson, *Hebrew and Aramaic Lexicon*: *smash, shatter*; Gesenius 1962: *zerschmettern (Bäume, Hörner, Bogen, Knochen, Masseben . . .), smash into fragments*.

between the source and target domains in the mapping of selected metaphorical expressions.

Passages of text that use the appropriate generic narrative structure in a conventional manner will be chosen in order to highlight the underlying tendencies and meanings generated within the Old Testament through the metaphor of the journey. Other metaphors, such as THE TORAH / LAW IS PROPERTY / VALUABLES, THE TORAH / LAW IS A BELOVED PERSON / OBJECT, THE TORAH / LAW IS A PLANT and THE TORAH / LAW IS SWEETNESS, will be described through metaphorical vehicles and structural correlations and correspondences that arise between the source and target domains in the mapping of selected verses.

2.1 THE CENTRAL CONCEPTUAL METAPHOR: THE TORAH / LAW IS A JOURNEY

The journey metaphor was first described by Lakoff and Johnson in *Metaphors We Live By*.[94] Johnson further identified the path image schema as one of the most common cognitive structures based on our physical experience, that is, our experience of movement in a space.[95] As the journey metaphor is anchored in this basic human physical and spatial experience, it is comprehensible across many languages and cultures and in many historical, linguistic and cultural contexts.

Examples of the journey metaphor are almost countless: LOVE IS A JOURNEY, LIFE IS A JOURNEY, CONFLICT IS A JOURNEY, INTERPRETING A TEXT IS A JOURNEY, EDUCATION IS A JOURNEY, DYING IS A JOURNEY, and so on. The following metaphorical expressions are a realisation of the conceptual metaphors LOVE IS A JOURNEY and AN ARGUMENT IS A JOURNEY:

Look *how far we've come.*
We're *at a crossroads.*
We'll just have *to go our separate ways.*
We can't *turn back now.*
I don't think this relationship is *going anywhere.*[96]
We have *set out* to prove that bats are birds.
When we get to the next point, we shall see that philosophy is dead.
So far, we've seen that no current theories will work.
We will *proceed* in a *step-by-step* fashion.
Our *goal is* to show that hummingbirds are essential to military defense.
This observation *points the way* to an elegant solution. We *have arrived at* a disturbing conclusion.[97]

---

94   Lakoff and Johnson, *Metaphors We Live By*, 44–45. Other authors speak of the path image schema as SOURCE--PATH–GOAL, or FROM–TO.
95   Johnson, *The Body in the Mind*, 113.
96   Lakoff and Johnson, *Metaphors We Live By*, 44 (italics in original).
97   Ibid., 90 (italics in original).

Lackoff and Johnson describe the words in italics as conceptual metaphors; in the Hebrew text, we refer to these kinds of expression as metaphorical vehicles.

The various components of the path image schema (the journey metaphor) can be highlighted to different degrees. For Lakoff and Johnson, the main accent is usually the target, but it can also be the starting point, the movement towards the target, or the time dimension of movement towards the target.[98] They nonetheless admit that this accent can be transferred to other components, such as a particular position within a path, to further characteristics of the path from the start to the finish, to the direction of movement (UP–DOWN; ASCENT–DESCENT), the speed of movement, and so on. We then talk about transformations of the path image schema. Components of the journey metaphor can be suppressed as well as accentuated. For example, a means of transport (*car, boat, train . . .*) in a particular metaphorical conceptualisation could be accented and the target suppressed.

In the wake of Lakoff and Johnson's pioneering work, case studies documenting the path image schema (journey metaphor) in different languages and contexts were developed in the fields of linguistics, culture theory, political science and sociology.

The metaphorical expression we find in Deuteronomy 8:6 (from the second introductory speech to the giving of the Law) could be considered a conventional use of the journey metaphor:

Deut 8:6 וּשְׁמַרְתָּ אֶת־מִצְוֹת יְהוָה אֱלֹהֶיךָ לָלֶכֶת בִּדְרָכָיו וּלְיִרְאָה אֹתוֹ׃

Therefore keep the commandments of the LORD your God,
by **walking in his ways** and by fearing him.

Use of the metaphor THE TORAH / LAW IS A JOURNEY is signaled by metaphorical vehicles: in this case, the verb root with preposition הלך + בּ (in Q *to go, to walk*) and the noun דרך (*way, road, journey*). The metaphorical conceptualisation of the source domain also includes the root verb שׁמר (in Q *to keep, to watch over, to take care of, to preserve, to protect*), but we will not consider this a metaphorical vehicle as the term frequently occurs in other contexts, in the sense of watching over a garden (Gen 2:15), watching over a herd (Gen 30:30), watching over grain stores (Gen 41:35), or watching over (keeping) a covenant (Gen 17:9–10).

In the metaphorical conceptualisation, the root verb שׁמר also connects correspondence in the target domain but its independent use does not signal *mapping* through the journey metaphor. In order to confirm use of the journey metaphor, other expressions must be present in the text which are unambiguously entities of the semantic area *Journey*. In Deuteronomy 18:19, 19:9 and 26:17, the noun דרך (*way, road, journey*) is such a metaphorical vehicle, just as it is in Deuteronomy 8:6.

---

98   Dirven and Vespoor speak of the hierarchy of the path schema in the human experience and refer to it as the *goal-over-source principle*. See René Dirven and Marjolijn Verspoor, eds., *Cognitive Exploration of Language and Linguistics* (Amsterdam: John Benjamins, 1999), 90.

The use of the journey metaphor in Deuteronomy 5:32 is signalled by the metaphorical vehicle סור (in Q *to turn aside, to go off, to retreat*) and is used in the spatial image schema—ימין שמאל RIGHT–LEFT:

Deut 5:32 ושמרתם לעשות כאשר צוה יהוה אלהיכם אתכם לא תסרו ימין ושמאל:

You must therefore be careful to do as the Lord your God has commanded you;
you shall not turn to the right or to the left.

The metaphor THE TORAH / LAW IS A JOURNEY in Deuteronomy 8:6 evokes the mental image of a person walking along a path and, colloquially speaking, *keeping a careful eye on where they are going*: where to put their feet, step by step, in order to maintain their direction and keep to the path. The core of the mental image is the movement people make when walking, watching to check the direction they are moving: just as people must walk correctly in order not to stray from the path, they must behave and act properly so as not to violate God's commandments (the regulations of the Torah). Right walking, in the right direction, is the right way according to the provisions of the Torah.

The generic narrative structure TO WALK ALONG THE PATH is reflected in the Hebrew text in the target conceptual area תורה *the Torah / Law*. People reading or listening to the Hebrew text are offered a metaphor for structural correlation (*living according to God's commandments* is like *walking along a path*) and correspondence: *watching over—obeying; watching over—living in fear of God; the path—the commandments of God; walking—living according to God's commandments; walking along the path—living in fear of God*. The journey metaphor in Deuteronomy 8:6 suggests that the readers are to understand obeying and living according to God's commandments and living in fear of God as a matter of "walking along a path," "watching every step," "watching where they are putting their feet," being mindful of where (and how) they are going.

Conventional use of the journey metaphor conveys the idea in metaphorical expressions that תורה *the Torah / Law* is **a straight and secure path** on which **one does not stumble or wander, and reaches the destination**. God himself **guards the paths** he has built and **guides** those who walk on these paths *in accordance with the Torah*. So, תורה *the Torah / Law* can be: **a path which leads to the temple**, the house where God himself dwells; **a path which leads to a castle or a fortified city**, a safe place to live; a road built by God (the king of his people Israel) in the land he gave to his people.

Thus, תורה *the Torah / Law* is actually the **infrastructure** of the promised land. God's people Israel are to **guard** the Torah, the ways of God, or the walls of God's city of Jerusalem (or the city itself), as an **inheritance** for future generations. As we shall see, the journey metaphor enters into the process of blending with other conceptual metaphors which together form a coherent system within the Hebrew biblical canon.

The Bible scholars Bancila, Jäkel, and Lam have all discussed metaphorical conceptualisation through the journey metaphor in the Old and New Testaments and developed theories of the conceptual metaphor using the methods of cognitive linguistics.[99]

Others have noted which target domains are conceptualised in biblical texts through the journey metaphor. Those most frequently mentioned are GOD, SOUL, HEREAFTER, LIFE, SPIRITUAL LIFE, and MORAL or METAPHYSICAL IDEAS. In variants of the journey metaphor, particular narratives incorporating path image schemas are also included in the mapping, such as the exodus from Egypt, crossing the Red Sea (or the Jordan), the journey in the wilderness, the journey to the promised land, the journey up to Jerusalem, and in the New Testament the journey to Damascus, the journey to Emmaus, and so on. One variant of the journey metaphor in the Bible regards passages that include the theological motif of homelessness and pilgrimage.

Based on his study of those components that are repeatedly accented in metaphorical expressions and the role of God in the journey schema, Jäkel describes several variants of the journey metaphor and suggests that metaphorical expressions in the Old Testament accent either the *way* aspect or the *traveller* aspect.[100] Variants with the *way* aspect accented include *moral journey*,[101] *God's way* (paths that are *straight, lead to [eternal] life*; they are ways through which God teaches or on which God guides),[102] and the *evil way* (*crooked, dark, slippery and full of obstacles*, paths leading to death).[103] Jäkel pays special attention to variants that arise through the roles given to God in the journey metaphor: *observer, teacher, guide, protector, enemy*.[104] Bancila notes other variants that arise from accenting the *speed* aspect, such as in Job 21:14, Psalm 119:59, Proverbs 1:15-16, Isaiah 41:3, and Jeremiah 18:15.[105]

Using examples from the Pentateuch, the Prophets and the Wisdom Literature, Bancilla recapitulates the use of the journey metaphor in the target domain *Righteous Life* and *Immoral Life*: "The common model of the journey of life, of life as a journey, acquires the significance of a moral journey: the target domain is moral behaviour, the path to be followed is God's commandments, a moral life is a journey on God's way, while unethical conduct is described as swerving, straying from it."[106]

Lam's *Patterns of Sin* is the most recent study on the journey metaphor in the Bible. Lam bases his work on Youngblood's 1978 study which suggested that the meaning of the verb roots חטא (in Q *to miss, to offend, to do wrong*), פשע (in Q *to behave disloyally, to behave as a criminal*), and עוה (in Q *to sin*) is connected to the idea of sin as deviation from a path or a given direction.

99 Maria Yvonne Bancila, *The Journey Metaphor in Old Testament Text* (2009), 365–373, http://www.diacronia.ro/ro/indexing/details/A34/pdf; Olaf Jäkel, "Hypotheses Revisited: The Cognitive Theory of Metaphor Applied to Religous Texts," *Metaphorik.de* (Feb 2002): 20–42, https://www.academia.edu/8706556/Hypotheses_Revisited_The_Cognitive_Theory_of_Metaphor_Applied_to_Religious_Texts; Joseph Lam, *Patterns of Sin in the Hebrew Bible. Metaphor, Culture, and the Making of a Religious Concept* (New York: Oxford University Press, 2016).

100 Jäkel "Hypotheses Revisited," 29–31.

101 Ibid., 25–27.

102 Ibid., 27–28.

103 Ibid., 28–29.

104 Ibid., 31–33.

105 Bancila, *Journey Metaphor*, 365–373.

106 Ibid., 370.

In support of Youngblood's hypothesis, Lam introduces a series of metaphorical expressions in which he identifies the use of the conceptual metaphors SIN IS A PATH and SIN IS A DIRECTION, and goes on to present a number of examples (mostly from the book of Proverbs) which demonstrate the lexicalisation of the journey metaphor in the Hebrew verb root חטא. The author also presents a range of other key terms that occur in the observed metaphorical expressions. We will refer to these expressions as metaphorical vehicles and will add to Lam's list.

Lam mentions the noun דרך (*way, road, journey*) as a key Hebrew term within the journey metaphor, and also the verb roots שוב (in Q *to turn back, to return, to turn away, to abandon*), שוב with the preposition מן (*to turn back, to return, to turn away, to abandon*), סור (in Q *to turn aside, to go off, to retreat, to fall down, to abandon, to desist, to stand aloof, to leave off, to stop*), and הלך (in Q *to go, to walk*), also sometimes in conjunction with the preposition ב. A large number of metaphorical conceptualisations concerning sin, morality and ethical guidelines are built, Lam suggests, through spatial and directional image schemas. This happens most often in Proverbs, but also elsewhere, such as Deuteronomy (Deut 5:32), 1 and 2 Kings (1 Kings 8:32; 2 Kings 10:31), and in the major and minor prophets (e.g. Isa 59:7; Jer 11:10; Mic 6:8; Zeph 1:17; Hos 6:8; 14:10).[107] The conceptual metaphor THE TORAH / LAW IS A JOURNEY[108] is a central concept that metaphorically structures the term תורה *the Torah / Law* and related concepts.[109] Most metaphorical expressions in the Pentateuch are conventional, but in the Wisdom Literature and the Prophets we find places where the journey metaphor is used in a unique or innovative way, sometimes with meanings that may even contradict the meaning of similar expressions in the Pentateuch. Prophetic criticism appears in the text as a redefining of תורה *the Torah / Law* and related terms. We will pay attention to the lexicalisation of the journey metaphor, that is, the "domestication" of other Hebrew expressions from the semantic area *Journey* in the semantic area *Torah / Law*. Youngblood and Lam highlighted the lexicalisation of the verb roots חטא (in Q *to miss, to offend, to do wrong*), פשע (in Q *to behave disloyally, to behave as a criminal*) and עון (in Q *to sin*) in the semantic areas *Righteous Life* and *Immoral Life*. Based on our own analysis and interpretation, other terms will be added. For example, the verb root שמר in the semantic area *Torah / Law* can also be said to be a lexicalised metaphor. Lexicalisation can be shown by many examples of when this verb is used to mean *to respect*, or *to obey* (the *Torah / Law*) in passages that are not metaphorical, such as in the Decalogue in Exodus 20:5–6:

Exo 20:5 לא־תשתחוה להם ולא תעבדם כי אנכי יהוה אלהיך

אל קנא פקד עון אבת על־בנים על־שלשים ועל־רבעים לשנאי׃

6 ועשה חסד לאלפים לאהבי ולשמרי מצותי׃

---

107 Lam, *Patterns of Sin*, 166–178.

108 On the metaphor of *the way* in the Hebrew text of the Old Testament, see: Øystein Lund, *Way Metaphors and Way Topics in Isaiah 40–55* (Tübingen: Mohr Siebeck, 2007); Markus Philipp Zehnder, *Wegmetaphorik im Alten Testament* (Berlin: Walter de Gruyter, 1999).

109 Terms related to תורה *the Torah / Law* include חק (*rule, regulation*), פקודים (*instructions, provisions*), מצוה (*commandment*) and משפט (*judgment, judicial decision, verdict*).

You shall not bow down to them or worship them;
for I the LORD your God am a jealous God,
punishing children for the iniquity of parents,
the third and the fourth generation of those who reject me,
but showing steadfast love to the thousandth generation of those
who love me and **keep**[110] my commandments.

Further examples of the lexicalisation of the verb root שׁמר (in Q *to keep, to watch over*) as a lexicalised metaphor (in Q *to respect, to obey*) include, among many others, Genesis 26:5 and Exodus 13:10; 15:26; 16:28 and 20:6. Standard dictionaries and lexicons give equivalents to שׁמר in Q: not only *to keep, to watch over, to take care of, to preserve, to protect*, but also *to respect*, or *to obey*. Moreover, lexicalisation will provide obvious proof of the *centrality* of the journey metaphor in the metaphorical conceptualisation of תורה *the Torah / Law* and related concepts in the Old Testament. The following tables provide an overview of metaphorical vehicles, that is, Hebrew expressions that are involved in the metaphorical conceptualisation of תורה *the Torah / Law* and related concepts.

Table 2.1

VERBS	
ישׁר	Q *to be straight, to be smooth, to be right* PI *to smooth, to go straight on, to observe carefully*; the nominative derivatives *uprightness, straightness*; and the adjectival derivatives *straight, right*
חלק	Q *to smooth, to slip* HI *to make smooth*
עקשׁ	PI *to twist, to be crooked*
נצר	Q *to keep watch, to watch over, to keep from, to protect, to preserve, to observe, to comply with*
הלך הלך + ב	Q *to go, to walk* PI *to go, to walk, to move about* HIT *to walk about*
בוא	Q *to come*
דרך	Q *to tread*
אשׁר	PI *to stride, to lead*
רוץ	Q *to run* POL *to run back and forth* HI *to cause to run, to fetch in a hurry*

---

110 In Hebrew, the verb root רמע rmv can be used in the sense of *to obey, to respect*.

מהר	PI *to hasten, to come quickly, to go quickly*
חוש	I. Q *to hurry* HI *to hurry, to hasten, to give way* II. Q *to care, to take notice*
רדף	Q *to pursue someone, to pursue, to follow after*
עזב	Q *to leave, to leave behind, to leave over*
רחק	HI *to stretch out, to spread out, to steer sideways, to guide away*
סור סור + מן	Q *to turn aside, to go off, to retreat, to fall down, to abandon, to desist, to stand aloof, to leave off, to stop* HI *to remove*
נטה	HI *to stretch out, to spread out, to steer sideways, to guide away*
עבר	Q *to pull along, to go to one's side, to move through, to pass over*
שוב[111] שוב + ל שוב + על שוב + אל שוב + מן	Q *to turn back, to return, to turn away, to abandon* PI *to bring back, to lead back, to turn around, to lead away, to lead astray, to pay back, to requite* HI *to bring back, to lead back*
שגה	Q *to stray* HI *to lead astray, to mislead*
שגג	Q *to go astray*
תעה	Q *to wander about*
נוד	Q *to sway, to be aimless, to be homeless* HITPO *to sway backwards, to sway backwards and forwards*
יצא	Q *to come out, to come forth, to go out, to go forth*
בוא	Q *to come*
בקש [35]	PI *to discover, to find, to attempt to do something, to try to possess, to demand, to require, to request*
דרש [35]	Q *to care for, to enquire about, to investigate, to require, to search*
ירה	HI *to direct (on the way)*
נחה	Q *to lead, to guide* HI *to lead, to guide, to bring*
דרך	HI *to tread down, to cause to tread upon, to cause to walk*

---

111   The verb roots שוב, דרש, בקש, דנא, נפל occur in contexts other than *journey* in the Old Testament, so to activate the journey metaphor and other generic narrative structures the presence of other metaphorical vehicles (nominal, adverbial or other) is necessary.

כשל כשל + ב [112]	Q *to stumble, to stagger* NI *to stumble, to stagger*
נפל [35] נפל + ב [113]	Q *to fall accidentally, to fall down, to throw oneself down* HI *to drop, to throw down, to cause to collapse*

Table 2.2

SUBSTANTIVES	
דרך	*way, road, journey*
נתיבה / נתיב	*pathway, path*
ארח	*way, ground, dam*
מסלה	*(main) road, highway, paved way, track*
מעגל	*wagon track, firm path*
צעד	*step, way*
מצעד	*step, footprint*
אשר	*step*
רגל	*foot, leg*
פח	*trapping net, thin plate of metal*
שוחה / שיחה / שחות / שיחה	*pit, trap*
חבל	*band, rope, cord, snare, length of rope*
מכשול	*offence*

Table 2.3

ADJECTIVES	
ישר	*straight / right (journey)*
חשך	*dark (journey)*

---

112 In the context of a *journey*, the conjunction ב in combination with the verb root כשל can refer to the obstacle on which a person stumbles (e.g. Lev 26:37) or the point at which they stumble (e.g. Jer 31:9). The preposition can also be followed by a time expression (e.g. "at noon" in Isa 59:10).

113 Because the verb root נפל occurs in contexts other than *journey*, to activate the journey metaphor and within it the generic narrative structure TO FALL DOWN ON THE PATH, the presence of other metaphorical vehicles (nominal, adverbial or other) is necessary. As with the verb root כשל, the conjunction ב in combination with the verb root נפל may refer, in the context of the road, to the obstacle or the stumbling point (Deut 22:4). In other contexts, however, it can refer to the cause of the fall (e.g. Num 14:43 *fall by the sword*, 1 Chron 5:10 *fall into the hands*), or the place of falling (e.g. *in the desert* in Num 14:32; *on the field* in Deut 21:1; *on the way* in Deut 21:1).

חלקלקות חלקלק	smooth (journey / place)
רחב	wide (journey)
משכה חדק	(journey) overgrown with thorns
הפכפך	crooked (journey)
עקש	twisted / crooked (journey)

Table 2.4

DEFINITION OF SPACE / DETERMINATION OF POSITION AND ORIENTATION	
שמאל–ימין	right–left
קרב	in the middle [of the journey]
תחלה	the beginning [of the journey]
קרוב	near
רחק רחוק	far away, far away from, from the distant

Metaphorical vehicles also guide the use of the generic narrative structure as apartial conceptual metaphor and create correspondence with the target domain expressions. In the tables, the structural correlations and correspondences are the basic guideline for explaining the metaphorical meaning of a verse.

As part of the metaphor THE TORAH / LAW IS A JOURNEY, we can identify the following eight generic narrative structures: TO WALK ALONG THE PATH; TO RUN ALONG THE PATH; TO LEAVE THE PATH / TO TURN FROM THE PATH; TO GO ASTRAY; TO RETURN; TO SEARCH FOR THE PATH / TO SEARCH ON THE PATH; TO TAKE ON / TO SHOW THE PATH; and TO FALL DOWN ON THE PATH. We assume that each generic narrative structure has its own narrative in the narrative structure that emerges from the source domains. We will also, therefore, mention non-metaphorical passages in which the narrative structure appears. For each generic narrative structure, we will give examples of its use in a metaphorical expression and show in a table the most important structural correlations and correspondences established during mapping.

Like conceptual metaphors, generic narrative structures can participate in mapping different target domains. They are abstract structures which as cognitive tools—tools of human perception, tools of memory, and ways or forms of understanding and experiencing reality—organise physical, mental, social and spiritual experiences. Where possible, we will give examples in which the generic narrative structure as a subset of the journey metaphor maps expressions of a semantic area other than *the Torah / Law.*

2.1.1 THE GENERIC NARRATIVE STRUCTURE TO WALK
ALONG THE PATH

Just as the THE TORAH / LAW IS A JOURNEY is the central metaphor which structures
the concept תורה *the Torah / Law* and related terms in the Old Testament Hebrew canon,
so the central generic narrative structure is clearly TO WALK ALONG THE PATH. Characteristic metaphorical vehicles or verb roots include הלך (in Q *to go, to walk*; in PI *to go, to
walk, to move about*; in HIT *to walk about*); בוא (in Q *to come*); אשר (in PI *to stride, to lead*);
and דרך (in Q *to march*). Other nouns, adjectives, adverbs, and so on, can add to these
verb expressions (see the table of metaphorical vehicles: table 2.5).

Verbs or verbal terms are usually determinative for generic narrative structures.
As we saw in the example from Deuteronomy 8:6, structural correlations are based
almost exclusively on verbal metaphorical vehicles: in Deut 8:6: *living* according to
God's commandments is like *walking* along a path; nominal and other expressions, and
exceptionally verb expressions, establish correspondence between source and target
domains (in Deut 8:6, for example, the correspondence between the expressions דרך
journey in the source domain and מצוה יהוה *commandments of the Lord* in the target domain). The metaphorical expression we find in Jeremiah 44:10 is an example of the
conventional use of the generic narrative structure TO WALK ALONG THE PATH:

> לא דכאו עד היום הזה ולא יראו ולא־הלכו בתורתי Jer 44:10
> ובחקתי אשר־נתתי לפניכם ולפני אבותיכם:
> They have shown no contrition or fear to this day,
> nor have they **walked in** my law
> and my statutes that I set before you and before your ancestors.

This metaphorical expression contains structural correlations (*to walk along the
path—to live in obedience to the Torah and its commandments—to live in the fear of God*)
which in the language and culture of ancient Israel consolidate numerous metaphorical expressions from a great many Old Testament texts. The verse Jeremiah 44:10 is
a strictly conventional way of applying the conceptual metaphor THE TORAH / LAW
IS A JOURNEY and the generic narrative structure TO WALK ALONG THE PATH. In this
context, the verb root הלך (in Q *to go, to walk*; in PI *to go, to walk, to move about*; in HIT
to walk about) works as a lexical metaphor (as in Lev 18:4; 19:16; 26:3; Deut 30:16, and
elsewhere).

The verb expression הלך (in Q *to go, to walk*) often appears in combination with
the preposition ב in metaphorical expressions within the generic narrative structure
TO WALK ALONG THE PATH, as in Jeremiah 26:4 and 44:10, Daniel 9:10, and here in
Psalm 119:1:

> אשרי תמימי־דר ההלכים בתורת יהוה: Ps 119:1
> Happy are those whose way is blameless, who **walk in** the law of the Lord.

The preposition ב can have several functions in relation to the verb הלך:

- It can specify the direction or destination of a journey. See Exodus 8:23: הלך + במדבר *into the wilderness.*
- It can demarcate the range or scope within which the person being referred to can move. See Leviticus 19:16: לא־תלך רכיל בעמיך *you shall not go about as a talebearer among your people.*
- It can delimit the trajectory of the movement and consequently of the journey (the path). See Genesis 42:38: בדרך אשר תלכו־בה *on the journey that you are to go on.*
- It can refer to a companion for the journey. See Exodus 10:9: בנערינו ובזקנינו נלך *we will go with our young and our old.*

In connection with the verb הלך, the preposition ב can even point to the driving force that sets human beings in motion, such as anger or defiance. See Leviticus 26:28: והלכתי עמכם בחמת *then I will walk contrary to you in fury.*

In the legal context, it is often assumed that the verb expression or phrase following the preposition[114] ב corresponds to *path* in the source domain, that is, the trajectory along which the person is walking, but none of the five options above is excluded.

The Hebrew term אמת *trustworthiness, constancy, faithfulness, truth* is conceptualised metaphorically in the following examples from Psalm 26:3 and 86:11 by means of the generic narrative structure TO WALK ALONG THE PATH, whose key metaphoric vehicle is the verb root הלך in conjunction with the preposition ב:

כי־חסדך לנגד עיני והתהלכתי באמתך: Ps 26:3
For your steadfast love is before my eyes, and **I walk in faithfulness** to you.

הורני יהוה דרך אהלך באמתך יחד לבבי ליראה שמך: Ps 86:11
Teach me your way, O Lord,
that I may **walk in your truth**;
give me an undivided heart to revere your name.

The generic narrative structure TO WALK ALONG THE PATH creates a narrative framework for the metaphorical conceptualisation of the Hebrew term תמים *complete, unscathed, without fault, perfect* in Psalm 84:12 and 101:6:

כי שמש ומגן יהוה אלהים חן וכבוד יתן יהוה לא ימנע־טוב להלכים בתמים: Ps 84:12
For the Lord God is a sun and shield; he bestows favour and honour.
No good thing does the Lord withhold from those who **walk** uprightly (verbatim: **in perfection**).

עיני בנאמני־ארץ לשבת עמדי הלך בדרך תמים הוא ישרתני: Ps 101:6
I will look with favour on the faithful in the land, so that they may live with me;
whoever **walks in the way that is blameless** shall minister to me.

---

114 Most commonly חק *due, prescribed task, law, regulation*; מצוה *order, commandment*; פקודים *instructions, procedures*; תורה *direction, instruction, law.*

The following table shows the most important structural correlations and correspondences established in mapping through the generic narrative structure of the journey in Jeremiah 44:10 and Psalms 26:3; 84:12; 86:11; 101:6 and 119:1.

Table 2.5

	source domain	target domain	location
structural correlation	**TO WALK ALONG THE PATH**		
	הלך + ב Q to go, to walk	to obey the Torah / Law	Jer 44:10
			Ps 119:1
			Ps 101:6
			Ps 26:3
		to be happy (אשרי)	Ps 119:1
		to live in the fear (ירא) of God	Jer 44:10 Ps 86:11
		to serve (שרת) God	Ps 101:6
		to live in truth	Ps 86:11
			Ps 26:3
other GNS	* to learn to walk	to learn to fear God to learn to live in truth	Ps 86:11
	* to show the way	to show / to allow the truth to be known	Ps 86:11
correspondance	way, road	Torah / Law (תורה)	Ps 119:1
			Ps 26:3
		steadfast love and faithfulness (חסד ואמתחסד)	Ps 26:3
	1. the direction / the destination of a journey 2. to demarcate the range / the scope **3. the way, the path, the journey** 4. a companion for the journey 5. the driving force	Torah / Law (תורה)	Jer 44:10
		dues, prescribed tasks, law, regulations (of the Torah) (חקה)	Jer 44:10
		complete, perfect (תמים) [life]	Ps 119:1 Ps 84:12 Ps 101:6
		truth, reliability, firmness (אמת)	Ps 86:11

correspondance	traveller	a happy person	Ps 119:1
		complete / perfect person (תמים)	Ps 84:12[115]
		God's servant	Ps 101:6
		psalmist	Ps 26:3
		Israel	Jer 44:10
	destination	a happy life (אשרי)	Ps 119:1
		complete / perfect life (תמים)	Ps 84:12
		God's house	Ps 101:6
		temple	Ps 101:6
		God	Ps 101:6
		welfare, good things (טוב)	Ps 84:12

The generic narrative structure TO WALK ALONG THE PATH is also found in the construction of meaning in metaphorical expressions in, for example, Exodus 16:4; 18:20; Leviticus 18:4; 20:23; 26:3; Deuteronomy 8:6; 10:12; 19:9; 26:17; 28:9; 28:14; 30:16; Joshua 1:7; Psalms 1:1; 15:2; 26:1; 78:10; 85:14; 89:31; 119:3,45; 125:5; Proverbs 2:13,20; 4:14,18; 6:12; 8:20; 10:9; 16:29; 20:7; 28:18; Isaiah 1:17; 2:3; 42:24; 48:17; 58:8; 59:8; 65:2; Jeremiah 9:12; 18:15; 26:4; 44:23; and Daniel 9:10.

The Hebrew expressions of the target domain establish further correspondences here, and other structural correlations emerge, some of which have already been mentioned. Correspondences with Hebrew adjectives that fill out a description of the path the person is walking along are relatively frequent: the paths of *the Torah* are *straight / right* (ישר), *wide* (רחב); some other paths, however, are *dark* (חשך), *smooth, slimy* (חלקלקות / חלקלק), *crooked* (הפכפך), *twisted / crooked* (עקש), or *(a path) overgrown with thorns* (משכה חדק), which in the target domain typically correspond to terms such as *injurious, evil* (רע), *fallible, sinful* (חטא), *blameless* (נקי), or *guilty, criminal* (חזר).

Numerous passages, some of them metaphorical, testify to the lexicalisation of the journey metaphor in the semantic area *Torah / Law*. In addition to the frequency of this generic narrative structure throughout the Hebrew canon, lexicalisation against a background of the generic narrative structure TO WALK ALONG THE PATH is also an expression of its central position among other generic narrative structures of the journey metaphor. Lexicalisation can be seen in the verb roots הלך, with a shift from *to go, to walk* towards *to respect, to obey*; נצר and שמר with a shift from *to keep, to watch over* towards *to respect, to obey*; and עקש, with a development from *to twist, to*

---

115   The phrase in Ps 84:11b is not a metaphorical expression; only the conceptual metaphors GOD IS THE SUN and GOD IS A SHIELD are present.

make crooked towards *to pervert.* Lexicalisation of the journey metaphor also affects the adjectives יָשָׁר, in which we note a shift from *straight* to *right*, and עָקֵשׁ, where the shift is from *crooked, twisted* to *virtueless*.

There can be a degree of inconsistency in the translation of lexicalised Hebrew expressions into other languages (within or between translations). Sometimes a metaphor is preserved in translation, at other times it is eliminated and translated by a lexeme belonging to the semantic area *Torah / Law*. An example of such fluctuation is the verse Exodus 15:26 and the translation of the verb roots אזן (in HI *to listen*) and שמר (in Q *to keep, to watch over*) into English:

> Saying: "If thou wilt hear the voice of the Lord thy God, and do what is right before him, and **obey** his commandments, and **keep** all his precepts, none of the evils that I laid upon Egypt, will I bring upon thee: for I am the Lord thy healer."
> *Douay-Rheims American Edition (1899)*[116]
>
> He said, "If you will listen carefully to the LORD your God and do what he considers right, if you **pay attention** to his commands and **obey** all his laws, I will never make you suffer any of the diseases I made the Egyptians suffer, because I am the LORD, who heals you."
> *God's Word to the Nations (1994–1995)*
>
> He said, "If you listen carefully to the voice of the LORD your God and do what is right in his eyes, if you **pay attention** to his commands and **keep** all his decrees, I will not bring on you any of the diseases I brought on the Egyptians, for I am the LORD, who heals you."
> *New International Version (1984)*
>
> He said, "If you will listen carefully to the voice of the LORD your God, and do what is right in his sight, and give **heed** to his commandments and **keep** all his statutes, I will not bring upon you any of the diseases that I brought upon the Egyptians; for I am the LORD who heals you."
> *New Revised Standard Version (1989)*

In standard dictionaries and lexicons of biblical Hebrew, lexicalised metaphors are usually given as the second or third meaning of the Hebrew term.

2.1.2 THE GENERIC NARRATIVE STRUCTURE TO RUN ALONG THE PATH

The generic narrative structure TO RUN ALONG THE PATH can be understood as a variant of the central generic narrative structure TO WALK ALONG THE PATH; on its own it is not central in the mapping of the journey metaphor. Here we see verb roots whose context of use varies considerably. The common element is running, but the motivation varies widely. Most often in metaphorical expressions, we find the verb root רוץ (in Q *to run*; in POL *to run back and forth*; in HI *to cause to run, to fetch in a hurry*), and much less frequently מהר (in PI *to hasten, to come quickly, to go quickly*). The verb root חוש

---

116   The Douay-Rheims Bible is a translation from the Latin Vulgate into English by members of the English College (*College des Grands Anglais*), a catholic seminary in Douai, France.

(in Q *to hurry*; in HI *to hurry, to hasten, to give away*) has mostly negative connotations: it is about running in fear of the enemy or impending danger and evokes a sense of escaping to save one's life. Standard dictionaries and lexicons of biblical Hebrew give the meanings: I. in Q *to hurry*, in HI *to hurry, to hasten, to give way*; II. in Q *to care, to take notice*. The meaning of the verb root רדף evokes an attacker or aggressor running; the meaning in Q is given as *to pursue someone, to pursue, to follow after*. These connotations are key to a satisfactory explanation of the metaphorical meaning generated by this generic narrative structure. As with all generic narrative structures, other nominal, adverbial and other expressions can be involved in mapping, together with verbal metaphorical vehicles. An example of the non-metaphorical application of this narrative structure with positive connotations (in this case רוץ) is Genesis 18:2, where running is a sign of politeness, respect or joy.

וישא עיניו וירא והנה שלשה אנשים נצבים עליו Gen 18:2

וירא וירץ לקראתם מפתח האהל וישתחו ארצה:

He looked up and saw three men standing near him. When he saw them, he **ran** from the tent entrance to meet them, and bowed down to the ground.

This narrative structure, with its connotations of joy, maps the metaphorical expression in Psalm 119:32.

דרך־מצותיך ארוץ כי תרחיב לבי: Ps 119:32

I **run the way** of your commandments, for you enlarge my understanding.

The basic structural correlation is similar to that generated through the generic narrative structure TO WALK ALONG THE PATH: *keeping the Torah's commandments* is to be seen as *walking along the path*. Conventional use of the journey metaphor follows the correspondence between the entities *the path* and תורה *Torah / Law* (*the commands of the Torah*). By contrast, negative connotations are evident in the use of the verb roots חוש (I. in Q *to hurry*; in HI *to hurry, to hasten, to give way*; II. in Q *to care, to take notice*) and רדף (in Q *to pursue someone, to pursue, to follow after*). An example of the non-metaphorical application of the narrative structure TO RUN ALONG THE PATH with negative connotations can be found in Leviticus 26:7.

ורדפתם את־איביכם ונפלו לפניכם לחרב: Lev 26:7

You shall **give chase to your enemies**, and they shall fall before you by the sword.

In the metaphorical expressions in Psalm 119:60 and Job 31:5, the generic narrative structure TO RUN ALONG THE PATH is activated via the metaphorical vehicle חוש (in Q *to hurry*) from the source domain *the Destination of the Running*.

In Psalm 119:60, this corresponds with מצוה *commandments* (by which we understand *commandments of the Torah*) in the target domain:

חשתי ולא התמהמהתי לשמר מצותיך: Ps 119:60

I **hurry** and do not delay to keep your commandments.

In Job 31:5, there is not only correspondence between the entities *the destination of the running* and מרמה *fraud, deceit*, but also between the entities *pursued prey* and מרמה *fraud, deceit*.

אם־הלכתי עם־שוא ותחש על־מרמה רגלי: Job 31:5

If I have walked with falsehood, and my **foot has hurried to** deceit.

The table below shows the most important structural correlations and correspondences established during mapping through the generic narrative structure TO RUN ALONG THE PATH in the above examples (Ps 119:32 and 119:60; Job 31:5).

Table 2.6

	source domain	target domain	location
TO RUN ALONG THE PATH			
structural correlation	to run along the path	to respect the Torah / Law (תורה)	Ps 119:32
			Ps 119:60
			Job 31:5
correspondence	way, journey, path	commandments (of the Torah / Law) (מצוה)	Ps 119:32
	the destination of the running	commandments (of the Torah / Law) (מצוה)	Ps 119:60
		fraud, deceit (מרמה)	Job 31:5
	pursued prey	fraud, deceit (מרמה)	Job 31:5
	traveller	psalmist	Ps 119:32
			Ps 119:60
		Job	Job 31:5

The generic narrative structure TO RUN ALONG THE PATH is also used in the construction of the meaning of the metaphorical expressions in Psalms 119:60 and 147:15, Proverbs 1:16, Isaiah 51:1 and 59:7, and elsewhere.

2.1.3 THE GENERIC NARRATIVE STRUCTURE TO LEAVE THE PATH / TO TURN FROM THE PATH

This is one of the central generic narrative structures of the journey metaphor and it is characterised by the verb roots עזב (in Q *to leave, to leave behind, to leave over*), רחק (in HI *to stretch out, to spread out, to steer sideways, to guide away*), נטה (in Q *to stretch out, to twist, to guide away*), מוש (in HI *to remove*), and עבר (in Q *to pull along, to go to one's side, to move through, to pass over*). In conjunction with other metaphorical vehicles, in particular רגל *foot, leg,* and דרך *way, road, journey,* the generic narrative structure TO LEAVE THE PATH / TO TURN FROM THE PATH is also connected to the verb root סור (in Q *to turn aside, to go off, to retreat, to fall down, to abandon, to desist, to stand aloof, to leave off, to stop;* in HI *to remove*) (Ps 119:29; Prov 4:27), and is sometimes seen in conjunction with the preposition מן (Mal 2:8). Again, these verb expressions can be placed with other nouns, adjectives or adverbs (see the table of metaphorical vehicles: table 2.7). In conjunction with other metaphorical vehicles, the verb root שוב, usually in conjunction with the preposition מן, meaning *to turn off,*[117] is also involved in the generic narrative structure TO LEAVE THE PATH / TO TURN FROM THE PATH.

An example of a non-metaphorical application of the generic narrative structure TO LEAVE THE PATH / TO TURN FROM THE PATH can be found in Deuteronomy 2:27.

אעברה בארצך בדרך בדרך אלך לא אסור ימין ושמאול: Deut 2:27

In mapping, this generic narrative structure generates the meaning of the verse in, for example, Deuteronomy 5:32.

ושמרתם לעשות כאשר צוה יהוה אלהיכם אתכם לא תסרו ימין ושמאל: Deut 5:32
You must therefore be careful to do as the Lord your God has commanded you;
you shall not turn to the right or to the left.

The same generic narrative structure is also used in a conventional way, for example in Psalm 119:150.

קרבו רדפי זמה מתורתך רחקו: Ps 119:150
Those who persecute me with evil purpose draw near; **they are far from** your law.

In this verse, two generic narrative structures that use the journey metaphor are seen when mapping: TO LEAVE THE PATH / TO TURN FROM THE PATH and TO RUN ALONG THE PATH (metaphorical vehicle רדף in Q *to pursue someone, to pursue, to follow after*). The metaphorical expression also demonstrates the spatial image schema FAR AWAY–NEAR. Spatial image schemas such as FAR AWAY–NEAR, UP–DOWN (see

---

117   The verb expression שוב in Q occurs in the Old Testament in contexts other than *the way,* so the presence of other metaphorical vehicles is necessary to activate this generic narrative structure.

Jer 30:14; 48:29), RIGHT-LEFT (see Deut 5:32), and BACK TO-FACE TO (see Jer 7:24) are commonly applied within the journey metaphor not only in the Hebrew text of the Old Testament but also in modern languages and across different cultures.

Other examples of the use of the generic narrative structure TO LEAVE THE PATH / TO TURN FROM THE PATH are the metaphorical expressions in Job 23:11–12 and Jeremiah 26:3–4 (in the latter, we see two generic narrative structures: TO LEAVE THE PATH / TO TURN FROM THE PATH and TO WALK ALONG THE PATH).

Job 23:11 באשרו אחזה רגלי דרכו שמרתי ולא־אט:

21 מצות שפתיו ולא אמיש מחקי צפנתי אמרי־פיו:

My **foot** has held fast to his **steps**;
I have kept his **way** and have **not turned aside**.
I have **not departed from** the commandment of his lips;
I have treasured in my bosom the words of his mouth.

Jer 26:3 אולי ישמעו וישבו איש מדרכו הרעה ונחמתי אל־הרעה אשר

אנכי חשב לעשות להם מפני רע מעלליהם:

4 ואמרת אליהם כה אמר יהוה אם־לא תשמעו אלי ללכת בתורתי אשר נתתי לפניכם:

It may be that they will listen, all of them, and will **turn from** their evil **way**,
that I may change my mind about the disaster
that I intend to bring on them because of their evil doings.
You shall say to them: Thus says the Lord:
If you will not listen to me, **to walk in** my law that I have set before you.

The metaphorical expression in Psalm 119:30 is an innovative application of the journey metaphor and within its generic narrative structure TO LEAVE THE PATH / TO TURN FROM THE PATH. Here, an important role is played by the metaphorical vehicle (verb root) בחר (in Q *to choose*), in conjunction with the noun דרך *way, road, journey*:

Ps 119:30 דרך־אמונה בחרתי משפטיך שויתי:

I have **chosen the way** of faithfulness; I set your ordinances before me.

The notion of space and movement behind this metaphorical expression is similar to that in Jeremiah 26:3–4. In both, the element of choice is foregrounded in the source domain, "path choice," and the target domain, "whether or not to obey the commands / decrees of the Torah," but while Psalm 119 thematises *obedience* to the Torah, Jeremiah 26 thematises *disobedience*.

The basic mental concept created by the generic narrative structure TO LEAVE THE PATH / TO TURN FROM THE PATH is clear from the examples given and from other metaphorical expressions: at least two paths open up before the person who stands at a crossroads; it is up to that person to choose which way to go. In the source domain, the entity *choice of the path* corresponds in the target domain to the entity *choice of obedience or disobedience to the Torah / Law*, that is, its *commands, rules* and *regulations*.

Table 2.7 shows the most important structural correlations and correspondences established during mapping through the generic narrative structure TO LEAVE THE PATH / TO TURN FROM THE PATH in the examples mentioned above (Deut 5:32; Job 23:11–12; Ps 119:30,150; Jer 26:3–4).

Table 2.7

		source domain	*target domain*	*location*
TO LEAVE THE PATH / TO TURN FROM THE PATH				
structural correlation		to turn off	*to violate the journey* (תורה)	Deut 5:32
		to run away		Ps 119:150
		to remove		Job 23:11–12
		to turn off	*to respect, to obey (the Torah / Law)*	Jer 26:3–4
		to choose the path	*to decide: respect or don't respect (the Torah / Law)*	Ps 119:30 Ps 119:30
correspondence		way, road	*the Torah / Law* (תורה)	Ps 119:150 Jer 26:3–4
			due, prescribed task, law, regulation (of the Torah / Law) (חק)	Job 23:11–12
			orders, commandments (מצוה)	Job 23:11–12
			the words of God's mouth (אמרי־פיו)	Job 23:11–12
			evil deeds	Jer 26:3–4
		traveller	Israel	Deut 5:32
				Jer 26:3–4
			Job	Job 23:11–12
			psalmist	Ps 119:30
				Ps 119:150

The table shows that the same generic narrative structure can be used in two metaphorical expressions in completely contradictory ways: *to turn from the path* meaning *to break the law* (Deut 5:32) or *turn from the path* meaning *changing one's way of thinking and way of life in the sense of repeated adherence to the commandments of the Law* (Jer 26:3–4; see also Zech 1:4). The ideas of space and movement are nonetheless the same in both cases.

The generic narrative structure TO LEAVE THE PATH / TO TURN FROM THE PATH is also applied in the construction of the meaning of metaphorical expressions in, for example, Exodus 23:2,6–7; Numbers 15:41; Deuteronomy 16:19; 24:17; 26:13; 27:19;

Psalms 89:31; 119:30,51,87,150–157; 141:4; Proverbs 2:13; 4:27; 15:10; 28:4; Isaiah 24:5; 40:27; 46:13; 58:2; 59:9; Jeremiah 5:22; 9:12; 25:5; 26:3; 32:40; 36:3; 44:5; Ezekiel 18:27,28,30; 33:18,19; Daniel 9:12,13; Jonah 3:10; Zechariah 1:4; and Malachi 2:6.

The Hebrew expressions of the target domain in these passages also establish further correspondence and create further structural correlations.

The generic narrative structure TO LEAVE THE PATH / TO TURN FROM THE PATH as a central generic narrative structure of the journey metaphor also participates in the metaphorical conceptualisation of Hebrew expressions from semantic areas other than *Torah / Law*, such as in Proverbs 9:6.

עזבו פתאים וחיו ואשרו בדרך בינה: Prov 9:6

Lay aside immaturity, and live, and walk in the way of insight.

Mapping allows for the same mental image as the verses mentioned above. The generic narrative structure TO LEAVE THE PATH / TO TURN FROM THE PATH is a framework for emerging structural correlations: in the source domain, *to choose from two (or more) paths*, or *to turn onto one of the paths* corresponds in the target domain to *choose simple-mindedness* or *simplicity*; *immaturity* (פתי) or *insight* (בינה).

2.1.4 THE GENERIC NARRATIVE STRUCTURE TO GO ASTRAY

This generic narrative structure is characterised by the verb roots שגה (in Q *to stray*; in HI *to lead astray, to mislead*), נוד (in Q *to sway, to be aimless, to be homeless*; in HITPO *to sway backwards, to sway backwards and forwards*), תעה (in Q *to wander about*), and שגג (in Q *to go astray*). For these last two, the journey metaphor lexicalises in the semantic area *Torah / Law*. Standard dictionaries give other meanings of תעה (in Q *to err, to stagger, to find oneself following the wrong course of action*), and שגג (in Q *to infringe, to break [the rules of the Torah], to make a mistake*). In addition to verbal metaphorical vehicles, other nominal expressions are also involved in the mapping of the semantic area *Torah / Law* through the generic narrative structure TO GO ASTRAY (see the table of metaphorical vehicles: table 2.8).

The meaning of the Hebrew noun שגגה, a derivative of the verb root שגג *to go astray*, is introduced in standard dictionaries and lexicons only as *inadvertent sin, unintentional mistake*. The lexicalisation of some key metaphorical vehicles and the frequency of this generic narrative structure throughout the Hebrew canon, as in the case of metaphorical vehicles in the generic narrative structure TO WALK ALONG THE PATH, indicates that the generic narrative structure TO GO ASTRAY is one of the central generic narrative structures within the journey metaphor. Lexicalisation of the journey metaphor in the semantic area *Torah / Law* is testified to by the Hebrew expressions mentioned above, which are used in verses that are evidently non-metaphorical (e.g. Lev 5:18).

Genesis 37:15 provides an example of a non-metaphorical verse in which we find the generic narrative structure TO GO ASTRAY:

וימצאהו איש והנה תעה בשדה וישאלהו האיש לאמר מה־תבקש: Gen 37:15

And a man found him **wandering** (verbatim: תעה in Q *to wander about*) in the fields; the man asked him, "What are you seeking?"

The metaphorical expression in Numbers 15:22 is an example of the conventional application of the generic narrative structure TO GO ASTRAY to the construction of meaning:

וכי תשגו ולא תעשו את כל־המצות האלה אשר־דבר יהוה אל־משה: Num 15:22

But if you (verbatim: **go astray** שגה) unintentionally fail to observe all these commandments that the Lord has spoken to Moses.

The same is true in Psalm 119:10.

בכל־לבי דרשתיך אל־תשגני ממצותיך: Ps 119:10

With my whole heart I seek you; **do not let me stray** from your commandments.

The metaphorical expression in Amos 2:4 is out of the conventional frame; the entity *guides* is included in the mapping from the source domain, which in the target domain corresponds to the Hebrew expression כזב *to lie*:

כה אמר יהוה על־שלשה פשעי יהודה ועל־ארבעה לא אשיבנו על־מאסם את־תורת יהוה Amos 2:4
וחקיו לא שמרו ויתעום כזביהם אשר־הלכו אבותם אחריהם:

Thus says the Lord: For three transgressions of Judah, and for four,
I will not revoke the punishment;
because they have rejected the law of the Lord, and have not kept his statutes,
but **they have been led astray** (תעה in HI *to stretch out, to spread out, to steer sideways, to guide away*)
by the same lies after which their ancestors walked.

The metaphorical expression in Jeremiah 31:18 is an example of mapping through two generic narrative structures: TO GO ASTRAY and TO RETURN (see 2.1.5 below):

שמוע שמעתי אפרים מתנודד יסרתני Jer 31:18
ואוסר כעגל לא למד השיבני ואשובה כי אתה יהוה אלהי:

Indeed I heard Ephraim pleading: "You disciplined me, and I took the discipline;
I was like a calf untrained. Bring me back, let me come back, for you are the Lord my God."

Finally, there are innovative structural correlations between *going astray* (נוד in HITPO *to sway backwards, to sway backwards and forwards*) and *God's punishment* (יסר in PI *to chastise, to rebuke, to teach*; in NI *to let oneself be instructed*).

The following table shows the most important structural correlations and correspondences established during mapping through the generic narrative structure TO GO ASTRAY in the examples used above (Num 15:22; Ps 119:10; Jer 31:18; Amos 2:4), where we find the stereotypical correlation: *breaking the Torah / Law* is like *straying*.

Table 2.8

	source domain	target domain	location
TO GO ASTRAY			
structural correlation	to go astray (שגה)	to infringe the commandments (of the Lord)	Num 15:22
			Ps 119:10
	to be led astray (תעה in HI)	to reject the Torah / Law	Amos 2:4
	to sway backwards and forwards (נוד in HITPO)	to reject the Torah / Law	Jer 31:18
		God's punishment	Jer 31:18
correspondence	way, road, journey (דרך)	commandments (מצוה)	Num 15:22
			Ps 119:10
		the Torah / Law (תורה)	Amos 2:4
		transgressions (פשע)	Amos 2:4
	traveller	Israel	Num 15:22
		psalmist	Ps 119:10
		Judea	Amos 2:4
		Ephraim	Jer 31:18
	guides	idols (כזב)	Amos 2:4

The generic narrative structure TO GO ASTRAY is also used in the construction of the meaning of metaphorical expressions in, for example, Numbers 15:28; Job 12:24; Psalms 58:4; 95:10; 119:21,67,110,118,176; Proverbs 12:26; 14:22; 28:10; and Isaiah 35:8.

It also contributes to the metaphorical conceptualisation of expressions in semantic areas other than *Torah / Law*, such as in Proverbs 19:27.

Prov 19:27 חדל־בני לשמע מוסר לשגות מאמרי־דעת:
Cease **straying**, my child, from the words of knowledge, in order that you may hear instruction.

In this case, straying / disobedience concerns not *the Torah / Law* but *knowledge* (דעת).

2.1.5 THE GENERIC NARRATIVE STRUCTURE TO RETURN

This generic narrative structure is somewhat peripheral to the mapping of expressions from the semantic area *Torah / Law* through the journey metaphor. It is activated by the verbal metaphorical vehicle שוב (in Q *to turn back, to return, to turn away, to abandon;*

in PI *to bring back, to lead back, to turn around, to lead away, to lead astray, to pay back, to requite*; in HI *to bring back, to lead back*), in conjunction with the prepositions עַל, לְ, or אל. Other verbal, nominal and adverbial metaphorical vehicles are also involved in mapping (see the table of metaphorical vehicles: table 2.9). The verbal expression שוב in Q occurs in contexts other than "path," so the presence of other metaphorical vehicles is necessary to activate this generic narrative structure.

Genesis 18:33 offers an example of a non-metaphorical passage of text where we see the generic narrative structure TO RETURN:

וילך יהוה כאשר כלה לדבר אל־אברהם ואברהם שב למקמו: Gen 18:33
And the Lord went his way, when he had finished speaking to Abraham; and Abraham **returned** to his place.

The same narrative structure is used in the metaphorical construction of meaning in, for example, Psalm 119:59 and Isaiah 45:23–24, blended with the metaphor GOD IS A SHEPHERD. Here, the verbal metaphorical vehicle שוב (in Q *to turn back, to return, to turn away, to abandon*) is key to identifying the generic narrative structure TO RETURN.

Other metaphorical vehicles are attached to it. In Psalm 119:59, these are the nouns דרך *way, road, journey* and רגל *foot, leg*;

חשבתי דרכי ואשיבה רגלי אל־עדתיך: Ps 119:59
When I think of your ways, **I turn** my feet to your decrees.

In Isaiah 45:23–24 they are the verb roots יצא (in Q *to come out, to come forth, to go out, to go forth*) and בוא (in Q *to come*).

בי נשבעתי יצא מפי צדקה דבר ולא ישוב כי־לי תכרע כל־ברך תשבע כל־לשון: Isa 45:23
By myself I have sworn, from my mouth **has gone forth** in righteousness a word
that shall **not return**: "To me every knee shall bow, every tongue shall swear."
Only in the Lord, it shall be said of me, are righteousness and strength;
all who were incensed against him shall **come** to him and be ashamed.

Metaphorical vehicles are related to the structural correlation expressions listed in the following table:

The generic narrative structure TO RETURN is also applied in the construction of the meanings of the metaphorical expressions in, for example, Deuteronomy 30:10; Psalm 51:45; Jeremiah 31:18; 36:7; Ezekiel 18:30; and Amos 2:4.

Table 2.9

	source domain	target domain	location
TO RETURN			
structural correlation	to return (to the path)	to respect, to obey (testimonies of the Torah / Law) (תורה)	Ps 119:59
	to return to the point of departure	to return to the Lord	Isa 45:23–24
correspondence	דרך way, road, journey	witnesses, testimonies (of the Torah / Law) (עדה)	Ps 119:59
	traveller	word (דבר) of the Lord	Isa 45:23–24
		righteousness (צדקה)	
		strength, power (עז)	
		all who were incensed against the Lord	
		Israelites in exile	Ezek 34:16
		psalmist	Ps 119:59
	point of departure	the Lord, mouth (פה) of the Lord	Isa 45:23–24

2.1.6 THE GENERIC NARRATIVE STRUCTURE TO SEARCH FOR THE PATH / TO SEARCH ON THE PATH

This generic narrative structure is also peripheral. Two verbal expressions are a key component: בקש (in PI to discover, to find, to attempt to do something, to try to possess, to demand, to require, to request); and דרש (in Q to care for, to enquire about, to investigate, to require, to search). Both of these verb roots also appear in contexts other than "journey" but do not in themselves create the mental image of a journey, so to map this generic narrative structure, additional metaphorical vehicles must be present in the verse.

Jeremiah 5:1 and 5:4 are examples of the use of the generic narrative structure TO SEARCH FOR THE PATH / TO SEARCH ON THE PATH in mapping Hebrew expressions in the semantic area *Torah / Law*:

Jer 5:1 שוטטו בחוצות ירושלם וראו־נא ודעו ובקשו ברחובותיה אם־תמצאו איש אם־יש עשה
משפט מבקש אמונה ואסלח לה:
Run to and fro through the streets of Jerusalem, look around and take note!
Search its squares and **see** if you can **find** one person who acts justly and **seeks** truth
—so that I may pardon Jerusalem . . .

Jer 5:4 ואני אמרתי אך־דלים הם נואלו כי לא ידעו דרך יהוה משפט אלהיהם:

... Then I said, "These are only the poor, they have no sense;

for **they do not know the way** of the Lord, the law of their God ..."

A structural correlation is established in the target domain through the conceptual metaphor THE TORAH / LAW IS A JOURNEY and the generic narrative structures TO SEARCH FOR THE PATH / TO SEARCH ON THE PATH and TO RUN ALONG THE PATH: *search for the path—run—judge* (עשה משפט)—*strive for righteousness and justice* in the land of Judah. This is a metaphorical metonymy, and the subject of the search in the verse is *the one who judges*, rather than *self-judgment* (משפט), or more commonly *righteousness and justice*. In the source domain, the time element, the urgency of the search (*running* rather than *walking*), and the visual aspect of the act of searching are all emphasised.

Similarly, the generic narrative structure TO SEARCH FOR THE PATH / TO SEARCH ON THE PATH can be seen in the metaphorical expression in Isaiah 58:2.

Isa 58:2 ואותי יום יום ידרשון ודעת דרכי יחפצון כגוי אשר־צדקה עשה

ומשפט אלהיו לא עזב ישאלוני משפטי־צדק קרבת אלהים יחפצון:

Yet day after day they **seek me and delight to know my ways**,

as if they were a nation that practised righteousness and did not forsake the ordinance of their God; **they ask of** me righteous judgments, they delight to draw near to God.

The table below lists the most important structural correlations and correspondences established during mapping through the generic narrative structure TO SEARCH FOR THE PATH / TO SEARCH ON THE PATH in the examples mentioned above (Isa 58:2 and Jer 5:1,4):

Table 2.10

	source domain	target domain	location
TO SEARCH FOR THE PATH / TO SEARCH ON THE PATH			
structural correlation	*to look for the path*	*judge* (עשה משפט) *or more commonly righteousness and justice*	Jer 5:1,4
			Isa 58:2
correspondence	*streets of Jerusalem*	*kingdom of Judah*	Jer 5:1,4
	way, road	*the Torah / Law* (תורה)	Jer 5:1,4
		righteousness (צדקה)	Isa 58:2
		justice of God (משפט אלהי)	Isa 58:2
		righteous judgments (משפטי־צדק)	Isa 58:2
	traveller	*residents of Judah*	Jer 5:1,4
			Isa 58:2

The generic narrative structure TO SEARCH FOR THE PATH / TO SEARCH ON THE PATH is also found in the construction of the meanings of metaphorical expressions in, for example, Psalms 35:14; 119:10,45,176; Jeremiah 2:33; and Micah 6:8.

2.1.7 THE GENERIC NARRATIVE STRUCTURE TO TAKE ON / SHOW THE PATH

This generic narrative structure comes into play through the verbal metaphorical vehicles נחה (in Q *to lead, to guide*; in HI *to lead, to guide, to bring*), דרך (in HI *to tread down, to cause to tread upon, to cause to walk*), and שוב (in PI *to bring back, to lead back, to turn around, to lead away, to lead astray, to pay back, to requite*; in HI *to bring back, to lead back*). The meaning of the verb root ירה (in HI *to direct [on the path]*) is a topic of much scholarly discussion.[118] The verb root עבר (in Q *to pull along, to go one's way, to move through, to pass over, to pass by, to go over*) is another metaphorical vehicle within this generic narrative structure, although standard Hebrew dictionaries and lexicons also indicate the meaning (in Q) *to infringe, to break (rules, the Torah / Law), to make a mistake*. We again see lexicalisation of the journey metaphor in the two key verbal terms ירה (in HI) and עבר (in Q). Lexicalisation of the latter can be seen as an argument in favour of Čech's "P-hypothesis"[119] concerning the etymology of the key Hebrew concept תורה *the Torah / Law* in the sense of *direction* (or *directions*) along the path, which would in turn prompt us to consider the generic narrative structure TO TAKE ON / SHOW THE PATH as a central generic narrative structure within the journey metaphor in the semantic area *Torah / Law*. Although the generic narrative structure TO WALK ALONG THE PATH is dominant with respect to frequency, its function in the journey metaphor is the same as that of the generic narrative structure TO TAKE ON / SHOW THE PATH.

Exodus 13:21 is an example of the non-metaphorical use of the generic narrative structure TO TAKE ON / SHOW THE PATH:

Exo 13:21 ויהוה הלך לפניהם יומם בעמוד ענן לנחתם הדרך

ולילה בעמוד אש להאיר להם ללכת יום ולילה:

The Lord went in front of them in a pillar of cloud by day,
to **lead** them along the **way**, and in a pillar of fire by night,
to give them light, so that they might **travel** by day and by night.

The use of the generic narrative structure TO TAKE ON / SHOW THE PATH when mapping Hebrew expressions from the semantic area *Torah / Law* is clear in Psalm 119:35.

Ps 119:35 הדריכני בנתיב מצותיך כי־בו חפצתי:

Lead me in the path of your commandments, for I delight in it.

---

118 Sometimes *to shoot, to throw* or *to teach.*
119 See Čech, "Zákon ve Starém zákonu," 163.

With respect to mapping, the metaphorical vehicle דרך (in HI *to tread down, to cause to tread upon, to cause to walk*) is central.

The journey metaphor is conceptually blended with the metaphor GOD IS A SHEPHERD (Ps 23:3), GOD IS A TEACHER (Ps 25:8–12; Mic 4:2), and GOD IS A JUDGE (Ps 67:5). The generic narrative structure TO TAKE ON / SHOW THE PATH participates in mapping throughout Psalm 25:8–12.

Ps 25:8 טוב־וישר יהוה על־כן יורה חטאים בדרך:

9 ידרך ענוים במשפט וילמד ענוים דרכו:

10 כל־ארחות יהוה חסד ואמת לנצרי בריתו ועדתיו:

11 למען־שמך יהוה וסלחת לעוני כי רב־הוא:

12 מי־זה האיש ירא יהוה יורנו בדרך יבחר:

Good and upright is the Lord; therefore **he instructs** (ירה in HI *shows the way*)
sinners in the way.
He leads the humble in what is right, and teaches the humble his **way**.
All the **paths** of the Lord are steadfast love and faithfulness,
for those who keep his covenant and his decrees.
For your name's sake, O Lord, pardon my guilt, for it is great.
Who are they that fear the Lord?
He **will teach** (ירה HI *will show the way*) them the way that they should choose.

In Micah 4:2, two generic narrative structures are involved in mapping: TO TAKE ON / SHOW THE PATH and TO WALK ALONG THE PATH. Conceptual blending of THE TORAH / Law IS A JOURNEY and the metaphor GOD IS A TEACHER also takes place.

Mic 4:2 והלכו גוים רבים ואמרו לכו ונעלה אל־הר־יהוה

ואל־בית אלהי יעקב ויורנו מדרכיו ונלכה בארחתיו כי מציון תצא תורה ודבר־יהוה מירושלם:

And many nations shall come and say:
"Come, let us go up to the mountain of the Lord, to the house of the God of Jacob;
that he may **teach** us his ways and that we may **walk in his paths**."
For out of Zion shall go forth **instruction**, and the word of the Lord from Jerusalem.

Conceptual blending of the metaphor THE TORAH / LAW IS A JOURNEY (generic narrative structure TO TAKE ON / SHOW THE PATH) and the metaphor GOD IS A SHEPHERD can be seen in Psalm 23:3.

Ps 23:3 נפשי ישובב ינחני במעגלי־צדק למען שמו:

He restores my soul. He **leads** me in **right paths** (verbatim: **in path—righteousness**) for his name's sake.

Again, the table shows the most important structural correlations and correspondences established during mapping through the generic narrative structure TO TAKE ON / SHOW THE PATH in the examples mentioned above (Ps 23:3; 25:8–12; 119:35; Mic 4:2):

Table 2.11

	source domain	target domain	location
TO TAKE ON / TO SHOW THE PATH			
structural correlation	to show the way / path	to teach to respect the covenant and the decrees, to teach to respect the Torah / Law (תורה)	Ps 25:8–12 Mic 4:2 Ps 119:35
		to keep alive	Ps 23:3
	to teach to walk	to teach to respect the covenant and the decrees, to teach to respect the Torah / Law	Ps 25:8–12 Mic 4:2
		to learn to choose (correctly)	
	to walk	to speak	Mic 4:2
correspondence	path, road, way	justice (משפט)	Ps 25:8–12
		steadfast love and faithfulness (חסד ואמת)	
		righteousness (צדק)	Ps 23:3
		commandments (מצוה)	Ps 119:35
	point of departure	mountain of the Lord, Zion, Jerusalem	Mic 4:2
	destination	mountain of the Lord, Zion, Jerusalem	Mic 4:2
		righteousness (צדק)	Ps 23:3
	traveller / travellers	a humble person	Ps 25:9
		sinners	Ps 25:8
		people who keep the covenant of the Lord	Ps 25:10
		psalmist	Ps 119:35 Psa 23:3 Ps 25:11
		many nations	Mic 4:2
		the Torah / Law (תורה)	Mic 4:2
		word of the Lord (דבר־יהוה)	Mic 4:2

The generic narrative structure TO TAKE ON / SHOW THE PATH is also used in constructing the meaning of the metaphorical expressions in Psalms 5:9; 25:5,9; 27:11; 67:5; Proverbs 11:3, and elsewhere.

2.1.8 THE GENERIC NARRATIVE STRUCTURE TO FALL DOWN
ON THE PATH

Verbal metaphorical vehicles of the generic narrative structure TO FALL DOWN ON THE PATH include the verb roots נפל (in Q *to fall accidentally, to fall down, to throw oneself down*; in HI *to drop, to throw down, to cause to collapse*) and כשל (in Q *to stumble, to stagger*; in NI *to stumble, to stagger*). Both verb roots also appear in contexts other than "journey," and in itself the mental image of the journey does not instruct this generic narrative structure to be activated when mapping: other metaphorical vehicles (especially nominal and adverbial) must be present in the passage. As we have already mentioned, the conjunction ב in connection with the verb root כשל can refer to an obstacle on a journey *due to which* or *on which* a person may stumble on the way (e.g. in Lev 26:37); it can also specify the site of the stumble (e.g. in Jer 31:9). A time reference sometimes follows the preposition (e.g. "at noon" in Isa 59:10), and the combination ב + נפל can also refer either to an obstacle or to the place where the fall occurs (Deut 22:4).[120]

The meaning of the noun derivative מכשול is presented in standard dictionaries and lexicons of biblical Hebrew as *offence* and is another example of lexicalisation of the journey metaphor in the semantic area *Torah / Law*.

Examples of the non-metaphorical application of this narrative structure can be found in Proverbs 26:27

Prov 26:27 כרה־שחת בה יפל וגלל אבן אליו תשוב:
Whoever digs a pit will **fall into** it, and a stone will come back on the one who starts it rolling.

and Nahum 3:3

Nah 3:3 פרש מעלה ולהב חרב וברק חנית ורב חלל וכבד פגר
ואין קצה לגויה [יכשלו] [וכשלו] בגויתם:
Horsemen charging, flashing sword and glittering spear, piles of dead, heaps of corpses, dead bodies without end – **they stumble over the bodies!**

The same narrative structure that we see here in Nahum generates the meaning of the metaphorical expression in, for example, Hosea 14:2.

Hos 14:2 שובה ישראל עד יהוה אלהיך כי כשלת בעונך:
Return, O Israel, to the Lord your God, for you have **stumbled** (verbatim: **you have stumbled over** your guilt / punishment) because of your iniquity.

---

120   As mentioned above, in other contexts, the combination can also refer to the cause or location of the fall.

The target domain entity עָוֺן *misdeed, sin, guilt caused by sin, punishment* corresponds in the source domain to something (or someone) that a person tripped over, to an obstacle along the way. The following example in Malachi 2:8 is structured in a similar way, with the source domain entity *to fall down on the path*, but surprisingly it corresponds in the target domain to the concept *Torah / Law*:

Mal 2:8 ואתם סרתם מן־הדרך הכשלתם רבים בתורה שחתם ברית הלוי אמר יהוה צבאות:

But you have turned aside from the way;

you have caused many **to stumble by** your instruction (verbatim: **to stumble over the Torah**);you have corrupted the covenant of Levi, says the Lord of hosts.

The final example of a conventional application of the generic narrative structure TO FALL DOWN ON THE PATH is the metaphorical expression in Psalm 5:11. The source domain entity *to fall down on the way* corresponds in the target domain *righteous life* and *immoral life* to the entity *advice, plans of culprits*:

Ps 5:11 האשים אלהים יפלו ממעצותיהם ברב פשעיהם הדיחמו כי־מרו בך:

Make them bear their guilt, O God; **let them fall by their own counsels**;

because of their many transgressions cast them out, for they have rebelled against you.

While the journey metaphor in Hosea 14:2 and Malachi 2:8 establishes a structural correlation between *fall down* and *violate the law* (iniquity or violation of the law is both called and understood as "a fall on the way"), the metaphorical expression in Psalm 5:11 establishes a structural correlation between *fall down* and *punishment for breaking the law*: the fall is not seen as breaking the law but as punishment for breaking it.

The following table lists the most important structural correlations and correspondences established during mapping through the generic narrative structure TO FALL DOWN ON THE PATH in the examples mentioned above (Ps 5:11; Hos 14:2; Mal 2:8):

The generic narrative structure TO FALL DOWN ON THE PATH is also applied in the construction of the meaning of the metaphorical expressions in, for example, Proverbs 4:19; 11:5,28; 17:20; 24:16; Isaiah 59:14; Ezekiel 33:12; and Hosea 5:5; 14:10.

Table 2.12

	source domain	target domain	location
TO FALL DOWN ON THE PATH			
structural correlation	to fall down	to break the law	Hos 14:2
			Mal 2:8
		to break the law	Ps 5:11
	to fall down	punishment for guilt	Ps 5:11

correspondence	*obstacle on the path / place of fall / reason for falling*[121]	*misdeed, punishment* (עָוֹן)	Hos 14:2
		the Torah / Law (תּוֹרָה)	Mal 2:8
		advice, counsel, plans (of culprits) (מוֹעֵצָה)	Ps 5:11
	travellers	*culprits*	Ps 5:11
		priests (כֹּהֲנִים)	Mal 2:8
		Israel	Hos 14:2

2.2 SUMMARY OF THE METAPHORICAL CONCEPTUALISATION OF תורה *THE TORAH / LAW* AND RELATED TERMS THROUGH THE JOURNEY METAPHOR

The conceptual metaphor THE TORAH / LAW IS A JOURNEY has been described through generic narrative structures and structural correlations and correspondences that arise during mapping in selected metaphorical expressions. We have sought to provide examples that show the usual way in which the journey metaphor works in the semantic area in metaphorical conceptualisation of *the Torah / Law*.

Generic narrative structures were presented as variants on the journey metaphor used to metaphorically conceptualise תורה *the Torah / Law* and related terms. They have also provided us with a means of classifying variants of the journey metaphor. The proposed classification of these variants contributes to the scholarly debate on a factually appropriate point of view according to which the variants of the journey metaphor in the Old Testament could be determined. Jäkel and Bancila both propose determining variants of the journey metaphor according to (i) those components that are repeatedly accented in metaphorical expressions and (ii) the role of God. Based on these two features, they describe several of those variants. The generic narrative structures presented here as variants of the journey metaphor offer an alternative proposal. The position by which the journey metaphor variants are determined does not come from outside (as with the role of God in Jäkel's journey metaphor schema) but directly from the logic of how metaphors work in mapping. We assume that the journey metaphor, at least in the Old Testament, is primarily a narrative scheme or structure. The partial positions of this scheme are therefore also narrative in nature. The core of the structures that metaphorically conceptualise the target domain and its entities are primarily verbal rather than nominal expressions (see the accented components to which nouns refer

---

121 It remains arguable whether the preposition b refers to an obstacle because of which or on which a person stumbles on his/her path, to the point where the fall took place, or possibly to some cause of the fall. The structural correlation in the metaphorical expression is clearly primary; the source domain entity that establishes correspondence in the target domain remains ambiguous.

in the English *way* and *traveller*; Jäkel). In narrative structures, nouns and other expressions are functionally linked to verbal expressions as entities of both source and target domains. It can be seen that defining the journey metaphor variants through generic narrative structures is factually more appropriate than using nominal expressions and provides a better match to how the metaphor works in conceptualisation in Old Testament texts.

Throughout the Old Testament corpus, the network of structural correlations and correspondences is immensely rich, interconnected and dynamic. It is beyond the scope of this book to fully express this dynamism, interconnectivity and richness but the underlying tendencies are very clear. Narrative structures with verbal expressions at their centre can be identified in both source and target domains. Within these structures, the Hebrew expressions of the source domain are functionally linked: they are part of a sequence of events, part of a narrative; they organise the target domains as generic narrative structures.

The resulting structural correlations and correspondences resemble a network. The meanings generated by metaphors are highly diverse, and within a single book or a literary circle, or in the whole canon, these meanings can be in dialogue with one another or even contradictory. The principle of meaning generation nonetheless remains the same. Narrative structures serve to organise experiences which may be individual or social, subjective or intersubjective, profane or religious, and even work in similar ways in metaphorical and non-metaphorical passages.

The following illustration seeks to express the rich and dynamic network of structural correlations and correspondences between source and target domains in the metaphorical conceptualisation of the semantic area *Torah / Law*.

Across the vast corpus of the Old Testament, aside from the "conventional" examples mentioned above, we find the journey metaphor in the semantic area *Torah / Law* in a series of metaphorical expressions that are "unconventional" and artistically unique. These are usually created either by conceptual blending (in single metaphorical expressions, more than one conceptual metaphor is used in one passage), or when mapping a rarely used source domain entity a detail from the source domain which does not commonly occur in metaphorical conceptualisations appears in the mapping (e.g. the entity שׁחר *light before dawn* in Isa 58:2). We have selected three examples of such innovative mapping in the semantic area *Torah / Law* and will analyse and interpret them in the next chapter.

The conceptual metaphor THE TORAH / LAW IS A JOURNEY is the central metaphor involved in the Old Testament conceptualisation of תורה *the Torah / Law* and related Hebrew terms. This is shown both by the frequency of its occurrence and by the lexicalisation of the metaphor through certain Hebrew verbal and nominal expressions. As we have already mentioned, in *Patterns of Sin in the Hebrew Bible*, Lam describes several metaphors used in the Old Testament to conceptualise sin, including SIN IS A PATH and SIN IS A DIRECTION. In this context, he supports Youngblood's hypothesis that the meaning of the Hebrew verb roots חטא (in Q *to miss, to offend, to do wrong*), פשׁע (in Q *to behave disloyally, to behave as a criminal*) and עוה (in Q *to sin*) is connected to the idea of

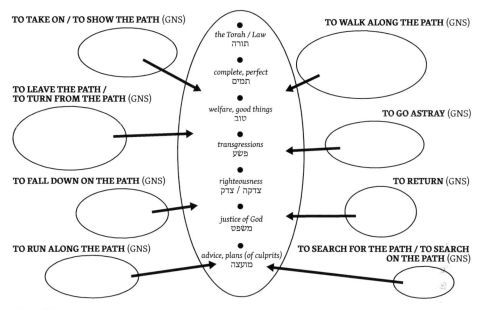

Figure 2.1

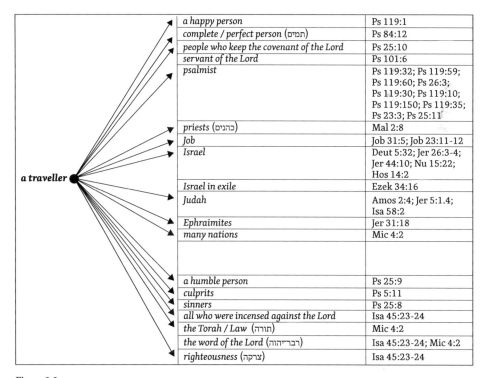

Figure 2.2

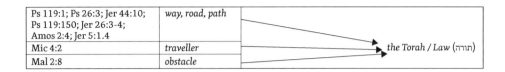

Figure 2.3

sin as deviation from a path or from a certain direction. One of Lam's key arguments in favour of Youngblood's hypothesis is the lexicalisation of the journey metaphor for the Hebrew verb root חטא. Based on our analysis of the metaphorical expressions used to conceptualise תורה *the Torah / Law* and related terms we can observe further lexicalisation of the journey metaphor. Other Hebrew expressions in which the journey metaphor is lexicalised are listed in the table below. The terms are associated with the generic narrative structures in which they appear. The first three nominal Hebrew expressions (*right*, *virtueless* and *intrigues*) are the exception. However, as we have already stated, the central component of generic narrative structures always consists primarily of verbal expressions; nominative, adverbial and other expressions are not usually tied to a specific generic narrative structure.

Table 2.13

LEXICALISATION of the journey metaphor in the semantic area *Torah / Law*		*basic meaning*	*metaphorical lexicalised meaning*
expressions that are not tied to a specific generic narrative structure	יָשָׁר	*straight*	*right*
	עָקֵשׁ	*crooked, twisted*	*virtueless*
	חֲלַקְלַקּוֹת חֲלַקְלַק	*smooth*	*intrigues*
	שָׁמַר	*to keep, to watch over*	*to respect, to obey*
	נָצַר	*to keep, to watch over*	*to respect, to obey*
TO TAKE ON / SHOW THE PATH	ירה	*HI to direct on the path*	*HI to teach*
	תורה	*direction*	*the Torah / Law*
	עבר	*Q to pull along, to go one's way, to move through, to pass over, to pass by, to go over*	*to infringe, to break (the rules of the Torah / Law), to make a mistake*

TO WALK ALONG THE PATH	הלך הלך+ב	to go, to walk	to respect, to obey
TO LEAVE THE PATH / TO TURN FROM THE PATH	עבר	Q to pull along, to go one's way, to move through, to pass over, to pass by, to go over	Q to infringe, to break (the rules of the Torah), to make a mistake
	עקש	PI to twist, to make crooked	PI to pervert
TO GO ASTRAY	שגג	Q to go astray	Q to infringe, to break (the rules of the Torah), to make a mistake
	derivative: שגגה	–	sin, mistake
	תעה	Q to wander about	Q to err, to stagger, to find oneself following the wrong course of action
TO FALL DOWN ON THE PATH	כשל	Q to stumble + ב to stumble over, to stagger, NI to stumble, to stagger	–
	derivative: מכשול	–	offence

The lexicalisation of the metaphor THE TORAH / LAW IS A JOURNEY in the semantic area *Torah / Law* is seen as proof that the metaphor is central to that semantic area. As most expressions in which the journey metaphor lexicalises can be classified in one of the generic narrative structures described above, these generic narrative structures can in turn be seen as central to the metaphor THE TORAH / LAW IS A JOURNEY.

Just as language categories have a centre and peripheries, so the conceptual metaphor THE TORAH / LAW IS A JOURNEY has a centre composed of the generic narrative structures TO TAKE ON / SHOW THE PATH, TO WALK ALONG THE PATH, TO LEAVE THE PATH / TO TURN FROM THE PATH, TO GO ASTRAY and TO FALL DOWN ON THE PATH and peripheries composed of the generic narrative structures TO RUN ALONG THE PATH, TO RETURN, and TO SEARCH FOR THE PATH / TO SEARCH ON THE PATH.

Table 2.14

Central generic narrative structures	*Peripheral generic narrative structures*
• TO TAKE ON / SHOW THE PATH	• TO RUN ALONG THE PATH
• TO WALK ALONG THE PATH	• TO RETURN
• TO LEAVE THE PATH / TO TURN FROM THE PATH	• TO SEARCH FOR THE PATH / TO SEARCH ON THE PATH
• TO GO ASTRAY	
• TO FALL DOWN ON THE PATH	

What are the theological implications of this? The dominance of the journey metaphor in the semantic area *Torah / Law* is significant because of its implicit theory of what it means to sin: to go astray through one's life, to turn from the good way or path, to fall, to slip. The journey metaphor "says" that sin in the Old Testament texts is mainly about falling, slipping, going astray and turning from the path, rather than "missing the target" (see 2.1.7 and the theory on the etymology of the central Hebrew expression תורה *the Torah / Law* based on the meaning of the verb root ירה in Q *to throw*, HI *to shoot, to throw*).

The journey metaphor is anchored in the general human experience of the human body moving in space and time and is not bound in its basic form to any one historical, social, cultural, geographical or religious context. This is its great advantage. It is readily available for the metaphorical conceptualisation of תורה *the Torah / Law* in numerous variants, contexts and communicative situations.

As we will see in the next chapter, even in linguistic (literal) translations of the Hebrew Old Testament text into modern languages, the journey metaphor can be understood without major problems. The conceptual metaphor THE TORAH / LAW IS A JOURNEY also has the status of a cardinal metaphor in the Old Testament. It conceptualises the whole conceptual area of תורה *the Torah / Law*; it is a theological statement, confession and testimony of the nature of the Torah and the role it plays in the personal lives of those who belong to the people of Israel and in the religion and culture of Judaism as a whole. The metaphor THE TORAH / LAW IS A JOURNEY has a central place in the construction of an extensive conceptual apparatus.

2.3 OTHER CONCEPTUAL METAPHORS

We have noted that the conceptual metaphor THE TORAH / LAW IS A JOURNEY is the central metaphor in the Old Testament conceptualisation of תורה *the Torah / Law* and related Hebrew terms. It is far from being the only metaphor, however. We will now present a basic overview of these other conceptual metaphors and describe how they may relate to the metaphor THE TORAH / LAW IS A JOURNEY. As a cardinal metaphor, THE TORAH / LAW IS A JOURNEY could combine with other Torah metaphors to create a coherent system or network of metaphors which interconnects in some way, and in which the correspondence between the individual concepts and the structural correlations could build on each other or even overlap to some extent.

Most Old Testament metaphors that play a part in the conceptualisation of תורה *the Torah / Law* and related Hebrew terms can be found in the Torah-Psalms (Pss 1, 19, and 119). Some of these expressions use a basic general metaphor, such as THE TORAH / LAW IS WATER; some use the same conceptual metaphor but in various sub-variants, such as THE TORAH / LAW IS A STREAM, THE TORAH / LAW IS A SOURCE, THE TORAH / LAW IS RAIN. The following overview of conceptual metaphors is not intended to be exhaustive.

2.3.1 OTHER METAPHORS INVOLVED IN THE CONCEPTUALISATION OF תורה *THE TORAH / LAW* IN THE OLD TESTAMENT

The conceptual metaphors THE TORAH / LAW IS LIGHT, THE TORAH / LAW IS WATER / MOISTURE and THE TORAH / LAW IS PROPERTY / VALUABLES can all be found in the background of metaphorical expressions in both general and particular forms (*rain, spring, stream, sea waves* as a form of *water*; *lamp, sun, morning star* as a form of *light* or *source of light*; and *gold, jewelry, heritage* as a form of *property* or *valuables*). They are also metaphors that could be considered variants of the more general conceptual metaphor THE TORAH / LAW IS THE SOURCE OF LIFE. Water plays a hugely significant role in the Middle East. A lack of water leads to soil infertility and drought; every living thing perishes without water. In both the Old and the New Testament, water is a symbol of life and blessing, and the conceptual metaphor THE TORAH / LAW IS WATER / MOISTURE also refers to such a symbol. The source domain of the metaphor THE TORAH / LAW IS LIGHT is light as a prerequisite for the life of plants and animals, for visual perception, and therefore for human orientation in the world. Light is also an important religious and cultural symbol throughout the Middle East.

Knowledge of the cultural, religious and social environment in which the relevant passages of text originated (the material and spiritual culture of the Middle East in general and of ancient Israel in particular) is key to understanding the meaning of many metaphorical expressions. Without such knowledge the meaning remains unclear.

The meaning of the following two metaphorical expressions from the Torah-Psalms is shaped against a background of the conceptual metaphor THE TORAH / LAW IS LIGHT. Here in Psalm 19:9 (NRSV 19:8), the verb root אור (in HI *to shine, to illuminate, to give light*) is signalled as a verbal metaphorical vehicle.

Ps 19:9 פקודי יהוה ישרים משמחי־לב מצות יהוה ברה מאירת עינים:
The precepts of the Lord are right, rejoicing the heart;
The commandment of the Lord is clear, **enlightening** the eyes;

In Ps 119:105, the metaphor of light is activated by the nominal derivative of the same verb root אור *daylight, light* and the noun נר *light, lamp*.

Ps 119:105 נר־לרגלי דברך ואור לנתיבתי:
Your word is a **lamp** to my feet and a **light** to my path.

Correspondences between the source and target domains arise between the following entities: *light—instructions of God; light—commandments of God; a lamp—the word of God; a light—the word of God*. Against the background of metaphorical conceptualisation in Psalm 19:9 we can observe a blending of the conceptual metaphors THE TORAH / LAW IS LIGHT, THE TORAH / LAW IS JOY (the metaphorical vehicle is the participle of the verb root שמח in PI *to gladden, to make someone merry*) and THE TORAH /

LAW IS GRAIN.[122] The meaning of the metaphorical expression in Psalm 119:105 is a product of the blending of the conceptual metaphors THE TORAH / LAW IS LIGHT and LIFE IS A JOURNEY; the coherence of these two metaphors is a feature of the Old Testament. Metaphors produce an interconnected metaphorical system in order to establish understanding of a specific aspect of the Torah. Metaphorical expressions mediate the experience of God's commandments, help people orient themselves in the world, and give them an opportunity to focus their lives on permanent and meaningful sources of life and joy. Thus, תורה the Torah / Law is a light on the path of life, allowing people to "live," that is, to "walk" safely, to live in accordance with God's will, and to "live" ("walk") through life towards the goals of justice, blessing, and so on. To those familiar with the Old Testament, the blending of the conceptual metaphors THE TORAH / LAW IS LIGHT and LIFE IS A JOURNEY evokes a wide range of other connotations.

The conceptual metaphor THE TORAH / LAW IS LIGHT can also be detected in the background of the metaphorical expressions in Psalms 37:6 and 119:130; Proverbs 4:18 and 6:23; Isaiah 8:20; 51:4; 58:8, 59:9,11; Hosea 6:5; Micah 7:9; and Malachi 3:20. The conceptual metaphors THE TORAH / LAW IS THE SUN (see Ps 37:6; Hos 5:15; 6:5; Mal 3:20) and THE TORAH / LAW IS A LAMP (Ps 119:105; Prov 6:23) can be viewed as variants of THE TORAH / LAW IS LIGHT.

Unique and innovative applications of conceptual metaphors can be found in passages which suggest the conceptual blending of two or more metaphors, or where in metaphorical conceptualisation some detail such as a rarely used element of the source domain comes to the fore. Isaiah 8:20, for example, makes use of an entity from the source domain, in this case the noun שחר *light before dawn*:

Isa 8:20 לתורה ולתעודה אם־לא יאמרו כדבר הזה אשר אין־לו שחר׃
"... for teaching and for instruction?" Surely, those who speak like this will have no dawn (verbatim: light before dawn [שחר])

The metaphor THE TORAH / LAW IS WATER / MOISTURE is surprisingly rare in the Old Testament,[123] but it makes an appearance in Amos 5:24 and Psalm 1:3. In the verse from Amos, the metaphorical vehicles מים *water, waters* and נהל *stream, small river* correspond in the target domain to the entities משפט *judgment, judicial decision, verdict* and צדקה *accuracy, the right thing, justice, justness*.

Amos 5:24 ויגל כמים משפט וצדקה כנחל איתן׃
But let justice roll down like **waters**, and righteousness like an ever-flowing **stream**

---

122 The Hebrew adjective רב can also be translated as the noun *grain*. It can also therefore be understood as a metaphorical vehicle that signals use of the conceptual metaphor THE TORAH / LAW IS GRAIN, or more generally as a vehicle of the conceptual metaphor THE TORAH / LAW IS THE SOURCE OF LIFE.
123 In metaphorical expressions in the Old Testament canon, the phrase מקור חיים *source of life* usually corresponds to the term יהוה *Lord* and related terms (Ps 18:29; 27:1; 118:27; Isa 60:19,20; Num 6:29, etc.).

Variants of the water / moisture metaphor include the conceptual metaphors THE
TORAH / LAW IS WAVES ON THE SEA (Isa 48:12) and THE TORAH / LAW IS RAIN / SNOW.
In addition to Isaiah 45:7, the latter appears in Isaiah 55:10–11,

כי כאשר ירד הגשם והשלג מן־השמים ושמה לא ישוב ^{Isa 55:10}
כי אם־הרוה את־הארץ והולידה והצמיחה ונתן זרע לזרע ולחם לאכל:
כן יהיה דברי אשר יצא מפי לא־ישוב אלי ריקם ¹¹
כי אם־עשה את־אשר חפצתי והצליח אשר שלחתיו:

For as the **rain** and the **snow** come down from heaven,
and do not return there until they have **watered** the earth,
making it bring forth and sprout, giving seed to the sower and bread to the eater,
so shall my word be that goes out from my mouth; it shall not return to me empty,
but it shall accomplish that which I purpose,
and succeed in the thing for which I sent it.

And by extension in Isaiah 56:1

כה אמר יהוה שמרו משפט ועשו צדקה כי־קרובה ישועתי לבוא וצדקתי להגלות: ^{Isa 56:1}
Thus says the Lord: Maintain justice, and do what is right,
for soon my salvation will come, and my deliverance be revealed.

In Isaiah 55, the metaphorical vehicles גשם *rain-shower*, *rain* and שלג *snow* correspond in the target domain to the entity דבר *word (of God)*, but these same (source domain) expressions also refer to the entire text of Isaiah 56:1–2, which has at its heart
the imperative *Maintain justice, and do what is right!* What is "harvested" in a area and
"irrigated" by law and justice, which in this sense are like rain (and where the "field"
entity corresponds to the *man* entity אנוש in the target domain), is salvation and justice,
keeping the commandments—specifically the Sabbath commandment (Isa 56:2)—and
doing what is right.

Metaphorical meaning is built in like manner through the natural vegetation metaphor in Amos 6:12, and here in Hosea 10:4.

דברו דברים אלות שוא כרת ברית ופרח כראש משפט על תלמי שדי: ^{Hos 10:4}
They utter mere words; with empty oaths they make covenants;
so litigation springs up like poisonous **weeds** in the furrows of the field.

Structural correlation organises the verbal metaphorical vehicle פרח (in Q *to sprout,
to shoot*). The noun ראש *wormwood* (NRSV "poisonous weeds") corresponds in the target
domain to the entity משפט *judgment, judicial decision*.

The conceptual metaphor THE TORAH / LAW IS PROPERTY / VALUABLES can be identified in numerous variants in the Old Testament. Conventional conceptualisations of
תורה *the Torah / Law* and related terms through this metaphor in the Torah-Psalms include Psalms 19:11a, 119:111, and here Psalm 119:127

עַל־כֵּן אָהַבְתִּי מִצְוֺתֶיךָ מִזָּהָב וּמִפָּז: Ps 119:127
Truly I love your commandments more than **gold**, more than **fine gold**.

As with the water / moisture and light metaphors, the metaphor THE TORAH / LAW IS PROPERTY / VALUABLES is applied in creative and unconventional ways either through conceptual blending or through correspondences between entities in the source and target domains. In the case of the water / moisture metaphor, the less common "details" of the entity are *stream, river, snow, rain* rather than the abstract *water*. In the case of the property / valuables metaphor, the less common entities that create correspondence with target domain expressions are nominal expressions such as *the temple treasury* (in Isa 33:5-6 when mapping the target domain *God*), *jewelry, headbands* (in Isa 25:5-6, again when mapping the target domain יהוה THE LORD), *gold rings*, and *an ornament of gold* (in Prov 25:12), *earnings* (in Isa 49:4 when mapping the target domain מִשְׁפָּט *judgment*), *inheritance* (in Ps 119:11), and *plunder* (in Ps 119:162).

The conceptual metaphor THE TORAH / LAW IS PROPERTY / VALUABLES forms the framework for the correspondence between the entities פְּעֻלָּה *reward* and מִשְׁפָּט *judgment, judicial decision* in the metaphorical expression in Isaiah 49:4

וַאֲנִי אָמַרְתִּי לְרִיק יָגַעְתִּי לְתֹהוּ וְהֶבֶל כֹּחִי כִלֵּיתִי אָכֵן מִשְׁפָּטִי אֶת־יְהוָה וּפְעֻלָּתִי אֶת־אֱלֹהָי: Isa 49:4
But I said, "I have laboured in vain, I have spent my strength for nothing and vanity; yet surely my cause is with the Lord, and my **reward** with my God."

Verbal metaphorical vehicles mainly establish structural correlations. On their own (without other, especially nominal metaphorical vehicles), verbal expressions rarely allow for the mapping of target domains in a unique or creative way. There are exceptions, however, such as the metaphorical expression in Hosea 2:20-21

וְכָרַתִּי לָהֶם בְּרִית בַּיּוֹם הַהוּא עִם־חַיַּת הַשָּׂדֶה וְעִם־עוֹף הַשָּׁמַיִם Hos 2:20
וְרֶמֶשׂ הָאֲדָמָה וְקֶשֶׁת וְחֶרֶב וּמִלְחָמָה אֶשְׁבּוֹר מִן־הָאָרֶץ וְהִשְׁכַּבְתִּים לָבֶטַח: 21
וְאֵרַשְׂתִּיךְ לִי לְעוֹלָם וְאֵרַשְׂתִּיךְ לִי בְּצֶדֶק וּבְמִשְׁפָּט וּבְחֶסֶד וּבְרַחֲמִים: 12
I will make for you a covenant on that day with the wild animals, the birds of the air, and the creeping things of the ground; and I will abolish the bow, the sword, and war from the land; and I will make you lie down in safety. And I will take you for my wife forever; I will take you for my wife (in Hebr. אשר + ב verbatim: for the bride price) in righteousness and in justice, in steadfast love, and in mercy.

In connection with the preposition ל the verbal expression ארשׂ (in PU *to become engaged, betrothed*) refers to the person (groom) to whom the girl / bride is engaged. The preposition ב refers to the *bride price*, the price the groom pays to the father or family of the bride. The verb root is used with both prepositions in, for example, 2 Samuel 3:14

וַיִּשְׁלַח דָּוִד מַלְאָכִים אֶל־אִישׁ־בֹּשֶׁת בֶּן־שָׁאוּל לֵאמֹר תְּנָה אֶת־אִשְׁתִּי אֶת־מִיכַל 2Sam 3:14
אֲשֶׁר אֵרַשְׂתִּי לִי בְּמֵאָה עָרְלוֹת פְּלִשְׁתִּים:

Then David sent messengers to Saul's son Ishbaal, saying, "Give me my wife Michal,
to whom **I became engaged at the price of** one hundred foreskins of the Philistines."

Correct identification of a generic narrative structure makes it possible to name
the correspondences between the source and target domains which establish the metaphorical expression in Hosea 2:20–21. The correspondences are shown in the table:

Table 2.15

	source domain	*target domain*
correspondence	espousal	renewal of obediance to the Torah
	groom	יהוה the Lord
	bride (mother of the sons of Judah and Israel)	Judah and Israel
	family of the bride	wild animals, the birds of the air, and the creeping things of the ground
	father of the bride	Baal
	bride price	righteousness, justice, love and mercy

A search of the Old Testament has so far unearthed the conceptual metaphor THE
TORAH / LAW IS SWEETNESS only in the Torah-Psalms, namely, Psalms 19:11b, 119:103
and 119:131. It is clearly a rare and unusual metaphor within the Old Testament Hebrew
canon. It is slightly different from the metaphors of light, water and property in that
the metaphorical conceptualisation of the source domain involves not the source of life
but the source of a higher quality of life, as here in Psalm 119:103

Ps 119:103 מה־נמלצו לחכי אמרתך מדבש לפי׃
. . . **sweeter also than honey, and drippings of the honeycomb**.
How **sweet** are your words to my taste, **sweeter than honey** to my mouth!

Psalm 119:131 represents an unconventional use of this metaphor. The metaphorical vehicles involved in the construction of meaning are פער (in Q *to open one's mouth*)
and שאף (in Q *to swallow, to pant*):

Ps 119:131 פי־פערתי ואשאפה כי למצותיך יאבתי׃
With open mouth I pant (verbatim: **I swallow**; or **I pant**),
because **I long for your** commandments.

In many metaphorical expressions, the Torah, like the Lord God of Israel, is seen
to be a source of joy (see Ps 19:9; 101:1; 119:143) or an object of praise (see Ps 97:8;
Ps 119:48,62,142,164; Isa 42:21). In all these cases, it is more appropriate to speak of
metaphorical metonymy, such as here in Psalm 119:48

Ps 119:48 ‏ואשא־כפי אל־מצותיך אשר אהבתי ואשיחה בחקיך:‏

I **revere** your commandments, which I love, and I will meditate on your statutes.

Metaphorical expressions in which the Torah is an object (or the subject) of love are a special case. Some metaphorical vehicles may specify the type of love—maternal, sexual, marital—that is part of the mapping process. The metaphorical vehicle that most frequently activates the conceptual metaphor THE TORAH IS THE BELOVED PERSON / OB-JECT in the Old Testament is the verb root ‏אהב‏ (in Q *to like, to love*), which contributes to the metaphorical conceptualisation of ‏תורה‏ *the Torah / Law* and related terms in, for example, Psalms 11:7; 33:5; 37:28; 45:8; 99:4; 119:47–48,97,113,119,127,140,159,163,165,167; and Isaiah 61:8. Here it is in Psalm 119:97

Ps 119:97 ‏מה־אהבתי תורתך כל־היום היא שיחתי:‏

Oh, how **I love** your law! It is my meditation all day long.

The metaphorical carrier ‏אהב‏ (in Q *to like, to love*) is involved in the mapping process: the source domain entity *a loved person / object* corresponds to the term in the target domain *Torah / Law*.

Another metaphorical vehicle that activates the conceptual metaphor THE TORAH / LAW IS A BELOVED PERSON / OBJECT is the verb root ‏חפץ‏ (in Q *to take pleasure in, to delight in*). It participates in the metaphorical conceptualisation of ‏תורה‏ *the Torah / Law* and related terms in, for example, Psalms 40:9; 112:1; 119:35; Isaiah 42:21; and Jeremiah 9:23. The verb root ‏שעע‏ (in PILP *to gladden, to delight, to enjoy oneself, to take delight in*) and its nominal derivatives (especially ‏שעשעים‏ *delight*) are involved in the conceptualisation of ‏תורה‏ *the Torah / Law* and related terms through maternal love for a child in, for example, Psalm 119:16,24,47,77,92,143,174. In Psalm 119:20,40,131, the Torah is even the object of fervent desire.

The importance of the metaphorical expression in Hosea 2:20–21 (already referred to above) is established in the process of the blending of the conceptual metaphors THE TORAH / LAW IS PROPERTY / VALUABLES and GOD'S PEOPLE ARE THE LORD'S BRIDE. A unique use of the conceptual metaphor THE TORAH IS A BELOVED PERSON can be found in Zephaniah 3:4. We will examine this phrase in more detail in the next chapter.

The conceptual metaphor THE TORAH / LAW IS A BELOVED PERSON forms part of the background to the meaning of the metaphorical expression in Psalm 85:11

Ps 85:11 ‏חסד־ואמת נפגשו צדק ושלום נשקו:‏

Steadfast love and faithfulness will meet;
righteousness and peace will **kiss each other**.

This unique and innovative application of this metaphor is probably a result of the personification of ‏חסד‏ *faithfulness*, ‏אמת‏ *truth, reliability, firmness*, ‏צדק‏ *righteousness*, and ‏שלום‏ *peace*. It is an interesting variant—a unique and creative act of the author—which uses the idea of friends meeting each other after a long time apart, welcoming each other and kissing each other in greeting (the verb root in the Hebrew text is נשׁק in Q *to kiss one another*).

The metaphor THE TORAH / LAW IS PILLARS OF THE THRONE has a very specific cultural and mythological background and contributes to the conceptualisation of תורה *the Torah / Law* and related terms in Psalms 89:15 and 97:2; Isaiah 9:6; and Proverbs 16:12 and 25:5. Here is Isaiah 9:6

Isa 9:6 [למרבה] [למרבהם] המשׂרה ולשׁלום אין־קץ על־כסא דוד ועל־ממלכתו
להכין אתה ולסעדה במשׁפט ובצדקה מעתה ועד־עולם קנאת יהוה צבאות תעשׂה־זאת:
His authority shall grow continually,
and there shall be endless peace for the throne of David and his kingdom.
He will establish and uphold it with justice and with righteousness from this time onward and forevermore.
The zeal of the Lord of hosts will do this.

Ringgren and Schmid both note that the language of Psalms 89 and 97 has its roots in Mesopotamian mythology where the goddesses *kittu* ("truth") and *mîšaru* ("righteousness") stand either side of the sun-god while he is pronouncing judgments.[124] The idea of a cosmic order in which the king is depicted as judge (the king sitting on a throne) seems to have been a notion shared right across the ancient Middle East. Cosmic order is upheld in society (and in nature) through the law and its commandments and is maintained (and restored) by observation and enforcement of that law. The guarantor of this law, this cosmic order, is the supreme God and, in turn, his earthly representative the king. Other guarantors traditionally include "inferior" gods (principles, ideas, concepts) such as justice, truth and mercy. In metaphorical expressions we then see these "inferior gods" (*kittu* and *mîšaru*, for example), or principles and concepts, corresponding to Hebrew terms: in Psalms 89:15 and 97:2 to משׁפט *judgment, judicial decision, verdict* and צדק *rigteousness, justice, justness*; in Isaiah 9:6 to משׁפט and צדקה; and in Proverbs 16:12 and 25:5 to צדקה. In Old Testament metaphorical expressions, these metaphorically conceptualised Hebrew expressions are presented through these "supporting" parts of the "furniture," in this case the royal throne.

We conclude our basic overview of Old Testament metaphors involved in the conceptualisation of תורה *the Torah / Law* and related terms with the list in the following table. The conceptual metaphors presented here are generally found only once in the Old Testament canon and as such are the unique work of the author of the particular text. The table gives an overview of the metaphors and verses identified through cognitive and culturally oriented linguistics:

---

124 Helmer Ringgren, *Word and Wisdom: Studies in the Hypostatization of Divine Qualities and Functions in the Ancient Near East* (Lund: Hakan Ohlssons, 1947), 53–54, 83–84; Hans Heinrich Schmid, *Gerechtigkeit als Weltordnung: Hintergrund und Geschichte des Alttestamentlichen Gerechtigkeitsbegriffe* (Tübingen: J. C. B. Mohr, 1968).

Table 2.16

	conceptual metaphor	location
	THE TORAH / LAW IS A JUDGE'S CLOTHING	Isa 11:5
	THE TORAH / LAW IS A WARRIOR'S CLOTHING	Isa 59:17
	THE TORAH / LAW IS THE INSTRUMENT OF THE BUILDER	Isa 28:17
	THE TORAH / LAW IS THE INSTRUMENT OF A HUSBANDMAN	Amos 5:7
	THE TORAH / LAW IS A PLANT	Amos 6:12 Amos 5:7 Isa 45:8
+ **personification**	THE TORAH / LAW IS THE CITIZENS (OF A TOWN)	Isa 1:21 Isa 59:14
	THE TORAH / LAW IS THE CITIZENS (OF A COUNTRY)	Ps 85:11
		Isa 32:16

As with all the examples given so far, we identified the conceptual metaphors on the basis of metaphorical vehicles. The next table shows the most important structural correlations and correspondences found during mapping. The correspondences established in the metaphorical expression in Isaiah 59:14 (not included in the table) will be discussed in more detail in the next chapter.

Table 2.17

	source domain	target domain	location
structural correlation	to get dressed (tie a belt)	judge fairly	Isa 11:5
	to dress for battle	God's wrath as a motive for punishing injustice	Isa 59:17
	measure length, height, width	God's judgment	Isa 28:17
	turn over on the other side (ploughing) [הפך in Q to overthrow, to overturn, to demolish, to turn back to front, to change]	court to cause injustice absence of law / court	Amos 5:7 Amos 6:12
	reap crops (collect bitter wormwood and leave a useful crop on the ground) [נוח II. in HI to place somewhere, to set, to lay]		
	to sprout, to put out buds [צמח in HI to make plants sprout, to cause to sprout]	establishment of the law	Isa 45:8
	joyful meeting of four friends [פגש in NI to meet one another, to encounter one another and נשק in Q to kiss]	justice and peace on the earth (salvation)	Ps 85:11

structural correlation	fornication	absence of court	Isa 1:21
	fertile land	justice and peace in the land	Isa 32:16
	populated land		
correspondence	waistcloth (אזור) [of God's judge]	righteousness (צדק)	Isa 11:5
		steadiness, reliability (אמונה)	
	warrior	God	Isa 59:17
	cloak (תלבשת, בגד)	God's wrath	
	scale / armour (שריון)	righteousness, justice (צדקה)	
	builder	God-judge	Isa 28:17
	measuring line (קו)	judgment, judicial decision, verdict (משפט)	
	instrument for horizontal accuracy (משקלת)	righteousness, justice (צדקה)	
	husbandman	Israel	Amos 5:7
	wormwood (לענה)	injustice	
	wormwood (לענה)	judgment, judicial decision, verdict (משפט)	
	spade / blade		
	cultivated crop (e.g. corn)	righteousness, justice (צדקה)	
	poisonous plant (ראש)	judgment, judicial decision, verdict (משפט)	Amos 6:12
	fruit (פרי)	righteousness, justice (צדקה)	
	wormwood (לענה)	righteousness, justice (צדקה)	
	shower from heavens	righteousness, justice (צדקה)	Isa 45:8
	rain		
	useful plants / crops		
	friends	righteousness, justice (צדק) + grace, faithfulness, peace (חסד ; אמת, שלום)	Ps 85:11
	citizens of the town	judgment, judicial decision, verdict (משפט)	Isa 1:21
		righteousness (צדק)	
	inhabitants of the land	judgment, judicial decision, verdict (משפט)	Isa 32:16
		righteousness, justice (צדקה)	

2.3.2 SUMMARY OF OTHER METAPHORS INVOLVED IN THE CONCEPTUALISATION OF תורה *THE TORAH / LAW* IN THE OLD TESTAMENT

As with many of the language categories and conceptual metaphors we have looked at in the semantic area *Torah / Law*, other metaphors have a centre and peripheries. The metaphor THE TORAH / LAW IS A JOURNEY clearly occupies centre stage, as evidenced by the frequency of its occurrence and its lexicalisation through numerous Hebrew verbal and nominal expressions. The metaphor is anchored in the human experience of movement in space and time, and in its basic form is not bound to any particular historical, social, cultural, geographical or religious context. The principal basis of all the other metaphorical conceptualisations in the semantic area *Torah / Law* which we have described above is physical, social and cultural experience. The metaphors are nonetheless linked to the specific socio-cultural, religious and geographical context of ancient Israel. Knowledge of the cultural, religious, social and geographical environment in which the text units originated is often a key to understanding their meaning. Knowledge of the connotations that arise from the whole material and spiritual culture is also crucial. This applies not only to the conceptual metaphor THE TORAH / LAW IS PILLARS OF THE THRONE but also to metaphors that at first sight are anchored only in the general human experience of darkness or light, rain, drought, and so on (e.g. THE TORAH / LAW IS LIGHT or THE TORAH / LAW IS WATER / MOISTURE.) The wide range of connotations is also related to the rich symbolism of water, the sun, the temple, and the king in the culture and religion not only of ancient Israel but also of the surrounding cultures of ancient Egypt, Mesopotamia and the rest of the ancient Middle East.

The conceptual metaphors THE TORAH / LAW IS LIGHT, THE TORAH / LAW IS WATER / MOISTURE and THE TORAH / LAW IS PROPERTY / VALUABLES can be found in the background of both general and specific metaphorical expressions (THE TORAH / LAW IS THE SUN, THE TORAH / LAW IS DEW, THE TORAH / LAW IS TEMPLE TREASURE, etc.). They are, as we have noted, also metaphors that could be considered variants of the more general conceptual metaphor THE TORAH / LAW IS THE SOURCE OF LIFE.

Other metaphors used in the conceptualisation of תורה *the Torah / Law* and related terms (THE TORAH / LAW IS JOY, THE TORAH / LAW IS SWEETNESS, THE TORAH / LAW IS AN OBJECT OF PRAISE, THE TORAH / LAW IS A BELOVED PERSON / OBJECT and THE TORAH / LAW IS A PLANT) occur only rarely in the Hebrew text of the Old Testament. The metaphorical expressions behind which these conceptual metaphors can be identified are innovative. In some cases, they could be considered some of the more common metaphors: THE TORAH / LAW IS SWEETNESS can be understood as a variant of THE TORAH / LAW IS FOOD, or more generally, THE TORAH / LAW IS THE SOURCE OF LIFE, using a specific entity which represents *the source of a higher quality of life* when mapping; likewise, THE TORAH / LAW IS A PLANT can be seen as a sub-variant of THE TORAH / LAW IS FOOD. Like the journey metaphor, the metaphor THE TORAH / LAW IS THE SOURCE OF LIFE conceptualises the entire conceptual area of תורה *the Torah / Law*, contributes significantly to the construction of a large conceptual apparatus, and has the status of a cardinal metaphor. It is a key theological statement which provides testimony to the importance of the Torah in the personal lives of those who belong to the people of Israel and to the status and function of the Torah in the religion and culture of Judaism.

One or at most two metaphorical expressions across the entire Old Testament canon were recorded in the metaphors THE TORAH / LAW IS THE CLOTHING OF THE JUDGE, THE TORAH / LAW IS THE CLOTHING OF A WARRIOR, THE TORAH / LAW IS AN INSTRUMENT OF THE BUILDER and THE TORAH / LAW IS THE INHABITANTS (OF THE LAND).

Despite the very narrow selection of specific metaphorical expressions, the network of structural correlations and correspondences is extremely rich, dynamic and often interconnected. We have seen a very wide range of conceptual blending. In general, however, we can state that unique or innovative applications of conceptual metaphors are found in passages which represent the conceptual blending of two or more metaphors, or where in metaphorical conceptualisation some detail such as a rarely used element of the source domain comes to the fore.

The following diagram graphically depicts and summarises the rich and dynamic network of structural correlations and correspondences between source and target domains in the metaphorical conceptualisation of the semantic area *Torah / Law*.

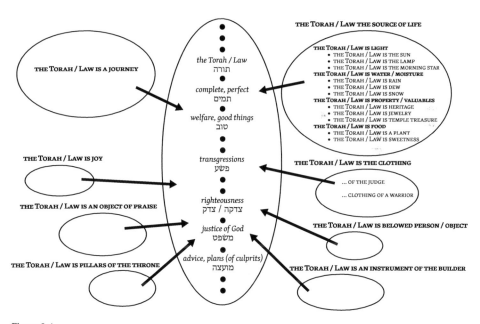

Figure 2.4

CHAPTER 3

USING COGNITIVE
AND CULTURAL-LINGUISTIC
ANALYSIS TO INTERPRET
AND TRANSLATE METAPHORICAL
EXPRESSIONS
IN THE OLD TESTAMENT

We have shown quite clearly that the methods of cognitive and culturally oriented linguistics are an effective tool in the analysis and interpretation of Old Testament metaphorical expressions, allowing us to reconstruct the mental image that is intended in the construction of the meaning of those expressions. Describing conceptual metaphors and their sub-variants using generic narrative structures and structural correlations and correspondences between entities of the source and target domains provides highly accurate descriptions of metaphorical meaning. Such an analysis of metaphorical meaning thus contributes to the exegesis of biblical texts and possibly to the scholarly debate over a number of thorny exegetical cases.

We have explained metaphorical meaning by naming the conceptual metaphors and generic narrative structures and noting (mostly in tables) the most important structural correlations and correspondences between the entities of the source and target domains. In this chapter, we will use examples from the book of Jeremiah to show how the journey metaphor and the spatial image schema can participate not only in the construction of the meaning of a metaphorical expression or a particular passage of text, but also in the formulation of key theological statements in larger passages of text such as a whole biblical book. We will also explain the meaning of metaphorical expressions in which the journey metaphor is used in the semantic area *Torah / Law* in an unconventional or innovative way. Here, we will use expressions from Proverbs 29:18 and Zephaniah 3:4.

Because any translation assumes a certain theological understanding of the original text, and is the realisation of this understanding, we use cognitive-linguistic analysis and interpretation in translation studies, within which (and within the work of exegesis) the translation of metaphorical expressions is a special case. A translation is always an expression of how the original was understood. However, the conceptualisation of the target domain against the background of the source domain in the original may not always be completely comprehensible to a reader from a different linguistic and cultural setting. The methods of analysing and interpreting the metaphorical expressions we present here can help us regain access to the cognitive function of a metaphor in the Hebrew text. These methods can also be used to re-examine translations by helping us to assess whether the author of an existing translation applied the metaphor used in the original or reworked it. In this chapter, we will use selected metaphorical expressions to explore the translation strategies deployed in the Greek Septuagint, the Latin Vulgate, and modern translations into English and Czech.

3.1 USING COGNITIVE-LINGUISTIC APPROACHES IN INTERPRETATION: THE JOURNEY METAPHOR AND SPATIAL IMAGE SCHEMAS IN THE BOOK OF JEREMIAH

In Jeremiah, the journey metaphor and the spatial image schemas within the framework of that metaphor will help us to conceptualise expressions from the semantic areas *Torah / Law* (our principal concern) and *Person, Character, Inner Self*,[125] and in so doing to speak about human mental qualities and processes. When a member of the people of God leaves or abandons the way of the Torah, leaves a life of obedience to God's commandments, this departure is related in some way to the person's behaviour, experiences, and emotional, mental and moral life. The semantic areas are connected, therefore, through a human agent, a participant—an Israelite. The journey metaphor allows us to discuss topics that today are dealt with in psychology, anthropology and philosophy. In the book of Jeremiah, the spatial image schemas contribute to the formulation of key theological statements about the causes of the exile and of the falling away of individuals and the whole people from the Lord, the God of Israel, but also about hope, and about God's promise to the exiles that they would return. The metaphorical expressions that work with the spatial image schemas we described in the previous chapters within the journey metaphor allow for an extremely effective conceptual grasp of the complex themes concerning the internal (spiritual) and external devastation of the lives of those exiled to Baylon: guilt, punishment, repentance, forgiveness, and, towards the end of the exile, the restoration of economic, social, cultural and religious life.

The main Hebrew expressions from the semantic area *Torah / Law* were introduced in chapter one. In Jeremiah, some of the key Hebrew anthropological expressions from the semantic area *Person, Personality, Inner Self* are the nouns נפש (*soul, life, living being*)[126] and לב / לבב (*heart, inner self, breast, conscience*). The two expressions are used metonymically in Jeremiah to denote a human individual. Hence the heart *perceives* (especially

---

125 The term נפש (*throat, breath, living being, people, life, soul, and so on*) appears 85 times in the book of Jeremiah. Most occurrences have the meaning *life, a living person, personality*; three times it has the meaning *self* (Jer 3:11; 13:17; 26:19). There is an extensive literature on the subject of the *soul*, which follows the subject either through the whole corpus of Christian Scripture in both Old and New Testaments or separately in the Old Testament and the New Testament. Other studies map the anthropology of the soul as presented in narrower literary circles such as the Psalms, the Wisdom Literature, or the Pentateuch.

126 The expression נפש (*soul, life, living being, human, etc.*), as the alternative meaning *throat, neck, breath* suggests, is associated with the neck, breathing and breath. The various verbal expressions in Jeremiah do not, however, connect the expression נפש with the neck (with the exception perhaps of Jer 2:24 and 4:10). If there is any connection between נפש and a particular vital or cognitive function, it is usually *breathing* (Jer 4:31; 15:9), *life* (Jer 4:10), *will* (Jer 2:24), *desire* (Jer 2:24; 44:14), or various emotions (*vengeance* Jer 5:9,29; *joy* Jer 32:41; *love* Jer 32:41; *sorrow* Jer 13:17; *fear* Jer 4:19; *resistance* Jer 14:19).

sees and *hears*: Jer 2:31; 23:18), *speaks* (Jer 13:22), *remembers, forgets,* and *pays / does not pay attention* to what is happening in the world.

In the Old Testament, a person is understood as an intricate, internally differentiated whole, a complex of limbs and organs and their specific vital functions.[127] Certain bodily organs (the heart, kidneys, eyes, ears, nose, etc.) are associated with particular emotional and cognitive processes, qualities of the will, and social and psychological conflicts.[128] Organs and body parts are seen as centres of activity associated with specific functions that in our modern European conception belong more to the person as a whole.[129]

Assmann[130] suggests that in the Old Testament, the heart (Hebrew לבב / לב)[131] is the central organ of human perception and cognition, bringing together all the parts of the body, the bodily organs and the cognitive functions into a single unit: the thoughts, feelings and blood vessels that connect the individual parts of the body come from the heart. But the *interior* (Hebrew קרב) and the *belly* (Hebrew מעיה / מעה, בטן and תוך) can have a similar connecting role to that of the heart in holding together the inner organs (especially the heart and the kidneys: Hebrew לבב / לב and כליה).

From our cognitive-linguistic analysis of Jeremiah, we suggest that לבב / לב *heart* is the organ which in the language of modern psychology would be associated with a person's personality, determining their motivations, qualities, temperament and character. The heart makes judgments and is also subject to moral judgment and the judgment of God (Jer 11:20; 17:10; 20:12). The Lord *gazes upon* a person's heart (Hebrew ראה in Q *to see, to look at, to inspect,* e.g. in Jer 20:12), *tests* (Hebrew בחן in Q *to test, to put to the test,* e.g. in Jer 11:20; 12:3; 17:10; 20:12), *explores, searches* (Hebrew חקר in Q *to explore, to search,* e.g. in Jer 17:10) and *judges* (in Hebrew שפט in Q *to pass judgment, to judge, to administer justice,* e.g. in Jer 11:20). What psychology calls a person's *mental qualities* (instincts, aptitudes, needs, interests and values as motives for human action) come from the heart; they "dwell" in the heart, but also "meet" and "clash" there.

The following metaphorical expression from Jeremiah 4:14 reflects the notion of the inner self (Hebrew קרב) in which false thoughts, false ideas (Hebrew מחשבה און) "live" (Hebrew verb root לין in Q *to remain overnight, to live, to dwell*).

Jer 4:14 כבסי מרעה לבך ירושלם למען תושעי עד־מתי תלין בקרבך מחשבות אונך:

Wash your heart clean of wickedness, O Jerusalem, that you may be rescued.

---

127 Emma Brunner-Traut, *Frühform des Erkennens am Beispiel Ägyptens* (Darmstadt: Wissenschaftliche Buchgesellschaft, 1992), 72.

128 In general, in the texts of the Old Testament Hebrew canon, the central anthropological concepts concerning the inner, mental life of a person include: נפש (*throat, breath, living being, people, life, soul*); לבב / לב (*heart, inner self, breast, conscience*); כליה (*kidneys, innermost being*); חי (*life, animateness, living being, people, soul*); רוח (*breeze, breath, wind, sense, mind*); מאד (*strength, power*); גבורה (*strength*); בטן (*belly, body cavity, womb, internal organs, bulging section*); תוך (*midst, in the middle*); קרב (*midst, inner parts, interior, the inward part of the body*); מעה / מעים (*entrails, intestines, inner being, stomach*); רחם (*womb*); מחשבה / מחשבת (*advice, counsel, plan, intent, invention*); מועצה (*advice, counsel, plan*); מזמה (*project, plan*); עין (*eye*); אזן (*ear*), and others.

129 In biblical Hebrew, *the ear hears, the eye looks, the legs walk, the mouth or the tongue speaks,* etc.

130 Jan Assmann, *Tod und Jenseit im Alten Ägypten* (Munich: C. H. Beck, 2001), 34.

131 *heart, inner self, breast, conscience,* and others.

How long will you harbour within you your evil designs?[132]
(**How long will your evil thoughts remain within your interior overnight?**)[133]

The most important structural correlations and correspondences established between the entities of the source and target domains by the metaphorical expression in Jeremiah 4:14 are shown in the table:

Table 3.1

structural correlation and correspondence	*source domain* **Living in an Abode**	*target domain* **Inner Mental and Spiritual Life**
	house	*heart*
	inhabitants of the house / guests in the house	*wicked thoughts*
	to spend the night in the house	*inner mental life of a person*

Because the heart, the inner self in modern terms, is also the centre of a person's character and temperament, the spatial image schema related to the inner self also provides the structure for the metaphorical expressions connected to behaviour. This is clear from Jeremiah 18:12

Jer 18:12 ‏ואמרו נואש כי־אחרי מחשבותינו נלך ואיש שררות לבו־הרע נעשה:
But they will say, "It is no use. We will keep on following our own plans;
each of us will act in the willfulness of his evil heart."[134]

Here we see again the metaphorical expressions structured in the background of the journey metaphor by means of metaphorical vehicles (see table 2.1), especially the verbs of motion, and also through Hebrew expressions for determining location, such as locating the heart in the inner self. In the metaphorical expression in Jeremiah 18:12, this is the verbal expression ‏הלך in combination with the preposition ‏אחר (*to follow, to keep on following*).

The Hebrew substantive ‏גאון (*pride, arrogance, superciliousness*) and the adjective ‏גאה (*proud, haughty*) come from nominal derivatives of the verb root ‏גאה (in Q *to rise up*); the spatial image schema behind these origins is very clear. In Jeremiah 48:29, this schema is used within a conceptual metaphor that suggests that the proud Moabites placed their hearts in a high place:

---

132 *Tanakh* (1985).
133 Literal translation.
134 *Tanakh* (1985).

Jer 48:29 שמענו גאון־מואב גאה מאד גבהו וגאונו וגאותו ורם לבו:
We have heard of the pride of Moab—he is very proud—of his loftiness,
his pride, and his arrogance, and the **haughtiness (height)** of his heart.

In Jeremiah, the heart is understood not only as the space within which the heart is located, but also as the space within which it moves. The notion of the movement of the heart within the inner self is probably based on physical experiences such as an accelerated, irregular or heavy pulse or heartbeat, accelerated breathing, or the tightening of the chest. The movement of the heart within this inner space, or rather this folk image of the movement of the heart, can then become the source domain for metaphorical and metonymic conceptualisations. In Czech, when someone is frightened, their heart can "jump out of their throat" or "fall into their trousers." This is also the case in the metaphorical expression in Jeremiah 4:19, where the (literally) *growling / moaning* heart is *surrounded by a wall* and cannot escape from the "space" of pain and fear:

Jer 4:19 מעי מעי [אחולה] [אוחילה] קירות לבי המה־לי לבי לא אחריש כי קול שופר [שמעתי] [שמעת] נפשי תרועת מלחמה:
My anguish, my anguish! I writhe in pain! Oh, the walls of my heart!
My heart is beating wildly [literally: is growling];
I cannot keep silent; for I hear the sound of the trumpet, the alarm of war.

The metaphorical expression in Jeremiah 4:18 is another example of how human behaviour can be metaphorically conceptualised through the journey metaphor (specifically the generic narrative structure TO TURN FROM THE PATH) against the spatial image of the *inner self* within which the heart *struck, collided with bitterness* (in Hebrew מר *bitter, bitterness*):

Jer 4:18 דרכך ומעלליך עשו אלה לך זאת רעתך כי מר כי נגע עד־לבך:
"Your ways and your doings have brought this upon you.
This is your doom; how bitter it is! It has reached your very heart!"
(verbatim: **Bitterness struck across your heart.**)

The meaning of this verse is shaped against the background of the image of a heart that has *diverted, departed from the way*—from *obedience to God*,[135] from the *way of truth, judgment and justice*.[136] The heart here is also a metonymy of the bearer, or of the *pars pro toto* of that person. The people of Jerusalem and the whole kingdom of Judah set off *on other ways—they performed deeds* (Hebrew מעלל) that were contrary to the deeds of a person who lives in obedience to God's commandments. On this (bad and dangerous) path, however, the enemy—*bitterness*—lay in wait for the heart. The heart (and hence the human person or the human soul) experiences pain and suffering (רעה) because it is *hurt, afflicted* (נגע) by the enemy—*bitterness* (מר).

---

135   This is clear from the context. See Jer 3:25.
136   Likewise, see Jer 4:2.

In the wider context of Jeremiah 4:1–18, alongside the metaphorical conceptualisation of the semantic areas *Torah / Law* and *Person, Personality, Inner Self*, other conceptual metaphors enter the blending process with the journey metaphor.[137] It is the
journey metaphor, however (in this section in its sub-variants—the generic narrative
structures TO WALK ALONG THE PATH, TO LEAVE THE PATH and TO GO ASTRAY), which
throughout the book of Jeremiah participates in the formulation of statements concerning the external and internal (spiritual) devastation of the life of the kingdom of
Judah and the causes and consequences of the turning away of individuals and all the
people from the Lord.[138]

The most important structural correlations and correspondences established
through the journey metaphor in Jeremiah 4:1–18 are listed in the table below, which
shows three target domains in which "journey" is conceptualised by the journey metaphor. The structural correlations and correspondences shown here fall across the
target domains. Through the journey metaphor, therefore, the author builds a link
between a person's heart and a person's deeds, a link between the devastation of the
hearts of the people of Judah, the legal and moral devastation of Judaic society, and
the destruction of the kingdom of Judah, which in turn leads to the invasion of enemy
troops.

In the older strata of the Old Testament biblical tradition, the concept of responsibility for idolatry, for turning away from the faith of Israel, from the Lord, and hence
the concept of guilt, is almost exclusively collective and connected to deeds. In this
respect, the exilic and post-exilic texts, including the book of Jeremiah, reflect a two-
fold turning. First, there is a turn from a purely collective concept of responsibility for
idolatry, for turning away from the faith of Israel, from the Lord, towards an individual
concept;[139] secondly, and related to the first turn, God's judgment is no longer con-
cerned simply with people's deeds, but also with the motivation for their deeds, with
their purposes and intentions. In the language of modern European law, the punishment for the offence is based on the offender's motivation, intention and purpose. The
judgment as to whether a person's deeds are "good" or "evil in the eyes of the Lord"[140]
includes God's consideration of a person's "inner self" ("heart", "soul"). This two-fold

---

137   For example, the conceptual metaphors THE HEART IS A DWELLING PLACE (Jer 4:13), THE HEART IS A FIELD (Jer
      4:3), GOD'S JUDGMENT IS FIRE (Jer 4:4), JUDGMENT IS HOT WIND (Jer 4:11). The conceptual metaphor THE HEART IS
      A FIELD establishes correspondence between entities as follows: *wasteland—hardened heart; field overgrown with
      thorns—hardened heart; ploughed field—repent; grain—the word of God; seed—hearing the word of God.*

138   In verse 18, the journey metaphor is activated by the metaphorical vehicle דרך *way, road, journey*; also involved
      in the construction of metaphorical meaning is the verbal expression נגע (in Q *touch, touch violently, strike*). The
      wider context includes other metaphorical vehicles: in verse 1, שוב (in Q *return*) and סור (in HI *remove*); and in
      verse 7, עלה (in Q *go up, go out*). The conceptual metaphor THE TORAH / LAW IS A JOURNEY includes use of the
      generic narrative structures TO WALK ALONG THE PATH (e.g. 4:18), TO LEAVE THE PATH (e.g. in verses 4:1 and 4:7)
      and TO GO ASTRAY (e.g. in 4:1).

139   Jer 31:29–30: "In those days they shall no longer say: 'The parents have eaten sour grapes, and the children's teeth
      are set on edge.' But all shall die for their own sins; the teeth of everyone who eats sour grapes shall be set on
      edge." A similar idea can be found in Ezek 18:2–4 (citation from Lam 5:7). See also Ex 20:5; 34:7; Deut 5:6, and
      elsewhere.

140   A formula typical of Deuteronomic literature (for a positive variant, see Deut 6:8; for a negative variant, see
      Deut 31:29).

aspect is anthropological, but also ethical, legal and theological. Human individuality and individual legal and moral responsibility are both connected to a person's inner self/heart/soul. In Jeremiah, this concept is formulated, inter alia, through the journey metaphor, and is

also connected to the concept of the new covenant (Hebrew ברית חדשה).[141] Part of the promise of salvation is the promise of the Torah, which will be "written on the heart" as on a scroll, as we read in Jeremiah 31:33.

Table 3.1

	source domain **Journey**	target domain I. **Inner Mental and Spiritual Life**	target domain II. **The Behaviour of the People of God with Regard to Legal, Religious and Ethical Standards**	target domain III. **Kingdom of Judah**
structural correlation	to walk along the path	to fear God	to swear: "As the LORD lives!"	
	to go astray in the sense of wandering aimlessly	to not fear God	idolatry	
	to return	to repent	deeds of truth, judgment and justice	
correspondence	traveller	the heart of the inhabitants of Jerusalem		
	the land	entrails (מעה)	people of Jerusalem / people of Judah	kingdom of Judah
	a journey (through the land)	repentance	deeds of truth, judgment and justice (אמת, נגע, צדקה)	
		obedience to God		
		obstinacy of the people of Jerusalem (מרה)	criminal deeds	
		wickedness		
	enemy on the way	bitterness	God's wrath	enemy army
			God's judgment	

---

141 Especially Jer 32:31–34.

כי זאת הברית אשר אכרת את־בית ישראל אחרי הימים ההם נאם־יהוה Jer 31:33

נתתי את־תורתי בקרבם ועל־לבם אכתבנה והייתי להם לאלהים והמה יהיו־לי לעם:

But this is the covenant that I will make with the house of Israel after those days, says the Lord: I will put my law **within them**, and I will write it **on their hearts**; and I will be their God, and they shall be my people.

The new covenant, the Torah "written on the heart," binds a person's vital centre—the centre of motivation, reason and emotion, everything that makes up a person's personality or inner self—to the Lord. In the background of the theologically key statement of Jeremiah 31:33, we detect the conceptual metaphor THE HEART IS A SCROLL OF THE TORAH.

The metaphorical expressions concerning the promised future—the return from exile, the renewal of the source of life, the renewal of life's flourishing—correspond to the revitalisation of the exiles' inner life. Just as we found a link between the devastation of the inner self, the legal and moral devastation of Judaic society, and the destruction of the kingdom of Judah, so the promise of salvation affects both the inner world of the heart (soul) . . .

their life [soul] shall be like a watered garden, and they shall languish no more (Jer 31:12)
I will water the life [soul] of the priests with fatness . . . (Jer 31:14)
. . . and the outside world, Judaic society, and the country to which it will return from exile:
...they shall come back from the land of the enemy (Jer 31:16)
With weeping they shall come, and with consolations I will lead them back,
I will let them walk by brooks of water,
in a straight path in which they shall not stumble (Jer 31:9)

This analogy is again built in the text, inter alia, through the journey metaphor and spatial image schemas. The metaphor therefore plays a significant role in the most important theological statements of the book of Jeremiah.

3.2 USING COGNITIVE AND CULTURALLY ORIENTED LINGUISTIC ANALYSIS AND INTERPRETATION IN TRANSLATION STUDIES

The issue of the translation of biblical texts has been addressed by biblical scholars, linguists, translators and lay people for many centuries. The form taken by any given translation is always a reflection of how the original text was interpreted. Each translation assumes a certain theological understanding of the original text and is the realisation of this understanding. It is not always possible, however, to preserve in a translation all the elements, expressions and meanings of the original text. With regard to the target language, or the communicative purpose or function in the target culture, some aspects of the source text may be highlighted, others suppressed. The decision as to which elements of the original text are retained, suppressed or modified is the translator's (or may be included in the translator's instructions). When translating metaphorical expressions, these initial parameters of the translated text include not only those words being used in a meaning of the word which is non-conventional or figurative.[142] Some metaphorical expressions, furthermore, are so embedded within the socio-cultural, religious and geographical context in which they originated that their translation into another language becomes a problem not only for translation but also for exegesis.

We will focus on modern translations from Hebrew into English and Czech of the metaphorical expressions in Proverbs 29:18 and Zephaniah 3:4, noting especially the strategies translators chose when translating these expressions. We will first of all be interested in whether the passages of text in the final translations are metaphorical, or the metaphor was eliminated and metaphorical conceptualisation of the semantic area *Torah / Law* abandoned for some reason. If the passage is also metaphorical in the translation, we will see if the translators kept the original metaphor or offered an alternative metaphorical conceptualisation.

More often than not, a (literal) linguistic translation of a metaphorical expression is not a translation of the metaphor but only a translation of the words involved in the metaphor. Literal (linguistic) translations of the Bible include *Young's Literal Translation of the Holy Bible* and *Český studijní překlad* (Czech study Bible). Part of the aim of so-called documentary translation,[143] undeniably the prevalent form of translation in modern biblical studies, is to make sure that the translation shows how the original text communicated its pragmatic content in the assumed former communicative context. Although the system of notes that accompanies a documentary translation draws attention to a metaphor and provides the information necessary to understand it, the translation itself cannot perform similar cognitive or aesthetic functions to the Hebrew original. A text with an extensive system of critical notes simply cannot function as a complex linguistic structure that is consistent in its content and at the same time fulfil the cognitive or aesthetic functions of the original. Eliminating a metaphor goes against the requirement of documentary translation because a significant aspect of the original has been suppressed or modified and the meaning has inevitably been flattened and distorted. These potential limitations of documentary (linguistic) translation must be taken into account.

---

142 According to substitution theory — the long-dominant theory with its origins in Aristotle's *Poetics* — THE essence of the metaphor is the use of a word in a non-conventional and figurative meaning: the basic principle is "seeing similarity," with the primary function being to adorn, diversify, impress, attract, emphasise, figuratively characterise, add emotional undertones, and so on. See, for example, Jiří Pavelka, *Anatomie metafory* (Brno: Blok, 1982).

143 Contemporary translation studies usually work with the term *equivalence*; Bible translations speak of either *formal* or *dynamic* equivalence (later also called *functional* equivalence), or *semantic* equivalence. Nord distinguishes two basic types of translation: documentary and instrumental. Linguistic translation is an example of the former. We will be using Nord's terminology. See Christine Nord, *Translating as a Purposeful Activity. Functionalist Approaches Explained*, Translation Theories Explained, 1 (Manchester: St. Jerome Publishing, 2007).

Other Bible translation projects past and present have placed different demands on the translation. Instrumental translation mainly takes into account communication in the target cultural environment. Translators aim to create a translation that is functionally appropriate to the expected communicative context. Typical examples of modern functional translations in English are *The Holy Bible New Living Translation*, the *Good News Bible*, and the *Contemporary English Version*, and in Czech *Slovo na cestu* (Word on the way) and *Bible 21. století* (Bible translations for the 21st century). In general, functional translation is more likely to preserve the cognitive functions of a metaphor in the target language and culture, but in doing so it should also respect a set of clearly defined constraints so that the adaptation of metaphorical expressions is neither arbitrary nor limitless.

In order to fulfil the cognitive function of the metaphor in a similar way to that realised through the original, the translator must of course first identify and understand the metaphor in the original—the mental image that the author of the text (and its first readers) would have been holding, the generic narrative structure projected into the target conceptual area, and the structural correlations and correspondences established by the metaphorical expression. If the cognitive function of the metaphor is to be preserved in the translation, the reader, like the reader of the Hebrew original, must be allowed to conceptualise the target domain against the background of the source domain. It will then be up to the translator to decide whether to preserve the conceptualisation behind the mental image that the original intended, that is, preserve in the translation the conceptual metaphor of the original and its generic narrative structure, or to opt for a different translation strategy.

The problems of metaphor translation have been dealt with by numerous authors, including by Peter Newmark in his *Approaches to Translation*.[144] Newmark saw literary language as the principal (though not the only) domain of metaphorical expressions, but like cognitive and culturally oriented linguists, he saw knowledge of connotations as key to the understanding of metaphors and proposed several strategies for translating them:

- Reproduce in the target language the mental image that the metaphor created in the original language.
- Replace a mental image that collides (is incomprehensible) in the target culture with a mental image that is common in the target language (and culture).
- Preserve the mental image from the source language even at the expense of losing the emotional character (the element of surprise, shock).
- Create a similar mental image, but add an interpretation.
- Eliminate the metaphor.
- Use the same metaphor in the target language and add an explanation. (Here Newmark is probably referring to documentary translation.)[145]

---

144   Peter Newmark, *Approaches to Translation*, Language Teaching Methodology Series (London: Prentice Hall, 1981).
145   See ibid., 84–96.

The issue of connotations is quite specific in biblical texts. Intertextuality, a feature of biblical texts,[146] contributes significantly to the construction of the meaning of individual terms, text units, books and whole literary circles. Newmark suggested that on the basis of connotations a mental image is built which forms the basis for creating metaphorical meaning. This image is often based on our physicality (such as our experience with objects or our orientation in a space) and tied to the socio-cultural, religious and geographical context of both the author and the first recipients of the Hebrew original. We understand the mental image as the basis of the metaphor, and as we have seen, it usually has a narrative structure, the core of which is a generic narrative structure as a partial position of a conceptual metaphor.

After focusing on modern translations of metaphorical expressions into English and Czech, we will explore the same metaphorical expressions in the Septuagint and the Vulgate. Even so-called modern translations are often influenced by these oldest versions of the biblical text. The first modern translations of the Old Testament into English are considered to be *Young's Literal Translation of the Holy Bible* (1863), the *English Revised Version* (1885), and the *American Standard Version* (1901). Translations into Czech made after 1900 will be considered modern.[147]

3.2.1 MODERN TRANSLATIONS OF THE BIBLE INTO ENGLISH AND CZECH

The first translations to be based on the original Hebrew and Greek texts rather than on the Latin Vulgate were produced during the Reformation. In the nineteenth and twentieth centuries, the missionary endeavours of churches and missionary and Bible societies provided an important impetus for the publication of the Bible and the commissioning of new translations into many hundreds of languages. Translation committees included scholars from different denominations who worked together on large-scale ecumenical Bible translation projects. Existing translations were revised as translators sought to take into account the results of text-critical research. "Confessional translations" (Jewish, Catholic, and so on) were produced in which translators developed the interpretative and translation tradition of their religion or denomination; some translations were made alongside liturgical reforms or efforts towards spiritual renewal. Some translations or revisions openly accept the emphases of a particular spiritual or theological stream within Christianity, and in their prefaces declare their intention to provide readers with a literal-linguistic, or sometimes "functionally equivalent" translation.

---

146 Meaning (not only metaphorical meaning) is always shaped in the context of whole texts or literary units or in the context of the whole canon of the Hebrew Old Testament.

147 Josef Bartoň, "Český starozákonní překlad po roce 1900. Kontexty, konfese, předloha, kánon," *Salve. Revue pro teologii a duchovní život* 2 (2013): 143–162.

Since the nineteenth century, attempts have been made to convey biblical texts to readers in a modern form of the target language. There has also been a recent move towards the use of "inclusive" language that is, for example, gender neutral. Some translations are "traditional"; others are "loose" or even paraphrased and addressed to specific groups of readers, such as children, young people, or people whose native language is different from the target language.

Given the vast array of modern translations of the Bible into English, we needed to select the translations we were to look at. The twenty-one translations we will work with are listed in the table below. They have all received official approval within, for example, the Jewish community or some of the larger Christian denominations or a particular ecumenical community, or are translations that have been generally accepted in English-speaking contexts, such as among evangelical Christians. We have provided basic information in the footnotes; for more detail, we refer you to other literature and bibliographies.[148]

Table 3.2

TRANSLATION AND YEAR ISSUED	ABBREVIATION
Young's Literal Translation of the Holy Bible[149] (1862)	YLT
English Revised Version[150] (1885)	ERV
American Standard Version[151] (1901)	ASV
Revised Standard Version[152] (1952)	RSV
New American Standard Bible with Code[153] (1977)	NAS

---

148   For example: Bruce Metzger, *The Bible in Translation* (Michigan: Baker Academic, 2001); David Daniell, *The Bible in English: Its History and Influence* (New Haven: Yale University Press, 2003).

149   The translation was made by Robert Young, who compiled *Young's Analytical Concordance to the Bible* and *Concise Critical Comments on the New Testament*. Young used the Textus Receptus and the Masoretic Text as the basis for his translation with the intention of creating a verbatim translation from the Hebrew and the Greek, even in terms of the grammatical and syntactic structure. Type of translation: formal equivalence.

150   This was the first translation that aimed to "purify" the original Greek and Hebrew text from "mistakes and appendages" in the light of developing textual criticism. It is a revision of the *King James Version*, but it is also regarded as the forerunner of the entire modern translation tradition. Two translation committees, British and American, both established in 1870, worked on the translation. Judging by the revisers' preface to the ERV, it seems as though they were asked to introduce as few alterations as possible to the text of the Authorised Version, to be consistent and faithful to it, and to match, as far as possible, the language of those alterations to that of the Authorised and earlier English versions. Type of translation: formal equivalence.

151   This is the American version of the *English Revised Version* of 1885, which was worked on by both English and American committees. "In English style the American revision introduced some distinct improvements over the British Revised Version." (Metzger, *Bible in Translation*, 103.) Type of translation: formal equivalence.

152   Revision of the 1901 *American Standard Version*. Type of translation (as declared by its translators): borderline formal equivalence and dynamic equivalence (according to Eugene Nida).

153   Revision of the 1971 *New American Standard Bible*. The impetus to create the *NASB* was originally provided by the Lockman Foundation (La Habra, California) in 1959. The *NASB* was a new translation based on the *American Standard Version* (1901). "Although the revisers of the NASB claim to have followed in most instances the text of

New American Standard Bible with Code (1995)	NAU
New Revised Standard Version[154] (1990)	NRS
English Standard Version[155] (2001)	ESV
New English Bible[156] (1970)	NEB
Revised English Bible[157] (1989)	REB
Tanakh[158] (1985)	TNK
Complete Jewish Bible[159] (1998)	CJB
Bible in Basic English[160] (1964)	BBE
New English Translation[161] (2001–2017)	NET
New Jerusalem Bible (1985)[162]	NJB

---

the twenty-third edition of the Nestle Greek New Testament, important deviations occur in the introduction of a number of verses that rest on doubtful manuscript authority." (Metzger, *Bible in Translation*, 150) The revisers declare formal equivalence, but "According to a detailed analysis comparing the NASB and the NASBU, the former contains 781,182 words and the latter 774,216 words. Changes introduced by the NASBU occur in 10,616 verses and directly affect 24,338 words in the NASB. There are only 4,704 changes in capitalization, 32 in spelling, and 30 in italics. This makes 19,572 corrections involving word omissions, additions, transpositions, or substitutions in the text of the NASB. The updated edition makes about 85 changes that introduce gender-inclusive language." (Metzger, *Bible in Translation*, 150–151).

154   Revision of the 1952 *Revised Standard Version*. Translation type: dynamic equivalence.
155   Another revision of the 1952 *Revised Standard Version*. Translation type: formal equivalence.
156   A new translation (not a revision of an older version) made at the instigation of the Church of Scotland. Translators from other major Protestant churches in Great Britain also joined the work on the translation. (Catholics were only observers.) The Old Testament Translators Group was coordinated by G. R. Driver from Oxford University. Translation type: formal equivalence.
157   Revision of the 1970 *New English Bible*. On this occasion, scholars from the Catholic church, the Salvation Army and Unitas Fratrum also participated in the revision. The translation therefore represents British Christianity in the late 20th century. Translation type: dynamic equivalence.
158   The translation was supported financially by the Jewish Publication Society. The editor-in-chief of the project was Harry M. Orlinsky of the Hebrew Union College. In 1999, a bilingual edition was published under the title *Hebrew-English Tanakh*.
159   Translation by David H. Stern, a Messianic Jew who lived first in America and then in Israel. Stern took the Old Testament and modified it on the basis of an English translation of the Old Testament, *The Holy Scriptures according to the Masoretic Text*, published in 1971 by the Jewish Society of America in Philadelphia. Translation type: dynamic equivalence.
160   Published in England in 1949. Written in simplified English, it was designed by the British writer and linguist C. K. Ogden and intended to be comprehensible to readers with only a basic knowledge of English. A revised translation was published in 1964. Type of translation as declared by its translators: functional equivalence.
161   A new online English translation / paraphrase with 60,932 translators' notes. Sponsored by the Biblical Studies Foundation and published by Biblical Studies Press. Translation type: borderline functional equivalence and dynamic equivalence.
162   The Dominican Thomas-Georges Chifflot from the Catholic publishing house Éditions du Cerf was the founder of the modern French translation of the Bible. He wanted the new translation to contribute to the spiritual renewal of France after the Second World War. The Jerusalem Bible School worked on the translation from 1946 to 1956. A revised translation into French, the *Bible de Jerusalem*, was published in 1973. The *Jerusalem Bible* (1966) is an English translation of the first French version. The *New Jerusalem Bible* (1985) is a translation of the French revision of 1973. Translation type: dynamic equivalence.

New American Bible[163] (1986)	NAB
Holy Bible, New Living Translation[164] (1996)	NLT
Good News Bible[165] (1976)	GNB
New International Version[166] (1984)	NIV
New King James Version[167] (1982)	NKJ
Contemporary English Version[168] (1995)	CEV

The fifteen translations into modern Czech that we will work with are presented in the following tables. A brief description of the translations is provided in the footnotes; once again we refer the reader to other scholarly literature on individual translations.[169] We will work with translations of the whole Old Testament, with the exception of the translations of the Pentateuch by the Chief Rabbis of Prague and the unfinished translation by the Roman Catholic theologian Václav Bogner.

---

163   The first Roman Catholic translation of the Bible from the original languages in the USA. A revision of the 1970 *New American Bible*. Translation type: formal and dynamic equivalence.

164   A revision of Taylor's *Living Bible Paraphrased*, published in 1971. (The *Living Bible Paraphrased* is a paraphrase of *The Living Bible*). This is not in fact a paraphrase, but a translation declaring dynamic equivalence and formal equivalence.

165   In 1966, a translation of the New Testament appeared with the title *Good News for Modern Man*. The translation was a response to many years of requests from American Bible Society from Africa to create a translation for readers for whom English was a foreign language. The translation is based on the principle of "dynamic equivalence" (according to Nida), later called "functional equivalence." The 1976 edition uses gender-neutral language, but the 1992 revision does not. Translation type: dynamic equivalence.

166   The impetus from American conservative protestants for the *New International Version* translation of the Bible came officially in 1956 from the Protestant Reformed Churches in America and in 1957 from the National Association of Evangelicals. Edwin H. Palmer became the Executive Secretary of the project in 1968. By 1978 the entire Bible had been completed. The publication was accompanied by an extensive advertising campaign that emphasised the ecumenical and international nature of the entire translation project. Several revisions have been made since. Translation type: formal equivalence.

167   The *New King James Version* revises the *King James Version* and preserves the classic style and literary beauty of the original 1611 version. Old Testament translators based their work on the 1967/1977 Stuttgart edition of the *Biblia Hebraica* and *The Mikraot Gedolot* of Ben Hayyim, which served as the textus receptus for the *King James Version* in 1611. Translation type: formal equivalence.

168   Published by American Bible Society in 1995. Leading personalities in the group of more than a hundred translators included B. M. Newman, Donald Johns and Steven Berneking. The Bible is a translation from the original languages, addressed to children. The translation is based on the principle of dynamic equivalence.

169   Bartoň, "Český starozákonní překlad."

Table 3.3

CZECH CATHOLIC translations		
TRANSLATION AND YEAR ISSUED	TRANSLATOR / HEAD OF THE TRANSLATION GROUP	ABBREVIATION
Bible česká (Czech Bible)[170] (1925) *Podlahova bible* (Podlaha Bible)[171] (1917–1925)	Jan Hejčl[172]	Hejčl
Písmo svaté Starého zákona (Holy Scripture of the Old Testament)[173] (1955, 1956, 1958)	Josef Heger[174]	Heger
Římskokatolický liturgický překlad (Roman Catholic liturgical translation)[175]		Bogner
Jeruzalémská bible (Jerusalem Bible) (2005, 2009)[176]		JB

Table 3.4

Translations of the Pentateuch by CZECH RABBIS[177]		
TRANSLATION AND YEAR ISSUED	TRANSLATOR / HEAD OF THE TRANSLATION GROUP	ABBREVIATION
Pět knih Mojžíšových (The five books of Moses) (1932–1950)	Isidor Hirsch, Gustav Sicher	Hirsch
Pět knih Mojžíšových. Včetně haftorot (The five books of Moses. Including the haftorot) (2012)	Karol Efraim Sidon	Sidon

170 Separate Old Testament.
171 Old Testament and New Testament together.
172 Jan Hejčl (1868–1935) was professor of Old Testament and Semitic languages at the Catholic Theological Faculty in Olomouc. Although his translation is officially based on the Vulgate (in the Czech context it was only possible to base the translation primarily on the Hebrew text after the publication of the papal encyclical *Divino afflante Spiritu* in 1943), Hejčl took the Hebrew and Septuagint text into account in his work. His intention was also to prepare a text in modern Czech.
173 Old Testament only, published gradually over the years stated. Heger's translation was published in book form only posthumously and his translation was edited by the Czech Catholic biblical scholars Jan Merell and František Kotalík.
174 Josef Heger (1885–1952) was professor of biblical studies at the Theological Faculty in Brno and at the Catholic Theological Faculty in Prague. He translated from Hebrew.
175 After the Second Vatican Council, the Czech Catholic biblical scholar Václav Bogner worked first on the translation of a lectionary and later on the translation of the relevant Old Testament texts. His work was continued and his translations revised by the Czech biblical scholars Josef Hřebík and Jaroslav Brož.
176 The translation of the Old Testament took from 1980 to 2009. It was worked on by theologians connected to the Dominican Order, but also by other theologians, biblical scholars and philologists (bohemists).
177 Translations of the Pentateuch by Jewish scholars and chief rabbis of Prague. An older translation by Isidor Hirsch (1864–1940) and Gustav Sicher (1880–1950) was published in parts—*The Five Books of Moses: In the Beginning* (1932), *The Five Books of Moses: The Second Book: "Names"* (1935), *The Five Books of Moses: The Third Book: "He Cried..."* (1938), *The Five Books of Moses: The Fourth Book: In the Desert* (1939) and *Moses' Speech. The Fifth Book of the Torah* (1950)—with explanations by Gustav Flusser. Karol Efaim Sidon made a more recent translation, published in 2012. The translation, which is a literal translation into Czech, accompanies the primary Hebrew text. Both translations serve as a literal translation into Czech and are auxiliary to the Hebrew text.

Table 3.5

The CZECH ECUMENICAL TRANSLATION and other translations		
TRANSLATION AND YEAR ISSUED	**TRANSLATOR / HEAD OF THE TRANSLATION GROUP**	**ABBREVIATION**
Písmo (The Scripture)[178] (1947, 1948, 1951, 1951)	Vladimír Šrámek[179] Vladimír Kajdoš[180]	Šrámek
Český ekumenický překlad (The Czech ecumenical translation)[181]		ČEP
Překlad nového světa (New world translation)[182] (1991)		PNS
Průvodce životem (The guide to life)[183] (1994–2003) *Slovo na cestu: Bible s poznámkami* (Word on the way: Annotated Bible)[184] (2011)	Jiří Dejnar	SC
Nová Bible kralická (New Kralice Bible)[185] (2002–2008)	Alexandr Flek Pavel Hoffman	NBK

---

178 The Old Testament with the same sequencing and length as the Palestinian canon, in four volumes. The text is divided into chapters only (not verses), and the translation was published without footnotes. The aim of the translators was to disregard the fact that the Old Testament was the sacred text of Jews and Christians and create a non-confessional, completely secular translation of an Old-Semitic literary relic with as little connection as possible to the established terms and expressions in the Jewish or Christian traditions.

179 Vladimír Šrámek (1893–1969) was a lawyer, actor, and translator of classical languages.

180 Vladimír Kajdoš (1893–1970) was a brigadier general in the Czechoslovak army, a politician, and a historian. He retired in December 1939. He returned to his unfinished study of philology and worked together with Vladimír Šrámek to translate the Old Testament.

181 Still the most widely published and widely used translation of the Bible in the Czech language, it was first published in 1979 and has been revised several times (1978–1984, 1998–2000). The translation originated between 1961 and 1979 with the collaboration of Catholic and evangelical biblical scholars. The Old Testament translation sought to be as literal as possible. In the evangelical context, the Czech ecumenical translation gradually replaced the Kralice Bible. It is a translation from the original languages with text-critical footnotes.

182 A translation written within the Jehovah's Witnesses Religious Society (in Czech NSSJ). The *Translation of Hebrew Scripts* was published in four samizdat volumes from 1983 to 1987. This confessional translation was first published in a single volume in 1991.

183 The Seventh-Day Adventist preacher Jiří Dejnar gathered around him an ecumenical group of around 15 evangelical Protestants who wished to remain anonymous in the publication. The aim was to create a kind of Czech *Living Bible*. The translators chose modern language tools: it is a rather free translation, and in some cases paraphrased. The New Testament is translated from Greek with only methodological inspiration from the *Living Bible*. The Old Testament is a translation from the English *Living Bible*.

184 The translation was first published in parts by International Bible Society and Luxpress between 1994 and 2003 under the title *Průvodce životem* (Guide to life). The later 1989 single-volume edition *Slovo na cestu* (Word on the way: The annotated Bible) is supplied with notes from the *Life Application Study Bible*, which was published in the US in a number of editions after the first in 1988.

185 The *Nová Bible kralická* (New Kralice Bible) translation of the New Testament was first published in 1998 and subsequently revised within the *Bible 21. století* (Bible translations for the 21st century). The leaders of the New Testament translation were Alexandr Flek and Pavel Hoffman.

Bible 21. století (21st century Bible)[186] (2009)	Alexander Flek Pavel Hoffman Jiří Hedánek	B21
Český studijní překlad (Czech study Bible)[187] (2009)		ČSP

In these selected modern translations into English and Czech, we will note which strategies were chosen when translating metaphorical expressions from the Hebrew, which aspects of the original text were retained, highlighted or suppressed, and how the chosen translation strategies affect the ability of the final text to fulfill the cognitive function of the metaphors used in the original. Other aspects of English and Czech translations, such as their dependence on the phraseology and syntax of the original language and the stylistic or aesthetic level of the translation will not be of interest unless they are directly related to the cognitive function of the metaphors used in the original Hebrew text.

3.2.2 ANALYSIS, INTERPRETATION AND TRANSLATION OF THE METAPHORICAL EXPRESSION IN DEUTERONOMY 8:6

We introduced the metaphorical expression from Deuteronomy 8:6 in the previous chapter as an example of the conventional use of the journey metaphor in structuring the semantic area *Torah / Law*. We now return to this verse to introduce the basic methods used in the analysis, interpretation and evaluation of strategies for translating metaphorical expressions into modern English and Czech. The method presented here will then be applied to passages of text which have a non-conventional way of applying the conceptual metaphors involved in the conceptualisation of תורה *the Torah / Law* and related Hebrew terms.

Identifying the conceptual metaphor (THE TORAH / LAW IS A JOURNEY), the generic narrative structure (TO WALK ALONG THE PATH), and the structural correlations and correspondences established by the journey metaphor is straightforward in Deuteronomy 8:6:

---

186 Bible 21. století (Bible translations for the 21st century) is a translation of the New Testament (previously published as *Nová Bible kralická* (New Kralice Bible), and the Old Testament. In the introduction, the translators claim to be following the functional equivalence of Eugene Nida, similar to the English translations *Holy Bible, New Living Translation* (1994), the *Good News Bible* (1976), and the *Contemporary English Version* (1995).
187 A translation from within Czech evangelical Christian circles under the patronage of the Czech *Christian Mission Society*. The translation seeks to be literal; the translators claim to be following formal equivalence. The translation is accompanied by notes, in many places interpretative, which clearly originate within the theology of evangelical Christianity.

Deut 8:6 וּשְׁמַרְתָּ אֶת־מִצְוֹת יְהוָה אֱלֹהֶיךָ לָלֶכֶת בִּדְרָכָיו וּלְיִרְאָה אֹתוֹ׃

Therefore keep the commandments of the LORD your God,
by **walking in his ways** and by fearing him.

The conceptual metaphor THE TORAH / LAW IS A JOURNEY signals the metaphorical vehicle, the noun דֶּרֶךְ (*way, road, journey*). The verb roots הלך with the preposition ב (in Q *to go, to walk*) and שׁמר (in Q *to keep, to watch over, to take care of, to preserve, to protect*) are also involved in the metaphorical conceptualisation. The latter verb root cannot be regarded as a metaphorical vehicle as it is commonly found in contexts other than the *way*, such as *guarding the garden* (Gen 2:15), *guarding the herd* (Gen 30:30), *guarding grain stores* (Gen 41:35) and *guarding (keeping) the covenant* (Gen 17:9,10). In the semantic area *Torah / Law*, this verb root is also a lexicalised metaphor with the meaning *to keep (the law), to respect, to obey*. It is also not exclusively tied to a single generic narrative structure in metaphorical expressions that are structured through the journey metaphor, as within the generic narrative structure TO WALK ALONG THE PATH in Genesis 18:9; 2 Samuel 22:22; 1 Kings 8:58, and here in 1 Kings 2:3–4:

1 Kings 2:3 וְשָׁמַרְתָּ אֶת־מִשְׁמֶרֶת יְהוָה אֱלֹהֶיךָ לָלֶכֶת בִּדְרָכָיו לִשְׁמֹר חֻקֹּתָיו מִצְוֹתָיו

וּמִשְׁפָּטָיו וְעֵדְוֹתָיו כַּכָּתוּב בְּתוֹרַת מֹשֶׁה לְמַעַן תַּשְׂכִּיל

אֵת כָּל־אֲשֶׁר תַּעֲשֶׂה וְאֵת כָּל־אֲשֶׁר תִּפְנֶה שָׁם׃

4 לְמַעַן יָקִים יְהוָה אֶת־דְּבָרוֹ אֲשֶׁר דִּבֶּר עָלַי לֵאמֹר אִם־יִשְׁמְרוּ בָנֶיךָ אֶת־דַּרְכָּם לָלֶכֶת לְפָנַי בֶּאֱמֶת

בְּכָל־לְבָבָם וּבְכָל־נַפְשָׁם לֵאמֹר לֹא־יִכָּרֵת לְךָ אִישׁ מֵעַל כִּסֵּא יִשְׂרָאֵל׃

And observe what the Lord your God requires:
Walk in his ways, and keep his decrees and commands, his laws and requirements,
as written in the Law of Moses,
so that you may prosper in all you do and wherever you go,
that the Lord may keep his promise to me:
"If your descendants watch how they live,
and if they walk faithfully before me with all their heart and soul,
you will never fail to have a man on the throne of Israel."

Likewise, the verb root occurs as a lexicalised metaphor in the sense of *to respect, to obey* in, for example, Job 23:11 within the generic narrative structure TO LEAVE THE PATH:

Job 23:11 בַּאֲשֻׁרוֹ אָחֲזָה רַגְלִי דַּרְכּוֹ שָׁמַרְתִּי וְלֹא־אָט׃

When he is at work in the north, I do not see him; when he turns to the south,
I catch no glimpse of him.

We have already suggested that the journey metaphor in Deuteronomy 8:6 offers the reader an understanding of a life lived in obedience to God's commands and in the fear of God against a backdrop of the mental image of "walking along a path," during which people "watch where they put their feet." The verse was presented as an example of a completely conventional application of the conceptual metaphor THE TORAH / LAW IS A JOURNEY, namely the generic narrative structure TO WALK ALONG THE PATH.

Although we could question the extent to which the original addressees of the Hebrew text perceived the text passage as metaphorical,[188] it clearly is, as indicated by the noun דֶּרֶךְ (*way, road, journey*).

The following table shows the structural correlations and correspondences between the source and target domains established by the conceptual metaphor THE TORAH / LAW IS A JOURNEY and the generic narrative structure TO WALK ALONG THE PATH in Deuteronomy 8:6.

Table 3.6

	source domain	target domain
TO WALK ALONG THE PATH		
structural correlation	to walk along the path	to obey the commandments (of the Torah)
	to guard (the path)	
	to walk along the path	to obey God
	to guard (the path)	
	to walk along the path	the fear of God
	to guard (the path)	
correspondence	traveller	Israel
	path, road	commandments of the Torah / Law (מצוה)

Although שׁמר and הלך + בּ are both lexicalised within the canon of the Hebrew Bible in the semantic area *Torah / Law*, and could not therefore be said to be metaphorical vehicles in Deuteronomy 8:6, both are important in determining which generic narrative structure is used and in reconstructing the mental image that the author of the text assumes when constructing the meaning of a metaphorical passage of text. To understand the metaphorical expressions in the other examples that we will analyse and interpret in this chapter, we will seek to identify both the conceptual metaphor and the generic narrative structure in order to reconstruct the mental image that the metaphor created in the original Hebrew text and to name the structural correlations and correspondences it established.

The verse Deuteronomy 8:6 is part of the second introductory speech of Moses (Deut 4:44–11:32), which precedes the Deuteronomic Code (chapters 12–26). The primary function of the whole passage is legal, and the author (authors, editors) certainly intended to make its meaning clear. However, even in a purely legal text, the meta-

---

188 Based on the analysis carried out in the previous chapter, we concluded that both verb roots (הלך in combination with the preposition בּ, and שׁמר) are lexicalised in the semantic area *Torah / Law* with the journey metaphor, and that in many texts in the Old Testament canon they are used in the sense of *to respect, to obey*.

phorical conceptualisation of the Hebrew term מצוה (*commandment*) has an important function. Although the journey metaphor is used in a completely conventional way, in the expressions used it tends to lexicalise, so the meaning is clear. However, the metaphor establishes new structural and dynamic relationships between the source domain and entities in the target domain (*God's commandments, obedience to the law,* etc.), thus enabling the target domain to be understood in a non-legal context. The metaphor significantly expands the range of connotations, and the source domain brings further intertextual references to the metaphorical meaning, for example through references to texts using the metaphor of God as a shepherd or king. In the Bible, "walking along the path" is not only about "obeying God's commandments" but also about "living". "Obedience to God's commandments" does not make sense in itself: it is like "wandering from somewhere to somewhere," and it has its causes and its meaning. The metaphor offers the reader a chance to think about the meaning of obeying God's commandments. Eliminating the metaphor and replacing the metaphorical expressions with purely legal terminology would distort and substantially "flatten" the meaning of the text.

The translation of Deuteronomy 8:6 into Greek (Septuagint) and Latin (Vulgate) and modern English and Czech indicates that translators of the Hebrew encountered few difficulties in understanding the metaphor. Even if the text unit is translated linguistically, the metaphor remains and is comprehensible. In the Septuagint, the Hebrew verse Deuteronomy 8:6 corresponds to:

καὶ **φυλάξῃ** τὰς ἐντολὰς κυρίου τοῦ θεοῦ
σου **πορεύεσθαι ἐν ταῖς ὁδοῖς αὐτοῦ** καὶ φοβεῖσθαι αὐτόν

The meaning of the Greek verb πορεύομαι is indicated in standard dictionaries and lexicons as *to go, to proceed, to travel,* etc. The meaning of the Greek verb φυλάσσω is given as *to keep watch; to keep guard; to watch, to guard, to defend; to protect.* Bauer[189] mentions an additional meaning, *to keep (a law),* and demonstrates its use among classical Greek authors such as Sophocles, as well as among the Greek Church Fathers and in the Septuagint. Thus, even in the form it takes in the Septuagint, the verb expression φυλάσσω appears as a lexicalised journey metaphor in the semantic area νόμος,[190] just like the verb root שׁמר in Hebrew. The Septuagint consistently uses νόμος in place of the Hebrew שׁמר, for example throughout Psalm 119, as well as in Leviticus 18:4 and 26:3, Deuteronomy 19:9, Joshua 1:7, Psalm 89:32, and elsewhere.

The Vulgate translates the Greek version of Deuteronomy 8:6 into Latin as:

ut **custodias** mandata Domini Dei tui et **ambules in viis eius** et timeas eum

189   See, for example, Walter Bauer, William F. Arndt, and F. Wilbur Gingrich, *A Greek-English Lexicon of the New Testament and Other Early Christian Literature,* 2nd ed. (Chicago: University of Chicago Press, 1979).

190   Septuagint variant of Hebrew תורה *Torah / Law.*

The meaning of the Latin verb *custodio* is given by standard English dictionaries as *to guard, to protect, to preserve, to watch over, to keep safe, to take a walk, to go on foot, to travel, to march*, and so on.

The Septuagint and Vulgate translators were alike in choosing a linguistic (literal) translation strategy for the Hebrew verse Deuteronomy 8:6. The journey metaphor is preserved in both versions, and understanding it in Greek and Latin is not problematic.

Thirteen of the twenty-one modern English versions translated the Hebrew verb root הלך (*to go, to walk*) in conjunction with the preposition ב and the noun דרך *way, road, journey*, by the English verb *to walk* in combination with *in his ways* (that is, *in the ways of the Lord*).[191] Translators of the *New Jerusalem Bible* chose the verb *to follow*.

Translators of the *Complete Jewish Bible*, the *New English Translation* and the *Good News Bible* interpreted the metaphor in the second half of the verse as follows:

> So obey the *mitzvot* of ADONAI your God, **living as he directs** and fearing him. (CJB)
> So you must keep his commandments, **live according to his standards**, and revere him. (NET)
> So then, do as the Lord has commanded you: **live according to his laws** and obey him. (GNB)

These translators did not replace הלך (in Q *to go, to walk*) with a legal expression, neither did they eliminate the metaphor. Rather, they interpreted and used the conceptual metaphors LIFE IS A JOURNEY and ACTIONS ARE A JOURNEY to build the meaning of the text unit.

In many parts of the Old Testament canon, the Hebrew verb root הלך (in Q *to go, to walk*) is involved in conceptualisation through the metaphors LIFE IS A JOURNEY (or MORAL LIFE IS A JOURNEY: as in Ps 91:11; 101:2; Prov 5:21 and elsewhere) or ACTIONS ARE A JOURNEY (as in Ps 77:14; 103:7; 145:17 and elsewhere).[192] The use of these metaphors in translation is therefore not only possible but appropriate as it takes into account the intertextuality and meaning of the entire passage of which the verse Deuteronomy 8:6 is a part.

The translators of the *New English Bible* and the *Revised English Bible* virtually eliminated the metaphor and used verbs from the semantic area *Law*: הלך (in Q *to go, to walk*) was translated as *to conform*, and שמר (in Q *to keep, to watch over, to take care of, to preserve, to protect*) as *to keep*.

> Keep the commandments of the LORD your God, **conforming to his ways** and fearing him.

In the interpretation of the metaphor THE TORAH / LAW IS A JOURNEY, the translators of the *Contemporary English Version* went furthest, narrowing the meaning of the verse considerably to "worship":

---

191   ERV, ASV, NAS, NAU, TNK, BBE, RSV, NRS, ESV, NAB, NLT, NIV and NJK.
192   Bancila, *Journey Metaphor*, 370.

Obey the commands the LORD your God has given you
and **worship him** with fear and trembling.

Sixteen of the twenty-one English translations of the Hebrew verb root שׁמר *to keep, to watch over, to take care of, to preserve, to protect* use the English verb *to keep*,[193] and three *to obey*.[194] The translators therefore either perceive the journey metaphor as a lexicalised metaphor or do not understand the expression as metaphorical at all.

The translators of the *New International Version* (1984) evidently sought the most literal translation: the Hebrew verb root שׁמר is translated as *to observe*, הלך in conjunction with the preposition ב as *to walk*, and the noun דרך as *way*. The journey metaphor can clearly be seen in the English version:

Observe the commands of the LORD your God, **walking in his ways** and revering him. (NIV)

Modern Czech translations of Deuteronomy 8:6 vary very little:

Proto budeš **dbát** na přikázání Hospodina, svého Boha,
chodit po jeho cestách a jeho se bát. (ČEP)
Dodržuj přikázání Jahva, svého Boha,
abys **kráčel po jeho cestách** a aby ses ho bál. (JB)
Zachovávej příkazy Hospodina, svého Boha,
abys **chodil po jeho cestách** a bál se ho. (ČSP)

The Hebrew verb root הלך (in Q *to go, to walk*) in conjunction with the preposition ב and the noun דרך (*way, road, journey*) are translated into Czech by expressions which in English correspond to the verbs *to walk, to go*. Only in the older rabbinic Czech translation do Sicher and Hirsch (in a similar way to the *New International Version* and the *Kralice Bible*[195]) translate the Hebrew verb root שׁמר using the Old Czech term *ostříhej* (in Czech also *hlídej, sleduj*, which in English can be translated as *to trail, to keep an eye*):[196]

---

193 YLT, ERV, ASV, NAS, NAU, NEB, REB, TNK, BBE, RSV, NRS, ESV, NET, NJB, NAB and NJK.

194 CJB, NLT and CEV.

195 The Kralice Bible was the first complete translation of the Old Testament and New Testament from the original languages into Czech and was translated and published by theologians and translators of the original Unitas Fratrum. The New Testament was first published in 1564 in Ivančice. The whole Bible was first published in six volumes with rich annotations (1579–1593), and later as a complete volume in 1596. According to tradition, the last revision was in 1613. The Kralice Bible was the Bible of the Czech-speaking Protestants until 1979, when it was replaced by the *Český ekumenický překlad* (Czech ecumenical translation). The Kralice translation of Deut 8:6 is: "A **ostříhej** přikázání Hospodina Boha svého, chodí po cestách jeho, a boje se jeho." (Guard the commandments of the LORD thy God, and walk along his paths, and fear him).

196 Old Czech *střežit* (guard closely), *hlídat* (guard), *opatrovat* (look after), *chránit* (protect), *pozorovat* (observe), *sledovat* (monitor, follow), *číhat na koho* (lie in wait for someone), *zachovávat co* (maintain something), *dbát čeho* (pay attention to something). See Jaromir Bělič, Adolf Kamiš, and Karel Kučera, *Malý staročeský slovník* (Prague: SPN, 1978).

Tak **ostříhej** příkazů Hospodina, Boha svého,
kráčeje po cestách jeho a maje ho ve zbožné úctě. (Sicher)

The metaphor was completely eliminated in *Slovo na cestu* (Word on the way),
where translators used only legal terminology:

Proto **respektujte** Boha a jeho nařízení a **jednejte v souladu** s jeho vůlí.[197]

The journey metaphor is used quite commonly in modern Czech and is by no
means attached only to the socio-cultural, religious and geographical context in which
the metaphorical expression originated. We suggest that there is therefore no need to
eliminate the metaphor here. Even the *New Living Translation*, which was the inspiration for *Slovo na cestu*, keeps it:[198]

So obey the commands of the LORD your God by **walking** in his **ways** and fearing him. (NLT)

The question arises as to whether for some reason the translators of *Slovo na cestu*
understood the metaphor as an archaic linguistic device or unnecessarily underesti-
mated their readers and assumed that keeping the metaphor would make the verse
more difficult to understand.

As we have said, the translation of Deuteronomy 8:6 into Greek (Septuagint) and
Latin (Vulgate) and into modern English and Czech indicates that translators of the
Hebrew encountered few difficulties in understanding the metaphor. Even if the verse
is translated linguistically, the metaphor remains intact and is comprehensible. This
is largely because the journey metaphor is anchored in the basic and universal human
experience of orientation and movement within a space and is therefore comprehensible across many languages and cultures and in many historical, linguistic and cultural
contexts. Another reason is the conventional use of metaphors in the lexicalisation of
verbal expressions. The attempt by some translators to interpret the journey metaphor
by involving the conceptual metaphors LIFE IS A JOURNEY (or MORAL LIFE IS A JOUR-
NEY) or ACTIONS ARE A JOURNEY is also a point of interest.

3.2.3 ANALYSIS, INTERPRETATION AND TRANSLATION
OF THE METAPHORICAL EXPRESSION IN PROVERBS 29:18

In contrast to Deuteronomy 8:6, the metaphorical expression in Proverbs 29:18 has
presented translators with problems of both translation and interpretation:

---

197 Therefore, respect God and His ordinances and act in accordance with His will.
198 At the same time, translators of *Slovo na cestu* (Word on the way) interpret God's commandments (Torah) as *His
(God's) will*, which is not entirely wrong, but such a translation loosens (perhaps even casts doubt upon) the close
connection between God's commandments (in the Torah) and God's will (the commandments of the Torah as
a revelation of God's will). This may, however, be the translator's intention.

באין חזון יפרע עם ושמר תורה אשרהו: Prov 29:18

For lack of vision a people [יפרע—**is let go**[199]], but happy is he who heeds the Torah.

Proverbs 29:18 is an example of antithetic parallelism. The problem is presented by the Hebrew verb יפרע (the verb root פרע in imperfect of Niphal stem). This is the only occurrence of this verb root in the Niphal in the whole corpus of the Hebrew Old Testament. Standard Hebrew dictionaries and lexicons disagree on both the etymology and the basic meaning of the Qal verb root. The meanings given in English are most often: in Qal *to let go, to let loose, to let alone*; in HI *to cause to refrain, to show a lack of restraint*,[200] I. *to surpass, to lead*, II. *to sprout*, III. *to let go, to loosen*,[201] *to let free, to let hair on the head hang unattended*,[202] Q *to loosen, to open, to let hair hang loose, to be hung loose, to let something go free, to deliver, to release, to go out of control, to allow to run wild, to be undisciplined, to let oneself go, to run wild, to ignore, to spurn* etc., NI *to let oneself go, to cast off restraint, to run wild, to rebel*, HI *to let lawlessness develop, to cause to go out of control, to cause to refrain (from doing)*, etc.[203]

In the Qal, this verb root refers in five text units to the styling, cutting or shaving of hair on the head (Lev 10:6; 13:45; 21:10; Num 5:18; Judges 5:2). In HI, the verb root פרע occurs twice in the context of violation of the law (Ex 5:4 and 2 Chron 28:19). In Proverbs, the verb root פרע in Q occurs five times (Prov 1:25; 4:15; 8:33; 13:18; 15:32), always in relation to avoiding discipline, a reprimand, or punishment.

Cognitive-linguistic analysis can offer us a key to understanding and interpreting Proverbs 29:18. In the spirit of this analysis, we assume that some of the meanings of the verb root פרע which are given in standard Hebrew dictionaries and lexicons may also include meanings derived from the use of that verb root in the metaphorical expression. Some of those meanings may be metaphorical, or they may be a lexicalised metaphor.[204] In English, these may be particularly the meanings *to run wild, to let hair hang loose, to rebel, to let lawlessness develop*,[205] *to show a lack of restraint*,[206] and others.

Analysis of the passages in which the verb root פרע occurs in the Hebrew Old Testament leads us to believe that the basic meaning of the verb root פרע in Q is *to let go, to loosen, to let loose*. Many of the other meanings mentioned above may be based on the use of this verb root within metaphorical passages of text, or derived from the basic meaning by other mechanisms.

---

199   Author's translation.
200   VanGemeren, *Dictionary of Old Testament Theology*.
201   Botterweck, Fabry, and Ringgren, *Theological Dictionary of the Old Testament*.
202   Gesenius 2013. In German: in Q *frei lassen, das Haar frei wachsen und herabhängen lassen, etwas ungeachtet lassen, vernachlässigen, nicht tun, sich entziehen*; NI *zuchtlos werden, verwilden*; HI *jemanden abhalten, Zügellosigkeit freien Lauf lassen, fliehen lassen*.
203   Clines, *Dictionary of Classical Hebrew*.
204   Repeated metaphorical use can lead to the lexicalisation of metaphors; dictionaries do not always distinguish between basic and metaphorical meanings. Cognitive-linguistic methods help to clarify the semantic development of phrases in many languages. This issue, and the role of metaphors, is studied within *historical cognitive linguistics* or *cognitive diachronic semantics*. For more on this, see Margaret Winters, Heli Tissari, and Kathryn Allan, eds., *Historical Cognitive Linguistics*, Cognitive Linguistics Research, 47 (Berlin: De Gruyter Mouton, 2010).
205   Clines, *Dictionary of Classical Hebrew*.
206   VanGemeren, *Dictionary of Old Testament Theology*.

Proverbs 29:18 can be seen as an innovative application of the semantic metaphor
THE TORAH / LAW IS A JOURNEY and the generic narrative structure TO TURN FROM
THE PATH. The following Hebrew expressions in particular are involved in the journey metaphor: the imperfect NI of the verb root פרע meaning *to let go, to be loosened, to
let loose*, and the participle of the verb root שמר in Q *to watch over* (primarily with the
eyes).[207] In the background of the metaphorical expression in Proverbs 29:18 we can
identify the mental image of going astray. Within this image, the Torah is the way that
the people of God are to follow, and the visions of the prophets have the power to keep
the people on this way. On the one hand, we see here the mental image of walking
along a path being likened to a life lived in obedience to the Torah, to receiving God's
discipline through the visions of the prophets; a journey on which the person knows
where they have come from and where they are going, and keeps an eye on both the
direction and the manner of walking—obeying the commandments of the Torah. On
the other hand, there is also life lived in disobedience of the Torah, rejecting God's
discipline as it is communicated through the visions of the prophets, and this leads to
going astray, losing one's way, going in the wrong direction, and losing the ultimate
destination. The previous verse (Prov 29:17) offers a similar image.

It is also possible to consider whether the verb expression פרע in NI also refers
to texts in which the gentile nations surrounding Israel—nations and their warriors that do not obey the commands of the Torah—are characterised as *people with
free-flowing hair* (see Ex 32:25; Deut 32:42; Judges 5:2). In that case, in the background
of Proverbs 29:18, we might also detect the idea of uncut or uncombed curly hair being reminiscent of wandering, of the uneven life paths of those who do not follow
the straight and upright ways—the ways of the Torah. The use of the verb root פרע in
Q as a lexicalised metaphor in Proverbs 1:25, 4:15 and 8:33 may also be explained in
this sense of *avoiding* the commandments of the Torah, avoiding reprimand, avoiding
punishment.

The text of Proverbs 29:18 in the Septuagint represents an interpretation of the
Hebrew text:

οὐ μὴ ὑπάρξῃ ἐξηγητὴς ἔθνει παρανόμῳ, ὁ δὲ φυλάσσων τὸν νόμον μακαριστός

The Hebrew verb root פרע in NI has no correspondence with any term in the Greek
text; the Greek wording is an interpretation of the Hebrew. Where the Hebrew has
a verb, the Septuagint has a noun and an adjective: παράνομος, ἔθνος. The English
meaning of the Greek adjective παράνομος, which characterises people (Greek ἔθνος)
as *lawless, acting contrary to law*,[208] is given as *acting contrary to the law, acting lawlessly*.
The same meaning can be found in the Greek of the Church Fathers.[209] The Hebrew

207 Although we stated in chapter two that the Hebrew text is probably already a lexicalised metaphor with the
meaning *to respect, to obey*, nonetheless in this case the original meaning of the verb root שמר (in Q *to watch over*)
could contribute to the meaning of the entire text unit.
208 Hebrew עם *people, nation*, etc.
209 Bauer, Arndt, and Gingrich, *Greek-English Lexicon*.

noun חזון *vision (of prophets)* is translated in the Septuagint as ἐξηγητής *expounder, interpreter*. The Hebrew verb שמר (in Q *to keep, to watch over*) is translated by the Greek verb φυλάσσω (*to keep watch, to guard*).[210] The Septuagint text is therefore a non-metaphorical interpretation of the Hebrew text.

The Vulgate translates Proverbs 29:18 as:

cum prophetia defecerit dissipabitur populus qui custodit legem beatus est

In contrast to the Greek, in the Latin text of the Vulgate, the Hebrew verb root פרע in NI corresponds to the verb *dissipabitur*.[211] The basic English meaning of the Latin verb *dissipo* is *to scatter, to disperse, to dissipate, to squander*.[212] The Greek verb φυλάσσω (*to keep watch, to guard*) is translated into Latin as *custodio* (I. *to guard, to protect, to watch over, to keep safe*, II. *to take heed or to care, to observe*, III. *to restrain*).

The Vulgate uses a shepherd metaphor (GOD IS A SHEPHERD), offering the reader a "prophetic vision" (the preaching of the prophets), with the Torah being set against the background of the shepherd's staff: the flock (Israel) guided by God. Those not "guided" by the vision of the prophets are not "guided" by the Torah but "dispersed" like a flock without the shepherd's guidance. Who it was that "dispersed the herd" is not made explicit. A reader could perceive "dispersion" as God's punishment for disobedience, but the text itself does not impose this idea. This appears to be a highly successful translation strategy and is fully in keeping with the hypothesis we outlined regarding the use of the semantic metaphor THE TORAH / LAW IS A JOURNEY in the Hebrew version of Proverbs 29:18 and the basic meaning of the verb root פרע.

The vast majority of modern English translations translate the text passage non-metaphorically. They interpret it, and in the second half of the verse use legal terminology. The Hebrew verb root שמר (in Q *to watch over, to respect, to obey*) is most often translated into English as *to keep the law*,[213] *to keep the Torah* (CJB), *to keep God's law* (GNB), or *to obey the law* (NLT, CEV). Only the rabbinic translation (TNK) keeps the original meaning: *to heed instructions*.

In two translations (*New English Bible* and *Revised English Bible*) we can observe the semanticisation of תורה *the Torah / Law* through the journey metaphor:

Where there is no authority, the people break loose,
but **the guardian of the law keeps them on the straight path**. (NEB)

With no one authority, the people throw off all restraint,
but **he who keeps God's law leads them on a straight path**. (REB)[214]

---

210   This is how the Septuagint usually (but not always) translates this Hebrew verb root.
211   Indicative future passive 3rd person singular.
212   I. *to scatter, to disperse, to dissipate, to squander*, II. *to destroy completely*, III. *to circulate*.
213   YLT, ERV, ASV, NAS, NAU, BBE, RSV, NRS, ESV, NET, NJB, NAB, NIV and NJK.
214   The Hebrew noun חזון *vision* is also interpreted as *authority*.

The Hebrew noun חזון *vision* appears in most translations as *vision*[215] (or with qualifications such as *prophetic vision*,[216] or simply *prophecy*,[217] or the more general *revelation*[218]).

Three modern English translations of the Bible which state their intention as carrying out a functionally equivalent translation (*Holy Bible: New Living Translation, Good News Bible* and *Contemporary English Version*) do not eliminate the journey metaphor but adapt the Hebrew metaphorical expression in modern English in a similar way to the Vulgate. The Hebrew noun חזון *vision* is translated as: *God's guidance* (GNB), *guidance from God's law* (CEV), and *do not accept divine guidance* (NLT). They attain the same mental image as translators into Latin, but by different linguistic means.

In general, however, English translations tend to be semanticised through the metaphor THE LAW IS A LIMITATION or THE LAW IS A SHACKLE, using the terms *to cast off restraint*[219] (or *to be unrestrained*,[220] *to lose restaint*,[221] *to throw off all restraint*)[222] or *to break loose*.[223]

> For lack of vision a **people lose restraint**, but happy is he who heeds instruction.

The *Bible in Basic English* and *New Jerusalem Bible* offer metaphorical semanticisation of תורה *the Torah / Law* through the semantic metaphor THE LAW IS A SUPERVISOR. The verb root פרע in NI is translated as *to get out of hand* (NJB) and *to be uncontrolled* (BBE):

> Where there is no vision the **people get out of hand**. (NJB)
> Where there is no vision, the **people are uncontrolled**. (BBE)

Other English translations offer the concept of the Torah as a tool for maintaining (or building) social order (GNB),[224] as a guarantee of the very existence of society (CEV),[225] or as an instrument for the moral and cultural cultivation of society (YLT, NAB, NLT).[226]

With translations into modern Czech, the Hebrew verb root שמר is usually translated using verb expressions from the semantic area *Law*, most often *zachovávat* (to keep), or *plnit* (to fulfil):

---

215 YLT, ERV, ASV, NAS, NAU, TNK, BBE and NJB.
216 CJB, NET and ESV.
217 RSV and NRS.
218 NIV and NKJ.
219 ERV, ASV, RSV, NRS, ESV, NET, NIV and NJK.
220 NAS and NAU.
221 TNK.
222 REB and CJB.
223 NEB.
224 A nation without God's guidance is a nation without order (GNB).
225 Without guidance from God, law and order disappear (CEV).
226 Without prophecy the people become demoralized (NAB); When people do not accept divine guidance (NLT); Without a Vision [sic] a people is made naked (YLT).

Chybějí-li vidění, žije lid bezuzdně; šťastný, kdo **zachovává** zákon. (JB)[227]
Kde chybí zjevení, lid ztrácí zábrany, kdo ale **plní** Zákon, ten je blažený. (B21)[228]

Only Šrámek uses *dbát* (to heed, to take heed of, to pay heed to):

Není-li zjevení, pustne i lid; kdo na zákon **dbá**, je šťasten. (Šrámek)[229]

Translations of the verb root פרע in NI vary widely. Throughout the book of Proverbs, the *Czech Ecumenical Translation* translates the verb expression פרע in Q as *vyhýbat se* (to avoid). Here in verse 18, however, the translators decided to interpret it:

Není-li žádného vidění, lid **pustne**, ale blaze tomu, kdo **zachovává** Zákon. (ČEP)[230]

Šrámek also uses *pustne* (becomes desolate), while Bogner and JB use *lid žije bezuzdně* (people live unbridled).[231] The Czech word *pustne* (becomes desolate) presents the reader with the idea of decline, of the disintegration of society, which brings with it disobedience and avoidance of the commandments of the Torah.[232] All this is probably against the background of the idea of a desolate, overgrown or arid landscape, an uncultivated field, or a shabbily presented (unwashed, ungroomed) person. Both mental images can be the basis for metaphorical semanticisation. The Catholic translations of Heger and Bogner appear to mean primarily the moral decline of society, and also perhaps the decline of the culture and the economy. A similar translation strategy was chosen by Heger and the translators of *Slovo na cestu* (Word on the way):

Není-li zjevení, **pokazí** se lid! Zdar tomu, kdo zákon zachovává![233] (Heger)
Nenaslouchá-li národ Božímu slovu, národ **upadá**![234]
Dobře se daří tam, kde zachovávají Hospodinův zákon.[235] (SC)

In terms of the journey metaphor, these translations develop the element of the *destination*. Within the JOURNEY schema, they shift the emphasis from *leave / go off the path* to *destination*, emphasising the destination people abandon by leaving the way of the Torah. In Czech translations, the goal is economic, agricultural, cultural or moral development. This translation strategy is undoubtedly closer to the Hebrew original than a purely literal translation such as in *Český studijní překlad* (Czech study Bible) or *Bible 21. století* (21st century Bible):

---

227   If vision is absent, the people live unbridled; happy is the one who keeps the law.
228   Where revelation is lacking, people lose their inhibitions, but the one who fulfils the Law is blissful.
229   If there is no revelation, the people will be desolate; the one who heeds the law is happy.
230   If there is no vision, the people will be desolate, but blissful is the one who keeps the Law.
231   "Bez zjevení se lid stává **bezuzdným**, šťastný však ten, kdo zachovává zákon." In the notes: "Bez zjevení"—bez zjeveného pravého náboženství lid propadá mravní zkáze.
232   Likewise, in Šrámek: "Není-li zjevení, **pustne** i lid; kdo na zákon **dbá**, je šťasten"
233   If there is no revelation, the people will go bad! Good luck to those who keep the law!
234   If the nation does not listen to God's Word, the nation falls!
235   They do well where they keep the law of the Lord.

Když není vidění, lid je **bez zábran**, ale šťastný je ten, kdo zachovává zákon. (ČSP)[236]
... lid **ztrácí zábrany** ... (B21)[237]

As we have seen, the semantic metaphor THE TORAH / LAW IS A JOURNEY and the generic narrative structure TO LEAVE THE PATH helped us to establish a hypothesis about the basic meaning of the verb root פרע in NI. The cognitive-semantic analysis also helped us to identify Proverbs 29:18 as a metaphorical expression, and thus to identify the semantic metaphor and generic narrative structure which stand behind it.

We can safely say that the journey metaphor has become a useful tool for evaluating the strategies chosen by translators of the Bible into modern Czech and English.

3.2.4 ANALYSIS, INTERPRETATION AND TRANSLATION OF THE METAPHORICAL EXPRESSION IN ZEPHANIAH 3:4

Here we will again analyse the semantic metaphors used in the original Hebrew text and note the strategies chosen by translators into English and Czech.

Zephaniah 3:4 is a reproach to the temple priests and prophets of Jerusalem.

Zeph 3:4 נביאיה פחזים אנשי בגדות כהניה חללו־קדש חמסו תורה:

A literal translation of the text would be:

Her[238] shameless prophets, treacherous husbands, her priests pierced[239] what was holy, they treated the Torah violently.[240]
Proroci její nestoudníci, manželé zrádní, její kněží prokláli, co je svaté, na Tóře se dopustili násilí.

We can also assume the use of synthetic *parallelismus membrorum* between the final two statements: כהניה חללו־קדש *her priests pierced what was holy* and חמסו תורה *they treated the Torah violently.*

The great diversity of modern translations into English and Czech, especially regarding the terms which describe the behaviour of the priests and prophets, bears testimony to the difficulties in understanding and translating this metaphorical expression.

Standard dictionaries and lexicons indicate the English meaning of the verb root פחז in Q (or direct participles in Q) as: *to be wanton, to be reckless,*[241] *to be insolent, to be*

---

236 When there is no vision, the people are uninhibited, but the one who keeps the law is happy.
237 The people lose their inhibitions.
238 The suffix נביאיה, **her** prophets, may refer to the *city* (Jerusalem) (see Zeph 3:1); עיר *city* is a feminine noun in Hebrew. It could also refer to the *Torah* (at the end of verse 4) as תורה is also feminine. I prefer the second option.
239 In the Hebrew text, a single verb expression חלל in PI.
240 My own working translation.
241 Gesenius 2013.

undisciplined,[242] to be reckless, to be arrogant,[243] and otherwise. German dictionaries and lexicons are similar.[244] Scholars usually assume that the basic meaning concerns amoral or immoral behaviour. Any behaviour contrary to religious regulations is denoted figuratively through the verb פחז and its derivatives. Indecent behaviour may or may not relate to the field of sexuality, but it is the primary connotation in many cultures with roots in Judaism and Christianity. In addition, however, in the Old Testament, worship directed towards a God other than the Lord, the God of Israel, is commonly described with expressions reserved for marital infidelity, adultery or sexual abandon. Likewise, in the New Testament, heresies and heretical doctrines (see 1 Cor 6; Rev 21:8 and elsewhere) are commonly described in this manner.

In Zephaniah, the main prophetic criticism with regard to Judaic religious practice and the practice of the Jerusalem temple and its priests is directed against the cult of Baal and Milcom, as here in Zephaniah 1:4–6:

> I will stretch out my hand against Judah, and against all the inhabitants of Jerusalem;
> and I will cut off from this place every remnant of Baal and the name of the idolatrous priests;
> those who bow down on the roofs to the host of the heavens;
> those who bow down and swear to the LORD, but also swear by Milcom;
> those who have turned back from following the LORD,
> who have not sought the LORD or inquired of Him.

In Zephaniah 3:4, the participle of the verb root פחז in Q will be understood in this way.

Zephaniah 3:4 is the only place the noun בגדות (in the phrase אנשי בגדות) occurs in the whole Old Testament canon. Its meaning cannot therefore be verified or backed up by other biblical texts. Standard dictionaries and lexicons indicate the English meaning as: men of treachery (in Q to act or to deal treacherously),[245] unfaithful, pernicious, disloyal, treacherous, traitorous (in Q to act faithlessly, treacherously, perfidiously).[246] Scholars agree that the basic meaning relates to a breach of contract, primarily a marriage contract. It is also possible to consider an allusion to the people in Zephaniah 1:8 who are wearing a foreign garment (Hebrew מלבוש נכרי) as בגדות and בגד (garment) derive from the same verb:

> And on the day of the LORD's sacrifice I will punish the officials and the king's sons
> and all who dress themselves in foreign attire. (Zeph 1:8)

---

242 Koehler, Baumgartner, and Richardson, Hebrew and Aramaic Lexicon.
243 VanGemeren, Dictionary of Old Testament Theology.
244 Leichtfertig, unzuverlässig sein (Gesenius 2013), I. leichtfertig, unzuverlässig, II. überschäumen (Gesenius 2013), and auftrumpfen, frech, zuchtlos sein, überwallen (Koehler, Baumgartner, and Richardson, Hebrew and Aramaic Lexicon). Pipal presents the Czech meanings: chvástat se, být neukázněný (English: to boast, to be undisciplined), participle chvastoun (English: boaster).
245 Gesenius 2013; Koehler, Baumgartner, and Richardson, Hebrew and Aramaic Lexicon.
246 VanGemeren, Dictionary of Old Testament Theology; Botterweck, Fabry, and Ringgren, Theological Dictionary of the Old Testament. German: Versteckheit, Treulosigkeit (Gesenius 2013); I. treulos, abtrünnig handeln, II. tückisch handeln, rauben, III. participle treulos, abtrünnig, betrügerisch (Gesenius 2013); Treulosigkeit, treulose [Frauen] (Koehler, Baumgartner, and Richardson, Hebrew and Aramaic Lexicon).

The meaning of the Hebrew verb חלל in PI is given in English as: *to bore, to pierce, to wound fatally*,[247] *I. to profane, II. to put into use*,[248] *to profane, to defile, to pollute, to make invalid.*[249] Domershausen[250] presents the original meaning of the Semitic verb root as *to hollow out, to pierce, to wound*; it is primarily about *killing, piercing* (with a sword, knife, or other sharp object). According to Domershausen, in the non-religious sense, the lexical root חלל in PI belongs to the semantic area *War* (see 1 Kings 11:15; 1 Sam 17:52; Lam 4:9 and elsewhere), but in Old Testament texts it also occurs in the sense of *committing a crime, murder* (such as in Deut 21:1–3).

In texts containing an element of myth, the verb חלל in PI has the meaning *to knock down* (a dragon, a monster; see Ps 89:11), or also *to kill*, where killing is understood as God's punishment (see Isa 53:5; Jer 51:52). In some Old Testament Hebrew texts, the verb חלל in PI is used in the sense of *to defile, to degrade* as in *to defile by non-legitimate sexual intercourse*, or *to defile by harlotry* (Lev 19:29; Deut 28:30; 1 Chron 5:1, and elsewhere). Modern standard dictionaries and lexicons give the metaphorical meaning *to profane, to defile* in relation to, for example, the temple, the altar, God's name.

In Zephaniah 3:4, the verb חלל in PI refers to how priests and prophets treat something that, or someone who, is "holy" (Hebrew noun קדש *what is holy, the holy*). There is no explicit mention of what or who is defiled or profaned, whether the temple itself, or objects that adorn the temple, or items used by the priests in the temple sacrifice. The noun קדש (*what is holy, the holy*) could refer to anyone or anything consecrated to the Lord, such as Jerusalem (explicitly mentioned in verse 1), or the Torah; the people of Jerusalem could also be in view.[251] In any case, it is clear that the actions of the priests are in direct contradiction to their "job description." Given that within Zephaniah 3:4 we anticipate the use of synthetic parallelism between the final two statements (כהניה חללו־קדש *her priests pierced what was holy* and תורה חמסו *they treated the Torah violently*), we understand the noun קדש *holiness* to be parallel to the concept תורה *the Torah / Law*.

The meaning of the verb root חמס in Q is given in English as *to treat violently* (bad behaviour—physical, ethical, or both),[252] *I. to treat violently, II. to devise*,[253] *to commit violence, treat violently, harm, oppress*,[254] *to commit violence* with an emphasis on physical violence and brutality.[255]

---

247 Gesenius 2013.
248 Koehler, Baumgartner, and Richardson, *Hebrew and Aramaic Lexicon*.
249 VanGemeren, *Dictionary of Old Testament Theology*. German: *I. entweihen, profanieren, II. durchbohren, verwunden, Flöte blasen Treulosigkeit* (Gesenius 2013); *I. entweihen, profanieren, II. in (profanen) Gebrauch nehmen* (Gesenius 2013); *entweihen, verstossen, in (profanen) Gebrauch nehmen* (Koehler, Baumgartner, and Richardson, *Hebrew and Aramaic Lexicon*).
250 See Botterweck, Fabry, and Ringgren, *Theological Dictionary of the Old Testament*.
251 The adjective קדוש often refers to the *Holy One—the God of Israel*, but the meaning of the nominal expression קדש is not clear here. The ambiguity may be intentional. Gesenius 2013.
252 Gesenius 2013.
253 Koehler, Baumgartner, and Richardson, *Hebrew and Aramaic Lexicon*.
254 VanGemeren, *Dictionary of Old Testament Theology*.
255 Koehler, Baumgartner, and Richardson, *Hebrew and Aramaic Lexicon*. In German: *gewalttätig behandeln, bedrücken* (Gesenius 2013); *I. entweihen, profanieren, II. in (profanen) Gebrauch nehmen* (Gesenius 2013); *entweihen, verstossen, in (profanen) Gebrauch nehmen* (Koehler, Baumgartner, and Richardson, *Hebrew and Aramaic Lexicon*).

We evaluated the verse Zephaniah 3:4 as a metaphorical expression based on the use of terms from multiple semantic areas: *Torah / Law*; *Contractual Obligation* (primarily marital); *Temple Worship*; *Violence* (general violence, but it could also be sexual violence or the violence of war). The key expressions of the target conceptual domain are clearly the Hebrew terms תורה *the Torah / Law*, נביא *prophet*, and כהן *priest*.

Intertextuality, connotations from a wide range of religious traditions within Judaism, especially concerning the Torah, also features in the construction of the metaphorical meaning of Zephaniah 3:4. These connotations could include the fact that biblical texts and later rabbinic texts created an image of the Torah as a bride, girl or woman loved by Israel (or by the Lord). This tradition is later anchored in the feasts of *Simchat Torah* (Rejoicing in the Torah) and *Shavuot* (Feast of Weeks).[256]

The verb expressions in Zephaniah 3:4 activate conceptual metaphors and build structural correlations between the target domain entities regarding the actions of the priests and prophets, especially their treatment of the Torah.

In Zephaniah, worship of the "foreign" deities Baal and Milcom is understood and presented against a background of marital infidelity through the conceptual metaphors used in Zephaniah 3:4. The *husband* (the prophets and priests in Jerusalem) is unfaithful to his *wife* (the Torah) with *a foreign woman* (Baal and Milcom). Correspondence need not, however, be reduced only to *a foreign woman*. In any case, the correspondence here between *the wife* and *the Torah* is an innovation. Traditionally, almost stereotypically, Old Testament texts present a correspondence between *the husband / the Lord* and *the wife (bride) / Israel (Jerusalem)*. In this respect, the metaphor in Zephaniah 3:4 is unique in the Hebrew Old Testament canon.

We see the following conceptual metaphors enter into the process of blending in Zephaniah 3:4: THE PRIEST IS A HUSBAND BREACHING THE MARRIAGE CONTRACT; THE PROPHET IS A HUSBAND BREACHING THE MARRIAGE CONTRACT; THE TORAH / LAW IS A WIFE; THE TORAH / LAW IS A MURDER VICTIM; THE TORAH / LAW IS A VICTIM OF VIOLENCE; THE PROPHET IS AN AGGRESSOR; THE PRIEST IS AN AGGRESSOR, and others.

Even in the previous verse (Zeph 3:3), the source area of the conceptual metaphors used is violence; the conceptual metaphors are THE OFFICIALS ARE BEASTS OF PREY and JUDGES ARE BEASTS OF PREY. Those who were entrusted with observance of the law and justice in society in fact violate justice and the law; those who were supposed to make sure that society did not resemble a jungle are themselves like jungle predators.

Likewise, in Zephaniah 3:4, the people for whom the Torah was to be a beloved life partner, a woman they esteemed and respected, in fact shamed, abandoned, and repudiated her; they betrayed the Torah with another woman and so deprived it of its position and thus of its power to be a source of law and justice. The priests and prophets, entrusted with what is holy (especially the Torah), the source of law and justice in the kingdom of Judah, are like an army bringing destruction and the devastation of all

---

256 See, for example, Marc Stern, *Svátky v životě Židů. Vzpomínání, slavení, vyprávění*, trans. A. Smutná (Prague: Vyšehrad, 2002), 117–118, 121–124. The person charged with reading the final verses of the Torah (Deut 33:37–34:12) during the Feast of Weeks is even called the Torah's *chatan* (groom).

political, religious and other guarantees. The keepers of the Torah / Law plunder and murder like criminals or a hostile army.

The most important structural correlations and correspondences established by the conceptual metaphors used in the Zephaniah 3:4 are shown in the table:

Table 3.7

	source domain I. **Marriage**	source domain II. **Violence**	target domain
structural correlation	adultery	to spear, to pierce to commit violence	treatment of that which is holy, treatment of the Torah (or worship of Baal and Milcom, or other)
correspondence	man —husband	assailant (even murderer)	priest prophet
	woman —wife	victim of violence	that which is holy the Torah
	marital infidelity, adultery	violence (even murder)	treatment of that which is holy, treatment of the Torah (or worship of Baal and Milcom, or other)
	another woman, possibly a prostitute	–	e.g. Baal and Milcom, or other
	marriage contract	–	obedience to the Torah

We certainly do not wish to reduce the meaning of the metaphorical expression in Zephaniah 3:4 to the structural correlations and correspondences shown in the table. Its construction is connected with connotations from source domains related to marital life, the relationship between husband and wife, intimacy, mutual devotion and trust, and obligations arising from the marriage contract. The second source domain is *Violence*. The construction of metaphorical meaning therefore entails the authors' and addressees' experience with violence in society, war, politics, and the family, and with sexual violence. As we have already stressed, meaning is also shaped by a wide range of religious traditions within Judaism, especially regarding the Torah. Nonetheless, the correspondences and structural correlations presented in the table define the basic framework within which the metaphorical expression can be interpreted.

The Septuagint interprets rather than translates the metaphor in Zephaniah 3:4

οἱ προφῆται αὐτῆς πνευματοφόροι, ἄνδρες καταφρονηταί οἱ ἱερεῖς αὐτῆς βεβηλοῦσιν τὰ ἅγια καὶ ἀσεβοῦσιν νόμον

We suggested in our analysis of translations of the metaphorical expression in Proverbs 29:18 that interpretation always results in a narrowing of meaning. However, after analysing and interpreting the conceptual metaphors used in the Hebrew text of Zephaniah 3:4, it should be said that the interpretation offered in the Septuagint is entirely in line with the intentions mentioned above.

The Greek term πνευματοφόρος (*he who has the spirit, a bearer of the spirit, spiritual [man]*) belongs to the target domain of the metaphorical expression. In place of the Hebrew participle פחזים *being wanton, being reckless, being insolent, being arrogant* (פחז in Q *to be wanton, to be reckless, to be insolent, to be arrogant*) the Septuagint uses καταφρονητής, in the phrase ἄνδρες καταφρονηταί, which can be translated into English as *despisers* or *scoffers*. This adjective is also used in the Septugint in Habakkuk 1:5 and 2:5 in the sense of *treacherous, arrogant*.

In place of the Hebrew verb expressions in the final parallelism (כהניה חללו־קדש *her priests pierced what was holy* and חמסו תורה *they treated the Torah violently*), the Septuagint has a pair of verbs: βεβηλόω (*to profane, to pollute, to defile*), which has clear connotations of worship, and ἀσεβέω (*to be impious, to act profanely, to commit sacrilege, to sin*). In general, therefore, it can be said that the Septuagint interprets the Hebrew metaphorical expression in Zephaniah 3:4 in a sense that corresponds to the conclusions of the analysis and interpretation we have made. Nonetheless, the metaphor is eliminated and the meaning narrowed and reduced.

The Vulgate translates the Greek version of Zephaniah 3:4 as:

> prophetae eius vesani viri infideles sacerdotes eius
> polluerunt sanctum iniuste egerunt contra legem

The adjective *vesanus* (*angry, violent, impetuous*) comes from the semantic area *Violence* and is probably a translation of the Hebrew participle פחזים (Hebrew verb root פחז in Q). From here, the Vulgate follows the Septuagint and is therefore an interpretation of the Hebrew.

The Greek phrase ἄνδρες καταφρονηταί (*despisers, scoffers*) is translated by the Vulgate as *viri infideles* (*betrayer, or traitor, religious infidel, pagan*) and the final pair of verb expressions from the fields of worship and religious law (purity of worship and obedience to the law) as *poluo* (*to pollute, to soil*) and *ago contra legem* (*to act against the law, to transgress the law*).

Modern translations into English and Czech have a relatively wide range of adjectives relating to the priests and prophets. In English, the most common pair of words is *reckless*[257] and *treacherous*,[258] which translators chose as the literal (linguistic) translation of the Hebrew expressions בגדות and פחזים. Similar translation solutions can be seen with other English adjectives that relate to immorality (not only sexual immorality): *wanton* (RSV), *light* (ERV, ASV), *insolent* (NAB, NKJ), *fickle* (ESV).

---

257 NAS, NAU, NEB, REB, CJB, TNK and NRS.
258 YLT, ERV, ASV, NAS, NAU, CJB, ESV, NAB, GNB, NIV and NJK.

Among Czech translations, the English translation mentioned above is closest to that of the Czech Jehovah's Witnesses: *nestoudní proroci a muži zrady* (insolent prophets and treacherous men).[259] The pair of adjectives *proradní* and *lehcí* (treacherous and light) in the secular and non-confessional translations by Šrámek and Kajdoš from the 1940s and 1950s are similar. No other adjectives in the English or Czech texts other than those mentioned above refer clearly to marital infidelity or the violation of the marriage contract.

Other adjectives for describing the behaviour of the priests and prophets are interpreted by translators of the *Revised Standard Version* and *New Revised Standard Version* using the conceptual metaphors THE PRIEST IS A HUSBAND BREACHING THE MARRIAGE CONTRACT and THE PROPHET IS A HUSBAND BREACHING THE MARRIAGE CONTRACT: *wanton / faithless*,[260] and *reckless / faithless*.[261] Other English connotations bring other variations into the text: *proud / deceitful*,[262] *arrogant / treacherous*,[263] *arrogant liars / seeking their own gain*,[264] *unstable / treachery*,[265] *good-for-nothing / full of deceit*[266] and the Czech *nesmyslní a nespolehliví* (nonsensical and unreliable),[267] *dobrodruzi a lidé prosáklí zradou* (adventurers and perfidious people),[268] *mluvkové a podvodní lidé* (talkers and deceitful people).[269] We can only hazard a guess as to whether the translators were struggling to understand the text passage or trying to interpret the metaphors they saw there.

The *New Jerusalem Bible* offers a highly specific interpretation of Zephaniah 3:4: *braggarts / impostors*. This is similar to the Czech version of the *Jerusalem Bible*: *chvastouni / podvodníci* (boaster, deceitful), and to other Czech translations: *chvastouni / podvodníci* (boaster, deceitful),[270] *namyšlenci a podvodníci* (proud and deceitful),[271] and *vychloubači a muži podvodu* (boasters and deceitful men).[272]

Our analysis of the final two parallel statements (כהניה חללו־קדש *her priests pierced what was holy* and תורה חמסו *they treated the Torah violently*) identified conceptualisation of the key Hebrew term תורה *the Torah / Law* through the conceptual metaphors THE PROPHET IS AN AGGRESSOR, THE PRIEST IS AN AGGRESSOR, THE TORAH / LAW IS A MURDER VICTIM and THE TORAH /LAW IS A VICTIM OF VIOLENCE. It is only Stern in his *Complete Jewish Bible* who does not translate the key phrase תורה *the Torah / Law*. The Rabbinic translation of the *Tanakh* uses the verb expression *ruling*, and two other

---

259 PNS.
260 RSV.
261 NRS.
262 NET.
263 NIV.
264 NLT.
265 YLT.
266 BBE.
267 Hejčl.
268 B21.
269 Bogner.
270 Sicher, ČEP and JB.
271 ČSP.
272 Heger.

versions use *God's instructions*[273] and *God's laws.*[274] Otherwise, most translations use the English word *the law*[275] (or the Law,[276] God's Law,[277] or the law of God[278]). Similarly, Czech translations translate the Hebrew concept of תורה *the Torah / Law* in the standard way, as either Law or law.

The Hebrew expression קדש (*the holy, what is holy*) is translated literally by half of the modern English translations in our study as *the holy,*[279] *what is holy,*[280] and the variation *what is sacred.*[281] In Czech translations, the English *holy / what is holy / what is sacred* corresponds to the Czech *co je svaté*[282] and *svaté věci*[283] (what is holy, holy things). However, nine of the twenty-one English translations[284] interpret (rather than translate) קדש (*the holy, what is holy*) and narrow its meaning to *the sanctuary, the Temple,*[285] *the holy place,*[286] or *the place of worship.*[287] Some Czech translations also interpret קדש as *temple* or *sanctuary.*[288]

All the English translations in our study eliminated the metaphorical semanticisation in the final two parallel statements; the semantic metaphors THE PROPHET IS AN AGGRESSOR, THE PRIEST IS AN AGGRESSOR, THE TORAH / LAW IS A MURDER VICTIM and THE TORAH / LAW IS A VICTIM OF VIOLENCE do not appear in the translations. Rather, the English verb expressions chosen are clearly cultural and legal. In fourteen of the twenty-one translations, the metaphor is interpreted. The Hebrew verb חלל in PI, which in the original text is connected to the semantic metaphor THE TORAH / LAW IS A MURDER VICTIM, is translated by the verb *to profane.*[289] Other translators also choose terminology connected to worship, and use the verb expressions *to defile,*[290] *to pollute,*[291] and *to make unclean.*[292]

Only the translators of the *Contemporary English Version* did not resort to worship terminology. Their use of the pair of verbs *to disgrace / to abuse* allows for the metaphorical semanticisation of the pair of expressions *place of worship / God's Law.* They thus fulfil the principles of formal equivalence, as they state in the introduction to their translation.

---

273 NLT.
274 NET.
275 YLT, ERV, ASV, NAS, NAU, NEB, REB, BBE, RSV, NRS, ESV, NAB, NIV and NJK.
276 NJB.
277 CEV.
278 GNB.
279 CJB.
280 TNK, ESV, NET, NJB and NAB.
281 RSV, NRS and GNB.
282 ČEP.
283 Hejčl, BJ and ČSP.
284 YLT, ERV, ASV, NAS, NAU, NEB, REB, NIV and NJK.
285 NLT.
286 BBE.
287 CEV.
288 B21.
289 ERV, ASV, NAS, NAU, NEB, REB, CJB, TNK, RSV, NRS, ESV, NJB, NAB and NIV.
290 NET, NLT and GNB.
291 YLT and NJK.
292 BBE.

Jerusalem's prophets are proud and not to be trusted.
The priests have **disgraced** the place of worship and **abused** God's Law.

In the Czech versions, a similar strategy was adopted by Catholic translators, who used the verb expressions *poskvrnit* (to defile) (Hejčl) and *zneuctít* (to dishonor) (BJ).

We evaluated the Hebrew verb root חמס in Q (*to commit violence*) as a metaphorical vehicle which by default enables semanticisation of the concept תורה *the Torah / Law* through the semantic metaphor THE TORAH / LAW IS A VICTIM OF VIOLENCE. Sixteen of the tweny-one English translations use a verb that fits into common legal terminology: *to do violence* (and the variants *to be violent, go violently*).[293] Legal terminology is followed in *The New English Translation*, which uses *to break (God's laws)*, and in *The Holy Bible: The New Living Translation*, which uses *to disobey*. Similarly, the English Rabbinic translation of the Tanakh has the following:

Her prophets are reckless, Faithless fellows;
Her priests profane what is holy, They give perverse rulings.

The original Hebrew text is also interpreted—rather than translated—by the translators of the *Good News Bible*:

The prophets are irresponsible and treacherous;
the priests defile what is sacred, and twist the law of God to their own advantage.

And the *Contemporary English Version*:

Jerusalem's prophets are proud and not to be trusted.
The priests have disgraced the place of worship and abused God's Law.

Most translators into modern Czech translate the verb expression חמס in Q (*to commit violence*) as *to rape* (Hejčl, Heger, Bogner, Sramek, ČEP, JB, ČSP, B21, PNS). Here is the *Czech Ecumenical Translation*:

Jeho proroci jsou chvastouni, muži věrolomní;
jeho kněží znesvěcují, co je svaté, **znásilňují** zákon.[294]

Czech translations semanticise the concept of תורה *the Torah / Law* against a background of a mental image similar to the Hebrew original: a background of sexual violence and adultery. In modern Czech, although the verb *rape* can also refer to mere helplessness, vulnerability, lack of liberty, or manipulation, its use allows the Czech reader to semanticise the Torah against a background of the mental image of a raped woman or girl. The non-confessional secular translations—*Písmo* (Scripture) by

---

293 YLT, ERV, ASV, NAS, NAU, NEB, REB, CJB, BBE, RSV, NRS, ESV, NJB, NAB, NIV and NJK.
294 His prophets are boasters, treacherous men. His priests desecrate what is holy, they rape the law.

Šrámek and Kajdoš, and *Překlad nového světa* (New world translation)—used yet another translation strategy which allowed the Czech reader to semanticise *the law* through the metaphor THE TORAH / LAW IS A VIOLATED GIRL / WOMAN:

> Věštci jeho jsou proradní, **lehcí**.
> A kněží—znesvětili **svůj** chrám a **znásilnili svůj** zákon. (Šrámek)[295]
> Jeho proroci byli **nestoudní**, byli muži zrady.
> I jeho kněží znesvěcovali, co bylo svaté; **znásilňovali** zákon. (PNS)[296]

We believe that the practice in most modern Czech translations of adapting the original metaphors by applying the semantic metaphor THE TORAH / LAW IS A VIOLATED GIRL / WOMAN is a highly creative and indeed successful solution to the problem. The basic parameters of and mental image behind the metaphorical semanticisation of the original survive in the translation. In particular, most of the key structural correlations and correspondences between the source domains and the target domain are retained. The phrases "the prophets raped their law" and "the shameless prophets raped the law" and the metaphor THE TORAH / LAW IS A VIOLATED GIRL / WOMAN in fact strengthen the semanticisation. In most modern Czech translations, the source domains of *Marriage* and *Violence* merge into a single source domain: *Sexual Violence*. The adaptations made by these translators are shown in the following (modified) table:

Table 3.8

	source domain I. *Marriage*	source domain II. *Violence*	target domain
structural correlation	adultery	to spear, to pierce	treatment of that which is holy, treatment of the Torah (or worship of Baal and Miclom, or other)
		commit violence	
	to commit sexual violence		
correspondence	man—husband	assailant (even murderer)	priest prophet
	man—sexual assailant		
	woman—wife	victim of violence	that which is holy, the Torah
	marital infidelity, adultery	violence (even murder)	treatment of that which is holy, treatment of the Torah (or worship of Baal and Milcom, or other)
	sexual violence		

---

295 His fortune-tellers are treacherous, light. And the priests—they desecrated their temple and raped their law.
296 His prophets were shameless, they were men of treachery. His priests also desecrated what was holy; they raped the law.

Since the end of the 1980s, a debate has continued between supporters of the theory of equivalence (Koller, Albrecht, etc.) and supporters of functionalist translation strategies (Reiß, Vermeer, Kußmaul, Hönig, Nord, etc.).[297] In the Czech context, Fišer[298] presents an overview of the current academic debate between functionalists and supporters of equivalence (consensus), and offers his own didactic model of creative translation. At the end of the 1970s and the beginning of the 1980s, Vermeer formulated the basis of the "functionalist" Skopos theory, which he and others later refined. By Skopos ("purpose"), Vermeer means the expected (predicted) functions of the target text (the translation), based on which the translator chooses the appropriate translation procedures.[299] The Skopos theory requires the translator to choose strategies that will function according to a precisely specified order with respect to the communicative functions that the translation will perform in the target culture. Skopos also sets clear limits on the translator's creativity. In *Překlad jako kreativní proces* (Translation as a creative process; 2009), Fišer formulates five basic principles of the didactic model of creative translation,[300] of which the first three are particularly relevant to our research into the translation of metaphorical expressions:

- The principle of Skopos, where Skopos is a translation function in the target communicative context which should be precisely formulated in a translation commission (brief).
- The principle of creating a translation that provides a creative solution to a problem.
- The principle of preserving semantic continuity between the original and the translation: continuity of information; the preservation of structured meaning complexes and functional continuity.[301] (Semantic continuity is of course a dynamic category which can be realised to varying degrees, as determined by Skopos, and at different levels of abstraction of the source and target texts.)

We believe that the important bearers of semantic continuity when translating metaphorical expressions is the reconstructed source mental image, with a generic narrative structure at its centre, and the key structural correlations and correspondences established in the original. It is clear from the table above that the phrases *znásilňují zákon* (they rape the law) and *znásilnili svůj zákon* (they raped their law)

297 According to Reiß, Vermeer, Kußmaul, Hönig, Nord, and others, equivalence (consensus) between the original text and the translation should be achieved on all or at least some of the following levels: lexical, textual, functional, pragmatic.
298 Fišer, *Překlad jako kreativní proces.*
299 The Skopos theory also has its share of opponents, whose main criticism is its lack of respect for the original. Critics regard functionalist translations as adaptations rather than translations. Fišer (himself a supporter of functionalist approaches) points out that the requirement of so-called equivalent translation (at any level—lexical, textual, functional or pragmatic) is impossible as the communicative contexts (and functions) of the original and the translation are rarely identical. For more on this debate, see Fišer, *Překlad jako kreativní proces,* 138, 140–147, 173–181.
300 Ibid., 183–185.
301 Ibid., 284–290.

preserved, although partially adapted, the source mental image in the translation of the metaphorical expression in Zephaniah. The adaptation consists mainly in the compression of two source domains into one. We can also say that the translation has changed the roles: the Torah is not the wife against whom the husband (the priests and prophets) commited infidelity with another woman. The basic structure of the meaning complex in the original nonetheless survives the translation so that the metaphorical expression can successfully fulfil its cognitive, religious (spiritual) and aesthetic functions in the modern-day Czech linguistic and cultural context.

3.3 SUMMARY

In the book of Jeremiah, we have seen how the journey metaphor, and within it the spatial image schema, is involved in formulating the central theological testimony of an extensive passage of text. Used in the semantic area *Torah / Law*, the "cardinal" journey metaphor allows an analogy to be made between a person's inner being and their outer actions; an analogy between the devastation of the inner lives of the people of Judah and the legal and moral devastation of the whole society and the destruction of the kingdom. The journey metaphor in Jeremiah also builds an analogy between the return of the exiles to their homeland, the revitalisation of their inner lives, and the restoration of the source of life.

The metaphorical expression in Deuteronomy 8:6 was presented as an example of the conventional use of the journey metaphor in the semantic area תורה *Torah / Law*. A comparison of the strategies used in its translation into modern English and Czech showed that when the metaphor is used conventionally, even linguistic translation allows for an understanding of the target domain against the background of the journey metaphor. We believe that this is because the journey metaphor is anchored in the universal physical human experience of orientation and movement within a space and is therefore comprehensible across historical, linguistic and cultural contexts. In some translations, we noted the involvement of a semantic metaphor not used in the original, namely GOD IS A SHEPHERD. The translators thus managed to incorporate intertextuality and connotations from a wide range of religious traditions within Judaism.

Cognitive-linguistic analysis and interpretation made it possible to identify the semantic metaphors used in the background of the metaphorical expressions of Proverbs 29:18 and Zephaniah 3:4, both of which have presented problems for translators. The semantic metaphor THE TORAH /LAW IS A JOURNEY in Proverbs 29:18 also became an appropriate framework for establishing a hypothesis for the basic meaning of the verb root פרע in NI *to let go, to loosen, to let loose,* and therefore contributed to the interpretation of this exegetically disputable verse. The journey metaphor also made it possible to assess the strategies chosen by some translators of this verse into modern Czech and English.

With Zephaniah 3:4, we noticed how some translators succeeded in conveying the mental image that the metaphor had built in the original language in a completely different historical, cultural and linguistic context. Nonetheless, eliminating the metaphor when translating this verse—and thereby significantly flattening and distorting the meaning—was still the most frequently chosen translation strategy. We believe that one of the important carriers of semantic continuity when translating such a metaphorical expression may be the reconstructed source mental image with a generic narrative structure at the centre, and also preservation of the key structural correlations and correspondences established in the original. As long as the semantic continuity between the original and the translation is preserved in such a way, the translator can adapt the metaphor and still preserve its cognitive function. In most of the modern Czech translations of Zephaniah 3:4, this kind of adaptation of the original semantic metaphors (the metaphors THE TORAH / LAW IS A WIFE, THE TORAH / LAW IS A MURDER VICTIM and THE TORAH / LAW IS A VICTIM OF VIOLENCE) was achieved with some success through the metaphor THE TORAH / LAW IS A VIOLATED GIRL / WOMAN.

CHAPTER 4

CASE STUDY
WHAT METAPHORS SAY
ABOUT HUMAN RIGHTS.
A COGNITIVE-SEMANTIC ANALYSIS
AND INTERPRETATION OF BIBLICAL
METAPHORS IN THE TEACHING
MATERIAL *COMPASS: MANUAL*
FOR HUMAN RIGHTS EDUCATION
WITH YOUNG PEOPLE.

In Paris in December 1948, the UN General Assembly approved the key human rights document the *Universal Declaration of Human Rights*. The rights enshrined in this and succeeding declarations have wide-ranging implications in the spheres of law and politics and in a broad range of discplines from philosophy, theology and history to education and journalism. Our aim here will be to use the methods of cognitive and culturally oriented linguistics to analyse the teaching manual *Compass: Manual for Human Rights Education with Young People*, which was created under the auspices of the Council of Europe as part of its Human Rights Education Youth Programme. We will note the metaphors involved in the conceptualisation of human rights and will consider their origins, inspiration, and the possible consequences of their having been used.

The metaphors and some of the concepts used in the manual bear undeniable signs of having been inspired by biblical texts and Christian teaching. The following analysis will therefore contribute to the debate on the biblical (Jewish and Christian) origins and nature of the whole idea and culture of human rights. Human rights are a subject of much academic debate and often sharp controversy. It is not uncommon for philosophers, theologians and legal theorists to aim to prove or disprove the Christian theological roots of the notion of human rights, but some key documents leave the issue open, and even question whether any kind of philosophical or theological justification of the idea of human rights is possible or even appropriate: the idea that human rights are universal makes it impossible to suggest that their origin can be attributed to any particular culture, philosophy or theology. Some authors even refuse in principle to justify the idea of human rights as by their very nature no such justification is required, like the laws of mechanical physics or in medieval Christian doctrine the so-called truth of faith.

4.1 CONCEPTUAL METAPHORS AND THEIR ROOTS IN BIBLICAL LANGUAGE

The Human Rights Education Youth Programme was launched in 2000 under the auspices of the Directorate for Youth and Sport of the Council of Europe. *Compass* was first published in 2002 and has its own website and tutorial portal.[302] Official translations of the manual into Arabic, German, French, Spanish, Russian, Ukrainian and Bulgarian are also posted on the Council of Europe website. (Other countries have published and printed translations of the manual and created their own websites.) In addition to a comprehensive set of activities and games (with instructions) for young people, the manual contains a wealth of information on the development of the idea of human rights and their protection in law, an overview of institutions, definitions of basic concepts and characteristics, and the whole text (or a summary) of key human rights documents. Some of the most important of these are: *Universal Declaration of Human Rights* (1948), *International Covenant on Civil and Political Rights* (1966),[303] *International Covenant on Economic, Social and Cultural Rights* (1966),[304] *Convention on the Elimination of Racism and Discrimination* (1969), *Convention on the Rights of the Child* (1989), *Convention on the Elimination of All Forms of Discrimination Against Women* (1979),[305] *Convention for the Protection of All Persons from Enforced Disappearance*,[306] *Convention on the Rights of Persons with Disabilities, European Convention on Human Rights*,[307] *European Social Charter*,[308] *Framework Convention for the Protection of National Minorities*,[309] *European Charter for Regional or Minority Languages*,[310] *Convention on Action against Trafficking in Human Beings*, and the 2017 *Council of Europe Charter on Education for Democratic Citizenship and Human Rights Education*.

In *Compass*, metaphorical expressions regarding human rights are found primarily in the prefaces and introductions to chapters one and four.[311] *Human rights* (or *human freedoms*[312]) are conceptualised through metaphors primarily in passages that deal with the purpose of the manual and the origins and meaning of human rights, and these metaphors reveal the kind of picture held by the authors of *Compass* regarding

---

302 Council of Europe, *Compass: Manual for Human Rights Education with Young People*, 2002, https://www.coe.int/en/web/compass/home.

303 The *International Covenant on Civil and Political Rights* is a multilateral treaty adopted by the United Nations General Assembly. Resolution 2200A (XXI) on 16 December 1966 came into effect on 23 March 1976 in accordance with Article 49 of the covenant.

304 The *International Covenant on Economic, Social and Cultural Rights* is a multilateral treaty also adopted by the United Nations General Assembly on 16 December 1966. Resolution 2200A (XXI) came into effect on 3 January 1976.

305 The *Convention on the Elimination of all Forms of Discrimination Against Women* was adopted by the United Nations General Assembly in 1979. It was instituted on 3 September in 1981 and has been ratified by 189 states.

306 The *International Convention for the Protection of All Persons from Enforced Disappearance* was adopted by the United Nations General Assembly on 20 December 2006 and opened for signatures on 6 February 2007. It entered into effect on 23 December 2010.

307 The *Convention on the Rights of Persons with Disabilities* was adopted by the United Nations General Assembly on 13 December 2006 and opened for signatures on 30 March 2007.

308 The *European Social Charter* was opened for signatures on 18 October 1961 and came into effect on 26 February 1965. The Charter was revised in 1996; the revision came into effect in 1999.

309 The *Framework Convention for the Protection of National Minorities* was adopted by the Committee of Ministers of the Council of Europe on 10 November 1994 and came into effect on 1 February 1998.

310 The *European Charter for Regional or Minority Languages* was adopted in 1992 under the auspices of the Council of Europe.

311 The author of the preface to the first edition of *Compass* (2002) was the Secretary General of the Council of Europe, Walter Schwimmer (1999–2004); the author of the second preface from 2012 was Thorbjørn Jagland, Secretary General from 2009 to 2019.

312 The terms *human rights* and *human freedoms* are used synonymously not only in the manual but in most human rights texts. For the sake of simplicity, we will use only the term *human rights*.

such origins and meaning.[313] Most of the conceptual metaphors used in *Compass* can be found elsewhere in journalistic output, political rhetoric and numerous historical, philosophical and theological texts, so our exploration of their origins and the inspiration that lies behind them can make a useful contribution to the discourse on human rights in the broader contemporary historical, social, cultural and political context. The central concepts used in *Compass* to conceptualise the term *human rights* are the conceptual metaphors HUMAN RIGHTS ARE THE LAW and HUMAN RIGHTS ARE A JOURNEY. Like laws and legal regulations, human rights are either **respected** (*to respect, to keep*) or **violated** (*to infringe, to violate*). Individual human rights are understood as *legal regulations*, or *commandments*, like the *commandments of the Torah*. This conceptualisation can be illustrated by the following passage:

> The message goes further in recalling that human rights are more than just inspiration: they are also moral and political **commands** that apply to the relations between states and people, as much as within states and amongst people.[314]

The use of HUMAN RIGHTS ARE A JOURNEY as a key metaphor for the whole manual is demonstrated by its very title:

> Like a COMPASS, this manual indicates different ways and directions in a journey through human rights.[315]

The journey metaphor constitutes a rich network of correspondence throughout the manual: human rights *point the way* (or *are the way*) to *world peace, freedom, equality*. Within the path image schema, the most commonly emphasised component is the *destination of the journey*. Like the source domain entity of *journey*, the *destination of the journey* usually corresponds to values within the idea of human rights that are assumed to be universal: *peace, humanity, human dignity, freedom,*[316] or, as in the following passage, the *culture of human rights*:

> ... there will also be different approaches to human rights education. There may be different views about the best or most appropriate **way to move towards a culture of human rights**, but that is as it should be. Individuals, groups of individuals, communities and cultures have different **starting points** and concerns. A culture of human rights ought to take into account and respect those differences.[317]

---

313 Key human rights documents and legal literature often try to avoid this very general theme of the origins and meaning of the idea of human rights.

314 *Compass*, chapter 1, section "Introducing human rights education," sub-section "Human rights education is a fundamental human right," 3rd paragraph.

315 From the preface to *Compass*.

316 The *United States Declaration of Independence*, one of the key documents regarding the birth of the idea of human rights, also mentions *happiness*.

317 *Compass*, chapter 1, section "Introducing human rights education," sub-section "Towards a culture of human rights," 4th paragraph.

Human rights are of course the core component of the "culture of human rights." The means of reaching the goal (a *culture of human rights*) must be *built* and *defended*. The correspondences *builders of the way—the General Assembly of the United Nations; builders of the way—the United Nations member states; to build the way—Human Rights Education* are established in the following passages:

> In 1994 the General Assembly of the United Nations declared the UN Decade of Human Rights Education (1995–2004) and urged all UN member states to promote "training dissemination and information aimed at the **building** of a universal culture of human rights."[318]
> The Council of Europe Charter on Education for Democratic Citizenship and Human Rights Education (2010) defines human rights education as education, training, awareness raising, information, practices and activities which aim, by equipping learners with knowledge, skills and understanding and developing their attitudes and behaviour, to empower learners to contribute **to the building and defence** of a universal culture of human rights in society, with a view to the promotion and **protection** of human rights and fundamental freedoms.[319]

In addition to the *destination of the journey*, the metaphorical conceptualisation uses the entity *signpost, indicator (on the way)*. In the following passage, the source domain entity the *indicator on the way* corresponds to the entity *conventions on human rights* in the target domain:

> The conventions on human rights . . . **orient us** in times of uncertainty and change.[320]

The metaphor HUMAN RIGHTS EDUCATION IS A JOURNEY is a variant of the conceptual metaphor HUMAN RIGHTS ARE A JOURNEY. Against the background of this conceptual metaphor, the manual is understood as *the beginning of the journey*:

> Compass . . . provides its users with important **starting points** and basic information.[321]

The same conceptual metaphor (HUMAN RIGHTS EDUCATION IS A JOURNEY) can also be identified in the passage below. Here the term *human rights culture* is metaphorically conceptualised by evoking the source domain entity *the journey: the destination of the journey*, specifically *Rome*. "Rome" carries important connotations in constructing the meaning of the metaphorical term. It evokes the idea of a city that has been the destination of Christian pilgrims for many centuries—the religious, political, cultural centre of Christian Europe:

> You can cut all the flowers but you cannot keep spring from coming—Pablo Neruda. "All roads lead to Rome" is a common idiom meaning that there are many ways of getting to your goal. Just

---

318 *Compass*, chapter 1, section "Introducing human rights education," sub-section "Defining human rights education," 1st paragraph.
319 Ibid., 3rd paragraph.
320 *Compass*, Foreword.
321 *Compass*, chapter 4, "Introduction," 4th paragraph.

as all roads lead to Rome, so there are many different ways to delivering human rights education. Thus, human rights education is perhaps best described in terms of what it sets out to achieve: the establishment of a culture where human rights are understood, defended and respected, or to paraphrase the participants of the 2009 Forum on Human Rights Education with Young People, "a culture where human rights are learned, lived and 'acted' for."[322]

In many Old Testament texts, the conceptual metaphors LIFE IS A JOURNEY and MORAL LIFE IS A JOURNEY are blended with the metaphor THE TORAH / LAW IS A JOURNEY.[323] Similarly, in the *Compass* manual, the same metaphor LIFE IS A JOURNEY is blended with the conceptual metaphor HUMAN RIGHTS ARE A JOURNEY. The following passage explicitly states this similarity:

> The People's Movement for Human Rights Learning prefers human rights *learning* to human rights education and places a special focus on **human rights as a way of life**. The emphasis on learning, instead of education, is also meant to draw on the individual process of discovery of human rights and apply them to the person's everyday life.[324]

In the Old and New Testaments, the conceptual metaphor THE TORAH / LAW IS A JOURNEY is the central metaphorical concept used in the conceptualisation of the semantic area *Law*. In chapter two, we stated that some terms from the semantic area *Way*, as lexicalised metaphors, became "domesticed" in the semantic area *Law*. The conceptual metaphor THE TORAH / LAW IS A JOURNEY also foreshadows the evolution of rabbinic Judaism into the concept of the *oral Torah*.[325] Also in chapter two we suggested that the journey metaphor is based on the universal human experience of orientation and movement within a space and is therefore comprehensible across many languages and cultures. Whether translating the Bible into Latin or a modern language, it is therefore possible to translate metaphorical terms connected to the law literally, from both Greek and Hebrew. Under the influence of biblical texts, the conceptual metaphor THE TORAH / LAW IS A JOURNEY played a significant role in the conceptualisation of the semantic area *Law* in modern European languages. The centrality of the journey metaphor in human rights is therefore very likely to have its roots in biblical language.

Compass creatively applies the journey metaphor in the learning activity *Path to Equality-land*, which addresses the issues of gender equality and elimination of discrimination against women. The players' first task is to draw a map of their journey from the "land of the present" to the "land of equality between men and women." They are then given an issue within the field of a particular human right and invited, for example, to think about how a *dark forest* may be used as a metaphor for evil. They should then suggest further correspondence to entities of the source domain: *mountains, riv-*

322 *Compass*, chapter 1, section "Introducing human rights education," sub-section "Towards a culture of human rights," 1st paragraph.
323 Bancila, *Journey Metaphor*, 368–373.
324 *Compass*, chapter 1, section "Introducing human rights education," sub-section "Defining human rights education," 7th paragraph.
325 In the Jewish tradition, this is also known as *halacha* (literally in English *course of action, way, walking*).

ers, forests, moorland, buildings, power cables. It is interesting to note some of the proposed correspondences: *moral strength / swimming across a fast flowing river; humility / helping a distressed animal;* and *temptation / a rosy red apple.* The biblical connotations are very clear. Besides *apple* and *temptation,* they are primarily the concepts of *coming out of the land of slavery into the promised land* and the function of the *law* (*human rights* and *the Ten Commandments*) as *signposts, indicators on the way* (*to the promised land*). These motifs are undoubtedly inspired by the central biblical concept of salvation and redemption. And just as the basic purpose of the Torah is to teach *God's ways* and pass them down from generation to generation, so it is with *human rights.*

Another important conceptual metaphor in *Compass* is HUMAN RIGHTS ARE KNOWLEDGE (KNOWLEDGE, SKILLS, ATTITUDES). Young people should be *taught* to *understand, appreciate, protect* and *respect* human rights. In the preface to the Czech version, published in 2006, Václav Havel[326] even speaks of *Compass* through the metaphor of the "ABC book" (in Czech *slabikář*), one of the first books Czech children use at school:

> And that is why I welcome and support the Council of Europe initiative which stands behind this "ABC book" of human rights, aimed primarily at young people, who unlike previous generations have not experienced what it is like when their human rights are overlooked or questioned.[327]

In the following passage, metaphorical conceptualisation of the term *human rights* takes place through the blending of two concepts in particular: HUMAN RIGHTS ARE KNOWLEDGE, SKILLS AND ATTITUDES;[328] A CULTURE OF HUMAN RIGHTS IS A CREATIVE WORK:

> **Knowing** about human rights is not enough; people must also develop **skills and attitudes** to act together to defend human rights, and they must use their heads, hearts and hands to bring about the personal and social changes necessary for the creation of a global culture of human rights.[329]

4.2 THE QUASI-RELIGION OF HUMAN RIGHTS

The authors of *Compass* have a serious ambition: just as Europe developed the Renaissance and Baroque cultures and the culture of the early Christian Middle Ages, we are

---

326 Václav Havel was president of the Czechoslovak Republic from 1989 to 1992 and president of the Czech Republic from 1993 to 2003. He died in December 2011.

327 "A proto vítám a podporuji iniciativu Rady Evropy, která stojí za tímto **'slabikářem'** lidských práv určeným především mladým lidem, kteří na rozdíl od předcházejících generací nezažili, jaké to je, když jsou jejich lidská práva přehlížena a zpochybňována." *Kompas—Manuál pro výchovu mládeže k lidským právům,* 10.

328 The language of the Czech Framework Educational Programmes and the school educational programmes is very clear here.

329 *Compass,* chapter 1, section "Approaches to human rights education in Compass," sub-section "The pedagogical basis of human rights education in Compass," 1st paragraph.

now building, living in and moving towards a *culture of human rights*. The idea of *human rights* calls for human rights to be a central shared value, a moral value, and the highest good for Europe and the whole world. The "highest value and good" has for many centuries been God. The culture of human rights therefore constitutes a secularised form of Christian culture.

The following lines are from the preamble to the *Charter of the United Nations*,[330] the founding statute of the UN and the key document immediately preceding the *Universal Declaration of Human Rights*. Here, we find a "confession of faith" in human rights, a "new Creed," a confession of faith in a European society rising from the ashes of the Second World War:

> WE THE PEOPLES OF THE UNITED NATIONS DETERMINED
> to save succeeding generations from the scourge of war, which twice in our lifetime has brought untold sorrow to mankind, and
> to reaffirm **faith in fundamental human rights**,
> in the dignity and worth of the human person, in the equal rights of men and women and of nations large and small . . .

The conceptual metaphor HUMAN RIGHTS ARE A DEITY has been widely used within the idea of human rights in connection with the *Charter of the United Nations*, and was developed in later human rights documents and other texts on the issue. The preamble to the UN Charter usually cites all later human rights declarations and conventions such as the *Universal Declaration of Human Rights*, the *International Covenant on Civil and Political Rights*, and others. Many of the metaphorical terms in *Compass* are an application of this conceptual metaphor.

In the metaphorical concept HUMAN RIGHTS ARE A DEITY, human rights are *valued* and *appreciated / not appreciated*; those who use this metaphor either consciously or unconsciously offer human rights as an object of faith, as the highest cultural and moral value.

> Human rights are best respected, protected and appreciated when all of us understand them, stand up for them and apply them in our actions.[331]

In Europe, for many centuries the object of faith was the God of the Old and New Testaments; since the time of the Enlightenment that object has been natural laws or reason ("Reason"). In *Lidská práva jako sekulární náboženství západu* (Human rights as a secular religion of the West), the Czech political scientist, writer and political commentator Jiří Pehe compares the status of human rights with that of basic physical laws.[332]

---

330   *Charter of the United Nations* (San Francisco, 1945).
331   *Compass*, "Foreword" by Thorbjørn Jagland.
332   Jiří Pehe, "Lidská práva jako sekulární náboženství Západu," in *Lidská práva. (Ne)smysl české politiky*, ed. Jiří Přibáň and Václav Bělohradský (Prague: Slon, 2015), 52.

According to Pehe, human rights are bound to the essence of humanity as "fundamental truths," as *natural* "laws of humanity." The aptness of his thesis can be illustrated by the following passage from *Compass*:

> Human rights are like . . . nature because they can be violated; and like the spirit because they cannot be destroyed. Like time, they treat us all in the same way—rich and poor, old and young, white and black, tall and short. They offer us respect, and they charge us to treat others with respect. Like goodness, truth and justice, we may sometimes disagree about their definition, but we recognise them when we see them.[333]

The suggestion is that like the *truths of faith (revealed truths)*, human rights need no justification in order to be universally recognised and respected.[334] During its long evolution, Christian theology has understood that rationality must not contradict spirituality, but also that the truths of faith can be justified by reason and through a dialogue with science; the quasi-theology of human rights remains at the stage of an ideology rather than a theology. Pehe and others point out that some politicians, human rights activists, educators, philosophers and journalists claim, whether consciously or unconsciously, that the idea of human rights is a secular revelation of universal truths about human beings. Such a notion makes human rights something of a dangerous ideology.[335] Most Christian theology would view the metaphor HUMAN RIGHTS ARE A DEITY as a dangerous exaggeration that runs the risk of profound error. While this is not the place to carry out a serious criticism of the use of this metaphor, a few other examples will at least serve to illustrate its use in *Compass*.

The culture of human rights as presented in *Compass* can in some respects be compared to worship. Human rights have their own *calendar*. While Easter is at the centre of the Christian liturgical calendar, the focus of the human rights calendar is 10 December, *Human Rights Day*, in honour of the adoption of the *Universal Declaration of Human Rights* on that day in 1948. *Compass* includes a calendar which lists the days when people around the world *commemorate* and *celebrate* human rights and those who fought for them:

> The following calendar is an updated attempt to compile a list of **days on which people worldwide commemorate human rights; fighters for rights are honoured**, abuses of human rights are remembered and hopes and joy are celebrated. . . . The challenge for you—the users of this manual—is to find new ways of **celebrating human rights** every single day of the year.[336]

---

333 *Compass*, chapter 4, section "Understanding human rights," sub-section "What are human rights?", 1st paragraph.

334 Pehe, "Lidská práva," 52.

335 Ibid., 55.

336 *Compass*, "Introduction" to "Human Rights Calendar" (https://www.coe.int/en/web/compass/human-rights-calendar).

Human rights thus have their "apostles, martyrs and missionaries" to countries where human rights have not yet been accepted or respected. "Holy wars," both violent and non-violent, are being waged in the interest of human rights. The "holy war" metaphor is very clear in the following passage:

> In April 2001, a resolution of the United Nations Commission on Human Rights rejected the notion that **fighting** terrorism could ever justify **sacrificing** human rights protections.[337]

Statements made by human rights activists are cited throughout the manual; the quotations are highlighted with use of graphics and then commented on by the authors of the manual. The layout resembles some Christian doctrinal writings in which quotations from the Bible or the Church Fathers are picked out graphically and accompanied by a commentary.

The battle metaphor can be seen in several passages in *Compass*, such as:

> In general terms we describe the outcome of human rights education in terms of knowledge and understanding, skills and attitudes: . . . Skills and abilities to fight for and defend your own and others' human rights such as awareness-raising, advocacy and campaigning, feeling able to contact the relevant authorities or the press (learning for human rights), and so on.[338]

Compass "recruits and trains" human rights fighters, for example through the teaching activity *Fighters for Rights* (see *Compass*, "List of activities").

The conceptual metaphor HUMAN RIGHTS ARE WAR ARMOUR can also be considered a partial position of the metaphor HUMAN RIGHTS ARE A DEITY, as we can see in the following passage:

> Human rights are like **armour**: they **protect** you; they are like rules, because they tell you how you can behave; and they are like judges, because you can appeal to them.[339]

The conceptual metaphor GOD IS A WARRIOR and its partial position GOD IS WAR ARMOUR are conventional biblical metaphors. In a culture anchored in the biblical tradition, the use of the metaphor HUMAN RIGHTS ARE WAR ARMOUR clearly has roots in the biblical and Christian faith, in both the Old Testament:

> The LORD is my strength and my shield; in him my heart trusts; so I am helped, and my heart exults, and with my song I give thanks to him.[340]

---

337 *Compass*, chapter 4, section "What are human rights?", sub-section "In the name of a good cause," last paragraph.
338 *Compass*, chapter 1, section "Approaches to human rights education in Compass," sub-section "Human rights education: process and outcome," 3rd paragraph.
339 *Compass*, chapter 4, section "Introducing human rights education, What are human rights?", 1st paragraph.
340 Ps 28:7. Similarly elsewhere: Deut 33:29; 2 Sam 22:31; 2 Kings 19:34; 20:6; Ps 7:11; 18:31; 84:12; 115:9–11; Isa 31:5; 37:35; 38:6; Zech 9:15; 12:8, etc.

Blessed be the LORD, my rock, who trains my hands for war, and my fingers for battle; my rock and my fortress, my stronghold and my deliverer, my shield, in whom I take refuge, who subdues the peoples under me.[341]

And the New Testament:

Therefore take up the whole armour of God, so that you may be able to withstand on that evil day, and having done everything, to stand firm. Stand therefore, and fasten the belt of truth around your waist, and put on the breastplate of righteousness. As shoes for your feet put on whatever will make you ready to proclaim the gospel of peace. With all of these, take the shield of faith, with which you will be able to quench all the flaming arrows of the evil one. Take the helmet of salvation, and the sword of the Spirit, which is the word of God.[342]

Another analogy between Christian theology and the discourse on human rights as we find it in *Compass* can be seen in passages that deal with the objectives of human rights education. Here there is a clear link to the ethics of Christian virtues. The idea of civic virtues is of course older than the Christian doctrine of virtues and vices. In European culture, however, the doctrine has been cultivated for many centuries and is deeply rooted. It is based on biblical texts and has found expression in ethics, systematic theology, literature, painting, sculpture and music. Thomas Aquinas gave the highest value to this Christian doctrine. The secular and rationalist variant of Christian virtues and vices is *civic virtues* and "vices." The English version of the manual does not use the term *civic virtues*, but the Czech authorised translation does.[343] The English text prefers the term *qualities (of a human rights culture)*. These *qualities* include democracy, tolerance, pluralism and non-discrimination:[344]

So how can we describe a human rights culture and what qualities would its adherents have? The authors of this manual worked on these questions and have formulated some (but not exclusive) answers. A human rights culture is one where people:

- Have knowledge about and respect for human rights and fundamental freedoms
- Have a sense of individual self-respect and respect for others; they value human dignity
- Demonstrate attitudes and behaviours that show respect for the rights of others
- Practise genuine gender equality in all spheres
- Show respect, understanding and appreciation of cultural diversity, particularly towards different national, ethnic, religious, linguistic and other minorities and communities
- Are empowered and active citizens
- Promote democracy, social justice, communal harmony, solidarity and friendship between people and nations

---

341 Ps 144:1–2.
342 Eph 6:13–17.
343 In Czech *občanské ctnosti.*
344 This example is from the first chapter of the manual (section "Towards a culture of human rights").

– Are active in furthering the activities of international institutions aimed at the creation of a culture of peace, based upon universal values of human rights, international understanding, tolerance and non-violence.

Compass also has a focus on vices. These include anti-semitism, discrimination, xenophobia, racism, homophobia, fanaticism, neo-Nazism, and extremism.

Just as Christianity has its key dogmas, so *Compass* puts forward its "religion of human rights." It is possible, for example, to apply the Christian doctrine of sin to the *Compass* manual's conceptualisation of human rights, although in a very simplified, reduced, or "flattened" form. In the source concept, the deepest cause of evil in the world is sin. According to Christian doctrine, sin has an individual, social and structural dimension. Sin originates in the human person's inner being, in human nature, but manifests itself in words, in concrete action, or in silence and passivity. The *Catechism of the Catholic Church* formulates this "source" doctrine as follows:

> Thus sin makes men accomplices of one another and causes concupiscence, violence, and injustice to reign among them. Sins give rise to social situations and institutions that are contrary to the divine goodness.[345]

We can see how *Compass* "reduces" the concept of sin through its metaphorical concept BREACHING HUMAN RIGHTS IS A SIN in the following passages:

> . . . we can see that almost every problem in the world today—poverty, pollution, climate change, economic inequality, AIDS, poor access to education, racism and wars—involves violations of human rights.[346]
>
> Peace education recognises many different forms of violence. For instance, physical or behavioural violence, including war; structural violence, that is, the poverty and deprivation that results from unjust and inequitable social and economic structures; political violence of oppressive systems that enslave, intimidate, and abuse dissenters as well as the poor, powerless and marginalised; cultural violence, the devaluing and destruction of particular human identities and ways of life; and the violence of racism, sexism, ethnocentrism, colonial ideology, and other forms of moral exclusion that rationalise aggression, domination, inequity, and oppression. Analysing all these forms of violence as violations of particular human rights standards provides a constructive way forward.[347]

One final example of the transfer between Christian doctrine and the concept of human rights, one that is applied regularly in key human rights documents and secondary literature, relates to the early Christian doctrine of the dual nature or essence of Christ. The *Chalcedonian Creed* of 451 states:

---

345 *Catechism of the Catholic Church 1992* (Citta del Vaticano: Libreria Editrice Vaticana, 1993), § 1869, http://www.vatican.va/archive/ENG0015/_INDEX.HTM.
346 *Compass*, Chapter 1, section "Approaches to human rights education in Compass," sub-section "Human rights education and other educational fields—Peace education," 1st paragraph.
347 Ibid., 3rd paragraph.

> . . . one and the same Christ, Son, Lord, only-begotten, to be acknowledged in two natures, **without confusion, without change, without division, without separation**; the distinction of natures being by no means taken away by the union, but rather the property of each nature being preserved, and concurring in one person and one subsistence, not parted or divided into two persons . . .[348]

This offers a striking reminder of the insistance that human rights are *inherent, inalienable, indivisible, unlimited, indestructible* and *universal*. In *Compass*, this mantra is rationalised as follows:

> Human rights are held by all persons **equally, universally and for ever**. Human rights are universal. . . . They are **inalienable, indivisible and interdependent, that is, they cannot be taken away**—ever; all rights are equally important and they are **complementary**.[349]
> Human rights are **indivisible, interdependent** and **interrelated** and it is not possible to pick and choose which human rights to accept and respect.[350]

Just as the expressions *without confusion, without change, without division, without separation* in the Chalcedonian confession are often graphically highlighted, so in *Compass* the expressions *indivisible, interdependent* and *interrelated* are highlighted in italics.

This insistance that human rights are natural, inalienable, indivisible, non-prescriptive, irrevocable and universal can be found in all human rights documents, and concerns first, second and third generation rights: fundamental rights, civil and political rights, and social, economic, cultural and collective rights. Such an insistance sounds factually inadequate, however, and even dogmatic.

We are not saying that the secular, humanistic, liberal idea of human rights is defective or ineffective in its practical application, but from the theological, philosophical and didactic point of view, conceptualisation of the term *human rights* through the metaphor HUMAN RIGHTS ARE A DEITY, in all its sub-positions, is at best problematic and debatable.

---

348 *Creed of Chalcedon:* ἕνα καὶ τὸν αὐτὸν Χριστόν, υἱόν, κύριον, μονογενῆ, ἐκ δύο φύσεων [ἐν δύο φύσεσιν], **ἀσυγχύτως, ἀτρέπτως, ἀδιαιρέτως, ἀχωρίστως** γνωριζόμενον οὐδαμοῦ τῆς τῶν φύσεων διαφορᾶς ἀνηρημένης διὰ τὴν ἕνωσιν, . . . *unum eundemque Christum, filium, Dominum, unigenitum, in duabus naturis* INCONFUSE, IMMUTABILIT-ER, INDIVISE, INSEPERABILITER *agnoscendum: nusquam sublata differentia naturarum propter unitionem, magisque salva proprietate utriusque naturæ, et in unam personam atque subsistentiam concurrente . . .*

349 *Compass,* chapter 4, section "Introducing human rights education," sub-section "What are human rights?", 3rd paragraph.

350 *Compass,* chapter 1, section "Approaches to human rights education in Compass," sub-section "Human rights education and other educational fields," 2nd paragraph.

CONCLUSION

It only makes sense to explore the "path"
when we also want to travel along this path.
(Wilfried Stinissen, *Wegen naar de waarheid*)

Outside Old Testament poetic texts, metaphorical expressions involved in the conceptualisation of תורה *the Torah / Law* and related Hebrew terms are mainly to be found in the preambles to the giving of the Law, where they reflect general questions such as the origin and meaning of the Law, the motivation for its observance or violation, and its universality or particularity. These are themes which today are studied within the fields of legal theory and the philosophy of law and related disciplines. A wide range of themes comes into play in the Psalms, Prophets and Wisdom Literature, and a wide spectrum of conceptual metaphors is applied. Some of these metaphors occur much more often than others, in various sub-variants; other metaphorical expressions are unique or innovative works of the author. With metaphors and their sub-variants, we can also usually determine a *centre* and *peripheries* of metaphorical conceptualisation, in our case in the semantic area *Torah / Law*.

In cognitive and cultural semantics, it is typical to use a prototypical concept of meaning. "Prototype" implies the existence of a "best example" within the relevant semantic category. For example, for birds, *eagle* is a better example than *penguin* or *kiwi* as the prototypical characteristics of birds include not only beak, feathers and wings, but also the ability to fly, which neither penguins nor kiwi possess.[351] The asymmetry within categories has been described at all levels of language: phonology, morphology, syntax and vocabulary. At the level of semantic categories, we talk about the centre and the peripheries, so as we have seen, metaphorical conceptualisation can also have a centre and peripheries. In this context, cognitive semantics also works with terms and theoretical concepts such as the *core of meaning, fundamental cognitive notion,* or

---

351 Barbara Lewandowska-Tomaszczyk, "Polysemy, Prototypes, and Radical Categories," in *The Oxford Handbook of Cognitive Linguistics*, ed. Dirk Geeraerts and Hubert Cuyckens (Oxford: Oxford University Press, 2007), 147–157.

prototype / stereotype theory.[352] The core of meaning and the central cognitive concept have also been shown to be appropriate models in the explanation of metaphorical meaning.

The cognitive approach to metaphors also takes into account a narrative aspect. Here, at the wider level of its conceptualisation, the narrative understanding of the metaphor is connected with the core of meaning, with the concept of central cognitive images. The centre of the metaphorical conceptualisation of the Hebrew expression תורה *the Torah / Law* and related terms in the Old Testament is formed by the conceptual metaphor THE TORAH / LAW IS A JOURNEY. We described this metaphor in chapter two using *metaphorical vehicles*, and in particular using sub-variants of the metaphor, which we have called *generic narrative structures*. Within the sub-positions of the conceptual metaphor THE TORAH / LAW IS A JOURNEY, we defined its centre in the generic narrative structures TO SHOW THE PATH, TO WALK ALONG THE PATH, TO LEAVE THE PATH/TURN FROM THE PATH, TO GO ASTRAY and TO FALL DOWN ON THE PATH.

On the periphery of metaphorical conceptualisation through the metaphor of the journey in the semantic area *Torah / Law* are, for example, the generic narrative structures TO RUN ALONG THE PATH, TO RETURN and TO SEARCH FOR THE PATH / SEARCH ON THE PATH. We have shown that in the semantic area *Torah / Law*, some key expressions of central generic narrative structures tend to become "domesticated" as lexicalised metaphors.

In chapter two, we used tables to describe the meaning of particular metaphorical expressions and these showed a network of the most important correspondences and structural correlations between the Hebrew expressions of the source and target domains using the journey metaphor. In addition to generic narrative structures, which define the central cognitive concept, these are the most important correspondences and structural correlations which form the core of the metaphorical meaning of a particular metaphorical expression.

In the second part of the chapter, we described other metaphors that are involved in the conceptualisation of תורה *the Torah / Law* and concepts related to the central metaphor THE TORAH / LAW IS A JOURNEY. Many of these are commonly found in the Old Testament as metaphors for the Lord, the God of Israel: the metaphors of light, water, food, or property and valuables. In metaphorical expressions, the Torah, like God Himself, is a source of joy and an object of love, reverence and praise; the Torah is understood as a manifestation of God, an instrument of the revelation of God's will, or of God Himself. This basic source of metonimic-metaphoric conceptualisations is also

---

352 Cognitively oriented sociology, sociolinguistics, ethnology, and cultural studies work with *stereotypes*. Stereotypes can have different positions and variants that exist in parallel in a given language and cultural sphere. For example, in the Czech context, Vaňková mentions four basic language stereotypes of a Gypsy: 1. The unfavourable, dangerously discriminatory stereotype which takes into account the image of a Gypsy as a dirty, disorderly, cunning person who is unwilling to work; who cheats, lies and steals; 2. The stereotype of a Gypsy woman— unfettered, wild, beautiful, lively, erotically attractive and passionate; 3. The stereotype of an old Gypsy who divines, conjures and reads palms; 4. The stereotype of a Gypsy woman as represented by masks at masquerade balls: a brunette dressed in colourful dresses and fringed scarves and decorated with shiny trinkets. See Vaňková et al., *Co na srdci*, 87.

evidenced by a number of other conceptual metaphors that we have described using some of the methods of cognitive and cultural linguistics, such as THE TORAH / LAW IS AN INSTRUMENT OF THE LORD-THE BUILDER and THE TORAH / LAW IS A GARMENT.

At the same time, the metaphors THE TORAH / LAW IS AN INSTRUMENT OF THE LORD-THE BUILDER and THE TORAH / LAW IS PILLARS OF THE THRONE can be interpreted as variants of the more general concept of the THE TORAH / LAW IS THE ABODE OF GOD-THE KING, in the sense of a temple or royal palace. The conceptual metaphor THE TORAH / LAW IS CLOTHING also forms a coherent system with the Lord-King metaphor. In concrete metaphorical expressions, the mental image of a king-warrior either who is himself clothed with armour/righteousness (Hebr. צדקה), a helmet/salvation (Hebr. ישועה), a robe/vengeance (Hebr. נקם) and a cloak/ardour (Hebr. קנאה) (Isa 59:17), or who dresses others, is projected into the target domain, thereby empowering and appointing his servants, the judge (Isa 11:5), or the priest (Ps 132:9).

Like the metaphor THE TORAH / LAW IS A JOURNEY and its sub-positions, other metaphors also form a coherent system. This system again has a centre and peripheries. The central concepts usually contain sub-variants: in the metaphor THE TORAH / LAW IS LIGHT, we find the variants THE TORAH / LAW IS THE SUN, THE TORAH / LAW IS A LAMP and THE TORAH / LAW IS THE MORNING STAR; in the the THE TORAH / LAW IS WATER / MOISTURE, we find the variants THE TORAH / LAW IS RAIN, THE TORAH / LAW IS DEW and THE TORAH / LAW IS SNOW; and in the metaphor THE TORAH / LAW IS PROPERTY / VALUABLES, we find the variants THE TORAH / LAW IS HERITAGE, THE TORAH / LAW IS JEWELRY and THE TORAH / LAW IS TEMPLE TREASURE. Although the central concepts do not include THE TORAH / LAW IS FOOD and THE TORAH / LAW IS CLOTHING, we nonetheless identified and described their sub-variants in the texts.

In chapter three we dealt first with the specific function of the journey metaphor in the semantic area *Torah / Law* in the book of Jeremiah. In this Old Testament book, the spatial image schemas contribute to the formulation of central theological statements concerning the causes of the apostasy of individuals and of the whole people and the causes and consequences of exile, and statements regarding hope and God's promise to return the exiles to their land.

We also introduced the possibility of using cognitive-linguistic analysis to explore the meaning of metaphorical expressions in Proverbs 29:18 and Zephaniah 3:4. Here, we were able to show that the methods used significantly refine the identification of conceptual metaphors and of passages of text as metaphorical expressions.

The system of enumerating metaphorical vehicles and generic narrative structures respects the narrative nature of metaphorical projection into the target domain. The core of the metaphorical meaning, formed by the central mental image, is explored quite clearly in the tables, which provide an overview of the most important structural correlations and correspondences between the entities of the source and target domains, as established during metaphorical mapping of a particular passage of text. A clear system of metaphorical vehicles, generic narrative structures, and correspondences and structural correlations shows that central conceptual metaphors very often form a coherent system in the closed corpus of the Old Testament. This is reinforced by the intertextual nature of the biblical text and also contributes to its formation. The methods used to analyse the metaphorical expressions made it possible to distinguish between conventional and unconventional (innovative) ways of using conceptual metaphors. It has also been shown that our method of analysis and interpretation can contribute to the linguistic and theological debate regarding exegetically controversial verses such as Proverbs 29:18 and Zephaniah 3:4.

Also in chapter three we introduced the possibile use of cognitive-linguistic analysis and interpretation in translation studies and translation practice. From the wide range of functions of a metaphor, the cognitive function was at the forefront of our interest as a tool which brings fresh knowledge and understanding to the target text.

Using the translations of two metaphorical expressions (in Prov 29:18 and Zeph 3:4) into modern English and Czech, we examined how the chosen translation strategies affect the ability of the translation to preserve the cognitive function of the original metaphor. We were interested in how translators managed to convey the mental image that the metaphor had built in the original language in a completely different historical, cultural and linguistic context.

If the metaphorical expression is tied to the specific socio-cultural and religious or geographical context in which it originated, its translation into another language presents a problem for both translation and exegesis. We believe that "literal" translation is not a translation of the metaphor and that the metaphorical expression needs to be adapted in the new context. One of the important bearers of semantic continuity in a translation that is also an adaptation can be the reconstructed initial mental image with a generic narrative structure at its centre. Preserving the key structural correlations and correspondences established in the source text also helps to maintain semantic continuity between the original and the translation.

The case study in chapter four presented another possible application of a cognitive-linguistic analysis of metaphorical expressions in the semantic area of *Law* and applied the theory described in chapters two and three to the contemporary context of human rights. The case study explored a cognitive-semantic analysis of the teaching material *Compass: Manual for Human Rights Education with Young People*, particularly the metaphors used in the manual to conceptualise the term *human rights*. The study illustrates the biblical (Old Testament) and Christian doctrinal roots of these metaphors.

The transfer of metaphors from the Torah (or the metaphors used in the New Testament and the Christian doctrinal tradition for Jesus Christ, the incarnate Word of God, the incarnate Torah) to human rights, not only sounds dogmatic, even manipulative, it is also factually questionable and can have serious social, cultural and political consequences. It is necessary to carefully consider which metaphors it is appropriate to use not only to interpret human rights issues but also to "build," "enforce" and "live" them. Sensitive and informed work with appropriate methods of cognitive semantics, such as those presented here for recognising the generic narrative structures in the metaphor, proves to be an appropriate tool for competent theological and lay reading and use of biblical texts in today's world.

BIBLIOGRAPHY

Bible Versions
American Standard Version, 1901. Available at https://ebible.org/asv.
Bible 21. století. Prague: Biblion, 2009.
Bible česká. Prague: Dědictví sv. Jana Nepomuckého, 1925.
Bible in Basic English. Cambridge: Cambridge University Press, 1964. Available at https://www.bible
    studytools.com/bbe.
Biblia Hebraica Stuttgartensia, ed. R. Kittel. 4th ed. In cooperation with H. P. Rüger and W. Rudolph.
    Stuttgart: Deutsche Bibelgeselschaft, 1990.
Biblia Sacra Iuxta Vulgatam Versionem. 3rd ed. Stuttgart: Deutsche Bibelgeselschaft, 1983.
Český ekumenický překlad. 14th ed. Prague: Česká biblická společnost, 2008.
Český katolický překlad. Prague: Česká biblická společnost, 2006.
Český studijní překlad. Prague: Nakladatelství KMS, 2009.
Complete Jewish Bible. Clarksville: Jewish New Testament Publications, 1998.
Contemporary English Version. Philadelphia: American Bible Society, 1995.
English Revised Version. 1885. Available at https://www.bible.com/versions/477-rv1885-revised-version
    -1885.
English Standard Version. Minneapolis: Crossway Bibles, 2001.
Good News Bible. New York: American Bible Society, 1976.
Jeruzalémská bible. Písmo svaté vydané Jeruzalémskou biblickou školou. Prague: Krystal OP, 2009.
New American Bible. 1986. Available at http://www.vatican.va/archive/ENG0839/_INDEX.HTM.
New American Standard Bible with Code. Illinois: The Lockman Foundation, 1977.
New American Standard Bible with Code. Illinois: The Lockman Foundation, 1995.
New English Bible. Oxford: Oxford University Press, 1970.
New English Translation. Biblical Studies Press, 2001–2017. Available at https://classic.biblegateway
    .com/versions/New-English-Translation-NET-Bible.
New International Version. New York: International Bible Society, 1984.
New Jerusalem Bible. Darton: Longman & Todd, 1985.
New King James Version. Nashville: Nelson, 1982.
New Living Translation. Chicago: Tyndale House Foundation, 1996.
New Revised Standard Version. Oxford: Oxford University Press, 1990.
Nová Bible kralická. 2002–2008. Available at https://ebible.org/cesnkb.
Pět knih Mojžíšových. Prague: Svaz pražských náboženských obcí židovských, 1932–1950.
Pět knih Mojžíšových. Včetně haftorot. Prague: Sefer, 2012.
Písmo. Edited by Vladimír Šrámek and Vladimíra Kajdoše. Prague: Melantrich, 1947–1951.
Písmo svaté Starého zákona. Prague: Česká katolická charita, 1955–1958.
Překlad nového světa Svatých písem. Brooklyn: Watchtower Bible and Tract Society, 1991.
Průvodce životem. Prague: International Bible Society, 1994–2003.

Revised English Bible. Cambridge: Cambridge University Press, 1989.

Revised Standard Version. Camden: Thomas Nelson & Sons, 1952.

Septuaginta. Vetus Testamentum graece iuxta LXX interpretes. Edited by A. Rahlfs. One-volume edition. Stuttgart: Deutsche Bibelgesellschaft, 1935, 1979.

Slovo na cestu. 2nd ed. Prague: Luxpress, 1990.

Slovo na cestu. Bible s poznámkami. Prague: Česká biblická společnost, 2011.

Tanakh. Philadelphia: Jewish Publication Society of America, 1985.

Young's Literal Translation of the Holy Bible. Edinburgh: A. Fullarton, 1862.

Other Primary Sources

Catechism of the Catholic Church. Citta del Vaticano: Libreria Editrice Vaticana, 1993. Available at http://www.vatican.va/archive/ENG0015/_INDEX.HTM.

Charter of the United Nations. San Francisco, 1945. Available at https://www.un.org/en/charter-united-nations/index.html.

Council of Europe. *Compass: Manual for Human Rights Education with Young People.* 2002. Available at https://www.coe.int/en/web/compass/home.

The Declaration of Independence. Washington DC, 1776. Available at http://www.ushistory.org/declaration/document.

The Universal Declaration of Human Rights. Paris, 1948. Available at https://www.un.org/en/universal-declaration-human-rights/index.html.

Secondary Sources

Allwood, Jens, and Peter Gärdenfors, eds. *Cognitive Semantics: Meaning and Cognition.* Amsterdam: John Benjamins, 1999.

Antalík, Dalibor, Jiří Starý, and Tomáš Vítek, eds. *Zákon a právo v archaických kulturách.* Prague: Filozofická fakulta Univerzity Karlovy, 2010.

Anusiewicz, Janusz. *Lingwistyka kulturowa. Zarys problematyki.* Wrocław: Wydawnictvo Uniwersytetu Wrosławskiego, 1995.

Assmann, Jan. *Tod und Jenseit im Alten Ägypten.* Munich: C. H. Beck, 2001.

Bancila, Maria Yvonne. *The Journey Metaphor in Old Testament Text*, 365–373. 2009. http://www.diacronia.ro/ro/indexing/details/A34/pdf.

Bartmiński, Jerzy. "Definicja kognitywna jako narzędzie opisu konotacji." In *Konotacja.* Czerwona seria instytutu filologii polskiej, 3, edited by Jerzy Bartmiński, 169–183. Lublin: Uniwersytet Marii Curie-Skłodowskiej, 1988.

Bartmiński, Jerzy. *Językowe podstawy obrazu świata.* Lublin: Uniwersytet Marii Curie-Skłodowskiej, 2007.

Bartmiński, Jerzy. "Narracyjny aspekt definicji kognitywnej." In *Narracyjność języka i kultury*, edited by Dorota Fillar and Dorota Piekarczyk, 99–115. Lublin: Wydawnictwo Uniwersytetu Marii Curie-Skłodowskiej, 2014.

Bartmiński, Jerzy. *Jazyk v kontextu kultury.* Prague: Karolinum, 2016.

Bartoň, Josef. "Český starozákonní překlad po roce 1900. Kontexty, konfese, předloha, kánon." *Salve. Revue pro teologii a duchovní život* 2 (2013): 143–162.

Bauer, Walter, William F. Arndt, and F. Wilbur Gingrich. *A Greek-English Lexicon of the New Testament and Other Early Christian Literature.* 2nd ed. Chicago: University of Chicago Press, 1979.

Bělič, Jaromír, Adolf Kamiš, and Karel Kučera. *Malý staročeský slovník.* Prague: SPN, 1978.

Berges, Ulrich. *Klagelieder.* Herders Theologischer Kommentar zum Alten Testament. Freiburg im Breisgau: Herder, 2002.

Bergmann, Claudia D. *Childbirth as a Metaphor for Crisis. Evidence from the Ancient Near East, the Hebrew Bible, and 1QH XI, 1–18.* Beihefte zur Zeitschrift für die alttestamentliche Wissenschaft, 382. Berlin: Walter de Gruyter, 2008.

Baicchi, Annalisa. "The Relevance of Conceptual Metaphor in Semantic Interpretation." *Rivisteweb. The Italian Platform for the Humanities and Social Sciences* 1 (2017): 155–170.

Black, Max. *Models and Metaphors. Studies in Language and Philosophy.* Ithaca: Cornell University Press, 1962.

Botterweck, Gerhard Johannes, Heinz-Josef Fabry, and Helmer Ringgren, eds. *Theological Dictionary of the Old Testament.* 15 vols. Translated by Douglas W. Stott. Grand Rapids: Eerdmans, 1991–2005.

Brunner-Traut, Emma. *Frühform des Erkennens am Beispiel Ägyptens.* Darmstadt: Wissenschaftliche Buchgesellschaft, 1992.

Cazelles, Henri. "Le Pentateuque comme Torah." In *Autour de l'Exode*, 136–137. Paris, 1987.

Čech, Pavel. "Zákon ve Starém zákonu." In *Zákon a právo v archaických kulturách*, edited by Dalibor Antalík, Jiří Starý, and Tomáš Vítek, 161–176. Prague: Filozofická fakulta Univerzity Karlovy, 2010.

Childs, Brevard S. *Old Testament Theology in a Canonical Context.* Philadelphia: Fortress Press, 1985.

Cienki, Alan. "An Image Schema and Its Metaphorical Extensions—Straight." *Cognitive Linguistics* 9 (1998): 107–149.

Cienki, Alan. "Metaphoric Gestures and Some of Their Relations to Verbal Metaphorical Expressions." In *Discourse and Cognition: Bridging the Gap*, edited by Jean-Pierre Koenig, 198–204. Stanford: CSLI, 1998.

Cienki, Alan, and Cornelia Müller. *Metaphor and Gesture.* Amsterdam: John Benjamins, 2008.

Clines, David J. A., ed. *The Dictionary of Classical Hebrew.* 4 vols. Sheffield: Sheffield Academic Press, 1998–2011.

Croft, William, and Alan Cruse. *Cognitive Linguistics.* Cambridge Textbooks in Linguistics. Cambridge: Cambridge University Press, 2004.

Crossan, John Dominic. *In Parables. The Challenge of the Historical Jesus.* San Francisco: Harper & Row, 1985.

Dancygier, Barbara, ed. *The Cambridge Handbook of Cognitive Linguistics.* Cambridge: Cambridge University Press, 2017.

Daniell, David. *The Bible in English: Its History and Influence.* New Haven: Yale University Press, 2003.

Deignan, Alice. *Metaphor and Corpus Linguistics.* Amsterdam: John Benjamins, 2005.

Delitzch, Friedrich. *Prolegomena eines neuen hebräisch-aramäisches Wörterbuch zum Alten Tesatment.* Leipzig, 1886.

Delitizch, Friedrich. *Assyrische Grammatik.* Berlin: Verlag von Reuther and Reichard, 1906.

Dirven, René, and Wolf Paprotté, eds. *The Ubiquity of Metaphor. Metaphor in Language and Thought.* Amsterdam: John Benjamins, 1985.

Dirven, René, and Marjolijn Verspoor, eds. *Cognitive Exploration of Language and Linguistics.* Amsterdam: John Benjamins, 1999.

Eidevall, Göran. "Spatial Metaphors in Lamentations 3:1–9." In *Metaphor in the Hebrew Bible*, edited by Pierre van Hecke, 133–137. Bibliotheca Ephemeridum Theologicarum Lovaniensium, 187. Leuven: Leuven University Press, 2005.

Eichrodt, Walther. *Theology of the Old Testament.* Philadelphia: Westminster Press, 1964.

Emerton, John A. "A Neglected Solution of a Problem in Psalm LXXVI 11." *Vetus Testamentum* 24 (1974): 136–146.

Evans, Vyvyan, and Melanie Green. *Cognitive Linguistics. An Introduction.* Edinburgh: Edinburgh University Press, 2006.

Fauconnier, Gilles, and Mark Turner. *The Way We Think: Conceptual Blending and the Mind's Hidden Complexities.* New York: Basic Books, 2003.

Fillar, Dorota. "Narracyjność w badaniach interdyscyplinarnych a kategorie narracyjne w semantyce." In *Narracyjność języka i kultury*, edited by Dorota Fillar and Dorota Piekarczyk, 13–33. Lublin: Wydawnictwo Uniwersytetu Marii Curie-Skłodowskiej, 2014.

Fišer, Zbyněk. *Překlad jako kreativní proces. Teorie a praxe funkcionalistického překládání.* Brno: Host, 2009.

Forceville, Charles J. "The Identification of Target and Source in Pictorial Metaphors." *Journal of Pragmatics* 34, no. 1 (2002): 1–14.

Garrett, Duane A., and Paul R. House. *Song of Songs, Lamentations.* Word Biblical Commentary 23B. Nashville: Thomas Nelson, 2004.

Geeraerts, Dirk, and Hubert Cuyckens, eds. *The Oxford Handbook of Cognitive Linguistics*. Oxford: Oxford University Press, 2007.

Gesenius, Wilhelm. *Hebräisches und Aramäisches Handwörterbuch über das Alte Testament*. 17th ed. Berlin: Springer, 1962.

Gesenius, Wilhelm. *Hebräisches und Aramäisches Handwörterbuch über das Alte Testament*. 18th ed. Berlin: Springer, 2013.

Glucksberg, Sam. "The Psycholinguistics of Metaphor." *Trends in Cognitive Sciences* 7, no. 2 (2003): 92–96.

Goulder, Michael D. *The Psalms of Asaph and the Pentateuch*. Studies in the Psalter, III. JSOT SS 33. Sheffield: Sheffield Academic Press, 1996.

Hanne, Michael, and Robert Weisberg, eds. *Narrative and Metaphor in the Law*. Cambridge: Cambridge University Press, 2018.

Hecke, Pierre van, ed. *Metaphor in the Hebrew Bible*. Bibliotheca Ephemeridum Theologicarum Lovaniensium, 187. Leuven: Leuven University Press, 2005.

Hillers, Delbert R. *Lamentations*. The Anchor Bible, 7a. New York: Doubleday, 1984.

Hossfeld, Frank-Lothar, and Erich Zenger. *Psalms*. Vol. 2. Minneapolis: Fortress, 2005.

Howe, Peter Bonnie. *Because You Bear This Name. Conceptual Metaphor and the Moral Meaning of 1 Peter*. Biblical Interpretation Series, 81. Leiden: Brill, 2006.

Hunziger-Rodewald, Regine. *Hirt und Herde. Ein Beitrag zum alttestamentlichen Gottesverständnis*. Beiträge zur Wissenschaft vom Alten und Neuen Testament, 8. Stuttgart: W. Kohlhammer, 2001.

Ishay, Micheline R. *The History of Human Rights. From Ancient Times to the Globalization Era*. Berkeley: University of California Press, 2008.

Jäkel, Olaf. "Hypotheses Revisited: The Cognitive Theory of Metaphor Applied to Religous Texts." *Metaphorik.de* (Feb 2002): 20–42. https://www.academia.edu/8706556/Hypotheses_Revisited_The _Cognitive_Theory_of_Metaphor_Applied_to_Religious_Texts.

Jensen, Joseph. *The Use of Tôrâ by Isaiah: His Debate with the Wisdom Tradition*. Catholic Biblical Quarterly. Monograph Series 3. Washington DC: Catholic Biblical Association, 1973.

Koehler, Ludwig, Walter Baumgartner, and M. E. J. Richardson. *The Hebrew and Aramaic Lexicon of the Old Testament. The New Koehler Baumgartner in English*. 4 vols. Translated by M. E. J. Richardson. Leiden: Brill, 1994–1999.

Kövecses, Zoltán. *Metaphors of Anger, Pride, and Love: A Lexical Approach to the Structure of Concepts*. Amsterdam: John Benjamins, 1986.

Kövecses, Zoltán. *Emotion Concepts*. New York: Springer, 1990.

Kövecses, Zoltán. *Metaphor and Emotion*. Cambridge: Cambridge University Press, 2000.

Kövecses, Zoltán. *Metaphor: A Practical Introduction*. Oxford: Oxford University Press, 2002.

Kövecses, Zoltán. *Metaphor in Culture. Universality and Variations*. Cambridge: Cambridge University Press, 2005.

Kövecses, Zoltán. *Where Metaphors Come From. Reconsidering Context in Metaphor*. Oxford: Oxford University Press, 2015.

Kövecses, Zoltán, and Peter Szabo. "Idioms: A View from Cognitive Semantics." *Applied Linguistics* 17, no. 3 (1996): 326–355.

Kraus, Hans-Joachim. *Psalmen 1. Psalmen 1–59*. Biblischer Kommentar Altes Testament, 15/1. 5th ed. Neukirchen-Vluyn: Neukirchener, 1978.

Krupa, Viktor. *Metafora na rozhraní vedeckých disciplín*. Okno, 67. Bratislava: Tatran, 1990.

Lakoff, George. *Women, Fire, and Dangerous Things. What Categories Reveal about the Mind*. Chicago: University of Chicago Press, 1987.

Lakoff, George, and Mark Johnson. *Metaphors We Live By*. Chicago: University of Chicago Press, 1980.

Lam, Joseph. *Patterns of Sin in the Hebrew Bible. Metaphor, Culture, and the Making of a Religious Concept*. New York: Oxford University Press, 2016.

Łebowska, Anna. "Pojęcie focus w narratologii—problem i inspiracje." In *Punkt widzenia w tekście i w dyskursie*, edited by Jerzy Bartmiński, Stanisława Niebrzegowska-Bartmińska, and Ryszard Nycz, 219–238. Lublin: Wydawnictwo Uniwersytetu Marii Curie-Skłodowskiej, 2014.

Lewandowska-Tomaszczyk, Barbara. "Polysemy, Prototypes, and Radical Categories." In *The Oxford Handbook of Cognitive Linguistics*, edited by Dirk Geeraerts and Hubert Cuyckens, 139–169. Oxford: Oxford University Press, 2007.

Lidell, Henry, Robert Scott, Henry Jones, and Roderick McKenzie, eds. *A Greek-English Lexicon*. Oxford: Clarendon Press, 1996.

Lund, Øystein. *Way Metaphors and Way Topics in Isaiah 40–55*. Tübingen: Mohr Siebeck, 2007.

Machová, Svatava, and Milena Švehlová. *Sémantika & pragmatická lingvistika*. Prague: Pedagogická fakulta Univerzity Karlovy, 2001.

Metzger, Bruce M. *The Bible in Translation*. Michigan: Baker Academic, 2001.

McFague, Sallie. *Metaphorical Theology: Models of God in Religious Language*. Philadelphia: Fortress Press, 1982.

Newmark, Peter. *Approaches to Translation*. Language Teaching Methodology Series. London: Prentice Hall, 1981.

Nord, Christiane. *Translating as a Purposeful Activity. Functionalist Approaches Explained*. Translation Theories Explained, 1. Manchester: St. Jerome Publishing, 1997.

Pavelka, Jiří. *Anatomie metafory*. Brno: Blok, 1982.

Pehe, Jiří. "Lidská práva jako sekulární náboženství Západu." In *Lidská práva. (Ne)smysl české politiky*, edited by Jiří Přibáň and Václav Bělohradský, 51–62. Prague: Slon, 2015.

Pípal, Blahoslav. *Hebrejsko-český slovník ke Starému zákonu*. 2nd ed. Prague: Ústřední církevní nakladatelství, 1974.

Preuss, Horst Dietrich. *Theologie des Alten Testaments*. Stuttgart: W. Kohlhammer, 1991.

Procházková, Ivana. *Hospodin je král. Starozákonní metafora ve světle kognitivní lingvistiky*. Prague: Česká biblická společnost, 2011.

Procházková, Ivana. "The Torah within the Heart, in the Feet, and on the Tongue: Law and Freedom in Psalm 119 from the Perspective of Cognitive Linguistics." *Communio Viatorum* 54, no. 1 (2012): 16–37.

Rad, Gerhard von. *Theologie des Alten Testament*. 2 vols. Munich: Chr. Kaiser, 1957–1967.

Rendtorff, Rolf. *Canonical Hebrew Bible. A Theology of the Old Testament*. Translated by D. E. Orton. Blandford Forum: Deo Publishing, 2005.

Ringgren, Helmer. *Word and Wisdom: Studies in the Hypostatization of Divine Qualities and Functions in the Ancient Near East*. Lund: Hakan Ohlssons, 1947.

Rosch, Eleanor. "Prototype Classification and Logical Classification: The Two Systems." In *New Trends in Cognitive Representation: Challenges to Piaget's Theory*, edited by E. Scholnick, 73–86. Hillsdale: Lawrence Erlbaum Associates, 1983.

Rosch, Eleanor, and Barbara Bloom Lloyd, eds. *Cognition and Categorization*. Oxford: Lawrence Erlbaum, 1978.

Saicová Římalová, Lucie. "Představová schémata a popis jazyka. Schéma cesty v češtině." *Bohemistyka* 9 (2009): 161–176.

Saicová Římalová, Lucie. *Vybraná slovesa pohybu v češtině. Studie z kognitivní lingvistiky*. Prague: Karolinum, 2010.

Schmid, Hans Heinrich. *Gerechtigkeit als Weltordnung: Hintergrund und Geschichte des Alttestamentlichen Gerechtigkeitsbegriffe*. Tübingen: J. C. B. Mohr, 1968.

Starý, Jiří, and Tomáš Vítek. "Zákon, právo a spravedlnost v archaickém myšlení." In *Zákon a právo v archaických kulturách*, edited by Dalibor Antalík, Jiří Starý, and Tomáš Vítek, 13–54. Prague: Filozofická fakulta Univerzity Karlovy, 2010.

Stern, Marc. *Svátky v životě Židů. Vzpomínání, slavení, vyprávění*. Translated by A. Smutná. Prague: Vyšehrad, 2002.

Strawn, Brent. *What Is Stronger than a Lion? Leonine Image and Metaphor in the Hebrew Bible and the Ancient Near East*. Orbis Biblicus et Orientalis, 212. Fribourg: Academic Press, 2005.

Sullivan, Karen. "Frame-Based Constraints on Lexical Choice in Metaphor." *Proceedings of the Annual Meeting of the Berkeley Linguistics Society* 32, no. 1 (2006): 387–399.

Sullivan, Karen. "Grammar in Metaphor. A Construction Grammar Account of Metaphoric Language." Doctoral dissertation, University of California, 2006.

Sullivan, Karen. *Mixed Metaphors: Their Use and Abuse*. London: Bloomsbury Academic, 2016.

Tendhal, Markus. *A Hybrid Theory of Metaphor: Relevance Theory and Cognitive Linguistics*. Basingstoke: Palgrave Macmillan, 2009.

Tesh, S. Edward, and Walter D. Zorn, eds. *The College Press NIV Commentary. Psalms*. Vol. 1. Joplin: College Press Publishing, 1999.

Turner, Mark. *The Literary Mind. The Origins of Thought and Language*. New York: Oxford University Press, 1996.

Ungerer, Friedrich, and Hans-Jörg Schmid. *An Introduction to Cognitive Linguistics*. New York: Longman, 2006.

VanGemeren, Willem. *Dictionary of Old Testament Theology, and Exegesis*. 5 vols. Grand Rapids: Zondervan, 1997.

Vaňková, Irena. *Nádoba plná řeči. Člověk, řeč a přirozený svět*. Prague: Karolinum, 2007.

Vaňková, Irena, Iva Nebeská, Lucie Saicová Římalová, and Jasňa Šlédrová. *Co na srdci, to na jazyku. Kapitoly z kognitivní lingvistiky*. Prague: Karolinum, 2005.

Vaňková, Irena, Jasňa Pacovská, and Jan Wiendel, eds. *Obraz člověka v jazyce a v literatuře*. Prague: Filozofická fakulta Univerzity Karlovy, 2010.

Vaňková, Irena, and Lucie Šťastná, eds. *Horizonty kognitivně-kulturní lingvistiky*. Vol. 2, *Metafory, stereotypy a kulturní rozrůzněnost jazyků jako obrazů světa*. Prague: Filozofická fakulta Univerzity Karlovy, 2018.

Vaňková, Irena, Veronika Vodrážková, and Radka Zbořilová, eds. *Horizonty kognitivně-kulturní lingvistiky*. Vol. 1, *Schémata, stereotypy v mluvených a znakových jazycích*. Prague: Filozofická fakulta Univerzity Karlovy, 2017.

Vaňková, Irena, and Jan Wiendel, eds. *Tělo, smysly, emoce v jazyce a v literature*. Prague: Filozofická fakulta Univerzity Karlovy, 2012.

Varela, Francisco, Evan Thompson, and Eleanor Rosch. *The Embodied Mind: Cognitive Science and Human Experience*. Cambridge: MIT Press, 1991.

Villanueva, Federico. *The "Uncertainty of a Hearing". A Study of the Sudden Change of Mood in the Psalms of Lament*. Supplements to Vetus Testamentum, 121. Leiden: Brill, 2008.

Wellhausen, Julius. *Skizen und Vorarbeiten*. Berlin: Georg Reimer, 1887.

Westermann, Claus. *Theologie des Alten Testament in Grundzugen*. Göttingen: Vandenhoeck & Ruprecht, 1985.

Westermann, Jenni. *Theologisches Handwörterbuch zum Alten Testament*. Munich: Chr. Kaiser, 1984.

Wiedl, Jan, ed. *Lidský život a každodennost v literatuře*. Prague: Filozofická fakulta Univerzity Karlovy, 2016.

Wierzbicka, Anna. *Emotions across Languages and Cultures. Diversity and Universals*. Studies in Emotion and Social Interaction. Second Series. Cambridge: Cambridge University Press, 1999.

Winters, Margaret, Heli Tissari, and Kathryn Allan, eds. *Historical Cognitive Linguistics*. Cognitive Linguistics Research, 47. Berlin: De Gruyter Mouton, 2010.

Zehnder, Markus Philipp. *Wegmetaphorik im Alten Testament*. Berlin: Walter de Gruyter, 1999.

NAME INDEX

SUBJECT INDEX